Copyright @ 2018 by Jeff Kolpack
Foreword by Steve Stark

All rights reserved. No part of this publication may be reproduced or transmitted in any form or by any means, electronic or mechanical, including photocopy, recording or any information storage or retrieval system, without prior permission in writing from the publisher, except of course in the cases of a critical (or non-critical) review of the book. In that case, have at it.

ISBN-13: 978-1984129734

ISBN-10: 198 4129732

Most excellent cover design (rich Red River Valley soil over the North Dakota state map) by Rob Beer, rbeer@forumcomm.com

Back cover photo (Bison football team practicing in a blizzard before December 2010 FCS playoff game at Montana State) by Dave Wallis. Title page photo of Collin Larsen by David Samson, dsamson@forumcomm.com

About the author photo by Kristi Ostendorf

To contact the author: jeff@kolpack.com

Twitter @FGOSPORTSWRITER

Special assistance and thanks to Uncle Brady Vick, retired professor extraordinaire, and Verna LaBounty, noted expert on the English language

Special thanks to all the writers and design editors at Forum Communications who worked thankless hours to bring the stories of the people to the people

Carson Wentz's Players' Tribune article used with permission from the Wentz family

First edition: First printing: 2018

Printed in the United States of America

North Dakota Tough

Collin Larsen, Central Cass High School, 2007

Unknown and Forgotten Stories from a Rural State

JEFF KOLPACK

To the reporters and editors who continue the great tradition of journalism in America. Don't stop.

Also from the author:

Available at www.Amazon.com
or Zandbroz Variety, Fargo, N.D

Foreword

When 24-year-old Theodore Roosevelt stepped foot into northern Dakota Territory to test his sport hunting skills, he never imagined the experience was a prologue to what he called "the romance of my life." Enraptured by the terrain and working among cowboys, settlers, lawmen and even a few tough hombres, he embraced wholeheartedly the challenges, vastness and values of the region and its inhabitants. He wrote three of his 35-odd books while nestled on his ranch in the badlands.

T.R. maintained a lifelong relationship to the region with over a dozen visits before, during and after his presidency. With earned filiation, the avid sportsman dubbed the people who lived here "the average Americans of the right type." A good call.

Writer Jeff Kolpack, with his latest book, has explored his native state for contemporary portraits of extraordinary talents displayed by present-day average Americans of the right type. I'd like to think T.R would find it a bully good read!

Jeff's talent, skills and regional acumen are well known and admired by three decades of The Forum of Fargo Moorhead newspaper readers. I knew and read his father's work, lionized sportswriter Ed Kolpack, years before I met Jeff. His brother Dave is another talented former Forum scribe turned brilliant writer for the Associated Press. The powerful three-man Kolpack crew have logged 110 years of collective press credentials, readers and admirers. While the Kolpacks won awards, their readers won *rewards* -- of solid writing, breadth of knowledge and old-fashioned professional journalism. You know, the good stuff.

Jeff's first book in 2016, "Horns Up: Inside the Greatest College Football Dynasty," was a worthy sequel of sorts to his dad's 1992 publication of the first book chronicling North Dakota State University football history. Both books are valued additions in my own library.

Jeff's observations, experience and ability to compose an adroit and powerful description of place, pace and personality are evidenced on these pages. Within this new collection he's mined story gems about some folks who have called North Dakota home. Some will be new names to you and some may be well known. They're all nuggets of determination, obstacles and triumph among people of the right type.

There's Steve Blehm, a basketball standout who set state records while playing at the North Dakota School for the Deaf in Devils Lake. Brad

Gjermundson was a wrestler and football player and then a real life rootin', tootin' bronc rider who is now in the North Dakota Cowboy Hall of Fame. There are other North Dakota farm-tough young men who also made hay in the sports fields on America's local, state, regional and national levels.

Among many more compelling subjects - there's story and insight of a rural North Dakota kid named Carson Wentz, who after leading the NDSU Bison to their fifth national Division 1 championship, is at this moment possibly the most famous NFL quarterback on the gridiron. You may be familiar with him. Yeah. North Dakota, America's most rural state has produced sports talent as fertile as our soil.

Associated primarily with athletics, Jeff's reporting career has chronicled nearly every sport from high school to the pros. Equally, his reporter's uncanny instincts of observation, explanation and dexterity with language have produced nearly countless news and feature stories. Newspaper reporters tally their stories by column inches and by that standard, I suspect his output over the years has accumulated column *miles* of newsprint print. I like to think that even the trees would approve with their contributions to the interesting reading Jeff has given us.

Newspaper reporting in America has always been an essential contribution our collective cultural literacy. Newspaper readers through the decades have always gravitated to their favorite categories. Sports and news have certainly been the highest draw to a majority of the varied newspaper readership often attracting eyes of different ages.

I once told Jeff, quite sincerely, that I likened his storytelling skills to the legendary Frank Deford, whose writing I also admired. He laughed. But to me they were in the same class - guys that could bounce effortlessly between flawless sports coverage and analysis and then easily compose a news story or biography on any given subject. Jeff has a legion of fans who follow his sports radio shows and podcasts. I relish watching my alma mater's Bison football on my treasured basement big screen and often follow Jeff's live game streaming on my iPad. I believe that every person has a story. Writers have captured personal sagas in novels and other prose.

But telling honest stories of the drama of human endeavor with honest empathy, detail and description has always been reserved for the finest of journalists who help draft history.

You have that in your hands right now. Enjoy.

Steve Stark

The Starting Lineup

I. The Cows Don't Care about Carson Wentz

II. The Kid on the Horse

III. Native Sons of Sakakawea

IV. Legend of Steve Blehm

V. Small Town Ball

VI. Farm Tough

VII. Cowboy Tough

VIII. JFK, Vietnam and Bison Football

IX. Gil

X. One Night in Madison

XI. 'When Cinderella Wore Spikes'

XII. The Skipper

XIII. State of N.D. vs. Don King

XIX. Epilogue

I. The Cows Don't Care About Carson Wentz

The first order of business demanded the proverbial photo at the corner of Haight and Ashbury, a 4x6 snapshot that hung on the refrigerator for years. On a trip in San Francisco that eventually took my wife Ruby and I to Napa and wine country, our sense of history had to be fed. Just walking around the area of the genesis of the hippie culture of the '60s and '70s, after all, emanated the feeling of the groovy lifestyle along with all the social unrest of those eras. A Summer of Love? Yes, it happened here. Jefferson Airplane, Grateful Dead ... they all walked the streets.

Back to the modern era, we walked into a nearby bar to watch the San Francisco Giants play the Detroit Tigers in a 2010 World Series game. The place was packed, like all the joints around San Francisco with their hometown team in the biggest baseball spectacle in the world. Yet, in a stroke of good timing, we found a couple of bar stools open and immediately grabbed them. After a day of trying not to act like tourists, even though we were, a cold beer on a warm day was the ticket. It wasn't long before we struck up a conversation with the gentleman one bar stool to the right of me.

His name was Chuck.

With Chuck, we got the real McCoy for a lesson in history. A member of the Oakland chapter of Hells Angels, he was at Altamont Speedway in the famous 1969 concert by the Rolling Stones when violence broke out killing a fan. The Stones incorporated the help of Hells Angels for their security, and Chuck took us through the whys and why nots of the evening. The intensity of it. Classic bands that played that night: Santana, Jefferson Airplane, Crosby, Stills, Nash & Young, and the Stones. The Grateful Dead were scheduled to play before things got out of hand. Chuck was a talking textbook of history of an evening that has been replayed for decades via documentaries and articles. The 24-hour period included three accidental deaths and, according to at least one published report, four live births on concert grounds.

Chuck's motorcycle group was a rough lot and by the time the Giants were in the 2010 World Series, not many were still around.

"How many?" I asked.
"Around five," he said.
"Five of how many?" I asked.
"Five of about 36," he said.
"You're not that old," I said.

Chuck bolted Hells Angels for a personal witness protection program of his own, packing up and living somewhere in Missouri for a lengthy bit of time. He needed to leave, most likely for his own survival. When things appeared settled down back in Frisco, he returned. He no longer had his nickname.

"What was your nickname?" I asked.
"Fuck'em Up Chuck," he said.
"How did you get that name?" I asked.
"When things needed to be taken care of, I would fuck 'em up," he said.

I'm pretty sure I knew what he meant but didn't pry further. The Giants won the game, the bar patrons were happy and we headed to Napa for a few days of serenity and wine tasting. Picturing Chuck back in his Hell's Angels days was a little tougher than I've experienced in my time.

But that doesn't mean my background is one of being a coddled cake eater. It's quite the opposite, actually. If you're somebody who grew up in North Dakota or lived there for an extended period of time, then you have more thickness to your skin than the rest of America. You don't have to "take care" of somebody in San Francisco to have veins of steel.

January on the calendar is 31 days long, even in North Dakota. It just seems like it's 62 days. If life is going too fast, here's some advice: move to North Dakota in January and it will slow down in a hurry.

Jessie Veeder, a writer and musician who lives in Watford City, North Dakota, probably put it best when she wrote about the weather in January.

"Our mutual annoyance with this long, cold month is what keeps us Northerners bonded together. January is the reason that there's an entire colony of North Dakotans who abandon ship and relocate to Arizona each season. And I would be jealous, except who can blame them? Especially when most of the Arizona-bound population has put in their years of earflap caps, long underwear and toddler mitten holes. Oh, but they come back eventually, usually around mid-May or June, when 42-below zero has become a distant memory, leaving only a scratchy little patch of frostbite you acquired on that one January night you had to walk home because you got the feed pickup stuck up to its floorboards in a snowbank. If only we could ship our cattle to Arizona for January as

North Dakota Tough

well. I'm sure they'd be pretty pissed if they knew there were cows in this world that have never had to lean in against 40 mph winds whipping ice pellets at them, so I haven't told them. No, we keep them blissfully unaware and fed each evening with giant bales of hay that smell like the beautiful, green, sunny summers we get up here."

Her words reminded me of the story of a high school boys' basketball coach from Edgeley, N.D., named Lon Ost. By day, a single farmer working the land near the small, central North Dakota town. By after school and night, a pretty good coach, who led the Rangers to one of the most unlikely Class B state championships in the state's history.

Edgeley came out of Region 5 and in those days, playing the champ from Region 5 was almost considered a first round bye by the rest of the state. The year was 1990; the tournament hosted by the Minot State Dome, which isn't really a dome but a rather large basketball venue that packed in the fans for the crown jewel of high school events in the state. The Class B tourney equaled North Dakota's Minnesota state hockey tournament or Indiana's state basketball tourney. If your home-town team wasn't in it, people went anyway.

Edgeley found itself in the title game against heavily-favored Dunseith, and for most of the game went as predicted. Eric Buckeye, Edgeley's scoring leader, had what he called "the worst game of my life" finishing 3 of 17 from the field. Starting guard Greg Braeger picked up three fouls in the first five minutes of the game and didn't come back until the third quarter. Guard Bryan Huber was 1 of 9 shooting.

But the three players didn't fold; the Rangers had other ideas then most of the 10,000 fans in attendance.

"These kids never gave up hope," Ost said. "The kids knew they had to dig deeper when the going got tough."

Braeger and sophomore guard Tyler Lamp combined for 19 of 24 fourth-quarter points. The game-winning hoop came on a Braeger basket off a nice pass from Huber with 25 seconds to play. On the other end, Buckeye forced a jump ball and the Rangers got the ball back on the alternating-possession rule leading by one point. Lamp added two free throws in the closing seconds.

Edgeley won with a dramatic rally, 78-75, erasing a 73-66 deficit in the last two minutes of the game. At the final horn, every Edgeley resident and former resident in attendance stormed the court in a celebratory jubilation that will never be forgotten. Lon Ost was in the middle of it. On Sunday, the team and fans caravanned back to town and a welcome-home celebration at the high school. It was Class B high school glory times 10.

By Monday morning, Ost was back on his farm, by himself, getting the land ready for planting. In his third year as the Edgeley head coach, he took over the family farm near Ortonville from his father 12 years prior, and the end of March is calving time.

"The first couple of weeks after the season ends, you go through withdrawal symptoms," Ost told Forum sports editor, Dennis Doeden. "You get a little extra nervous energy about 3 o'clock in the afternoon. You kind of want to go to the gym but you can't. It's over with. Until spring work comes, you're kind of preoccupied with memories of the season."

The headline in The Forum on Doeden's column: "Rangers are Class B champs, but will the cows care?"

Those cows didn't know the weather in Arizona is nicer in March than it is in North Dakota, either.

The weather.

Around the small-town cafes and bigger-town convenience stores, it's usually the first subject of conversation. San Diego always seems like it's 75 degrees, so why even talk about it? In Edgeley and the state of North Dakota in general, the variance in climate is huge, perhaps the widest in North America. The extremes in the Great Plains are greater than any other region in the lower 48. In 2017, weather records documented that western North Dakota and eastern Montana had the greatest extreme of temperature from coldest to warmest.

"There is actually more variability here," said John Wheeler, the senior meteorologist at WDAY-TV in Fargo. "From summer to winter, from season to season and day to day, it's because we are in the middle of the continent and the marine influence on our weather is limited."

One other factor makes weather such a common topic: the mere longitude and latitude of the state. The jet stream runs close to North Dakota for most of the year and storms often form around the jet stream. A sinking feeling occurs when the weather forecast on TV show the jet stream dipping into the southern states. That means nothing stops the arctic air from Canada making an unwelcomed visit. The state welcomes Canadians because they come down to shop and contribute tax dollars. We hate it when they bring their weather. Especially Alberta. The phrase "Alberta Clipper" from a weatherman makes people want to stay in bed the next day. Those winds penetrate right through the GORE-TEX winter jacket, or whatever technologically-advanced gear works in the bitter cold.

"North Dakota, especially eastern North Dakota, has more constant cold weather in the winter than any other place outside the tops of mountains," Wheeler said. "We have fewer days above 40 than most places. We have fewer days above freezing than most places not on the tops of mountains. Of course, North Dakota would win any wind chill contest."

Oh, the wind chill.

There are two types of temperatures: the actual number on the thermometer and the wind chill temp, the latter being a computation taking the wind and cold into account. The latter sucks.

"Because of the open terrain, flatness, and lack of trees, it's a place where the wind can just blow freely," Wheeler said. "If all you're doing is driving in your car, it has no effect. But if you're outside, it gets to you. It does."

Wheeler is a proponent that weather alone does not make you tough. You can go anywhere in the country and make that argument, whether it's the summer humidity in Houston or the constant winter rain and drizzle in Seattle.

But there is a mindset to it. Anybody who has ever played a spring sport in North Dakota understands the obstacles. I was a sophomore playing baseball at North Dakota State in the 1980s when we started a doubleheader in Grand Forks with the University of North Dakota under pretty good conditions, considering the time of year. The sun was out. UND college students were heckling us; it was all good. By the time the second game got going, you could see the horizon bearing down on us, in the form of a snirt storm. Snirt is a term only North Dakotans would know – a combination of snow and dirt in one word that makes for a blizzard-like condition as unique as it gets. In this case, the snow was light so we kept playing in the light snowfall. Yes, playing baseball in the middle of snow flurries, or snirt flurries, whatever you want to call it. We finished the game – and I was sneezing dirt and pulling it out of my ears for two days.

It happens. In 2018, a week after the scheduled opening game of the Fargo North High School baseball team, a brigade of a parents including me formed a snowplowing army to clear the Spartans' field of compacted snow. It was a brutal spring for all sports, with the first 10 days of April the coldest first 10 days of April in the history of recorded weather.

Bison softball players know that feeling, too. This is a program that for the longest time had some of the worst Division I facilities in the country and yet produced one of the winningest programs. The head coach, Darren Mueller, a Fargo North graduate, found recruits mostly in California and molded them into North Dakotans. They practiced in February and perhaps some of March with a batting cage on the stage at old Bentson Bunker Fieldhouse on the NDSU campus. Caves in the Black Hills have better lighting than that cage did. They did drills on the wood volleyball and basketball floor. Every movement with the bat or on the wood floor was scrutinized. Ask a softball player what they're most looking forward to before they board a plane for somewhere warm, and most will say "dirt."

Never were they more resilient than in 2009. A historic flood that spring hit the Red River Valley, bringing back memories of a 1997 flood that almost destroyed the city of Grand Forks still somewhat fresh in the mind. Folks furiously sandbagged residents' back yards to the Red River to save their homes. At one point, a voluntary evacuation order was given in Fargo. Yet, in May, the NDSU softball team won the Summit League postseason tournament and ventured to the NCAA regional in Norman, Oklahoma, the home of the University of Oklahoma. The Bison upset the Sooners and defeated the University of Tulsa to qualify for the Super Regional in Tempe, Arizona.

The following season, I did a story on the Bison outfielders that perhaps shed some light on how Mueller found players and didn't let the Fargo climate get in the way. They all had roots to California with hometowns like Laguna Hills, Pacifica, and San Mateo. Hardly the picture of places like most towns in North Dakota. But Taylor Lynn, Elisa Victa, Richel Briones and Taylor Mortensen carried the nickname "Worker Bees" and for a good reason: "They really don't take a day off," Mueller said.

A 24-hour, seven-day-a-week softball mentality was a big reason the Bison reached the NCAA Super Regional in 2009. The Worker Bees had the common denominator of good speed and good defensive skills. That's the way Mueller recruited positions like shortstop, second base and the outfield. If given the choice of recruiting a good hitter and teaching said player to play defense or a recruiting a good defender and teaching her to hit, he took the latter every time. Lynn was from San Mateo, Briones from Pacifica, and Victa from Laguna Hills. Mortensen grew up in California before moving to Sioux Falls, S.D.

Credit the nickname to assistant coach Jamie Trachsel. Whereas the infield was called the "Queen Bees" because they tended to be flashier with the quick throws, a good outfield that plays virtually error-free usually isn't noticed. Hence, the Worker Bees.

Lynn exhibited a typical reaction when Mueller first approached her during recruiting. She was at a tournament in Huntington Beach, California, when Mueller talked to her and gave her his business card. When she got home, she logged on to the Internet and searched for NDSU. Same with Victa.

"My travel coach asked me what I thought about North Dakota State and I'm like, 'Who?'" Lynn said. "But I trusted what the coaches said about the team. And I'm glad I did."

Glad despite the less-than-ideal practice facilities. Trachsel, who worked with the outfielders, used alternative methods like tennis balls from a racquetball racquet in the Bentson Bunker Fieldhouse.

"We don't complain," Lynn said. "We always have that attitude that whenever we come to practice, we come ready to work. What we have is what we have, but we don't make excuses for the obstacles that we might come across."

Weather can be a routine obstacle for any sport or activity in the spring. The Fargo Marathon that annually attracts thousands of entrants is run every May, meaning those running from the Upper Midwest usually start training in January. And during the string of days when the temperature rarely gets above zero, they cannot take those days off. They gotta get their miles in, so they invest in better running gear and learn the layering system.

"Most people in the country would skip the training day," Wheeler said. "But here, if it's 15 below, you go ahead. I've run in 30 below wind chills."

I once ran a 10K in Bismarck in the winter that had the slogan "Up Hill and Into the Wind. Both Ways."

Now that's tough. That's "North Dakota Tough."

NFL football coach Jon Gruden made it a cool term in the fall of 2017. In his time as the analyst for Monday Night Football, he gave quarterback Carson Wentz the label during one of the telecasts: October 24, 2017, Washington Redskins at the Philadelphia Eagles. During the game, Gruden blurted out his assessment of Wentz, a graduate of Bismarck Century High School and NDSU:

"Carson Wentz is what I like to call 'North Dakota tough,'" Gruden said. It wasn't the only time he said it that night, either. He repeated "Carson Wentz is not just tough, he's North Dakota tough."

Boom! A catchphrase throughout the state was born. Eleven words from a former head coach-turned-analyst-turned-head coach again captivated the native folks. Wentz was sharp that game, finishing 17 of 25 for 268 yards and four touchdowns. Not everybody was enamored with the telecast. Obviously, Redskins fans were having a tough night. One poster on the Redskins fan board wrote "last night if I heard Jon Gruden say 'North Dakota tough' one more time, I was going to puncture my eardrums with an ice pick."

Sports columnist Phil Heron of the Delaware Daily County Times took note, perhaps writing the best description of one play in which Gruden made reference to Wentz's home state:

"Wentz, who was under siege most of the night, combined 'North Dakota tough' and a Houdini-like escapability to once again dazzle. He went onto a national stage on Monday Night Football and basked in the limelight. He pulled off a play that will now reside beside a similar piece of QB lore pulled off by Randall Cunningham, also on a Monday night game, in which he appeared to be in the grasp of several Redskins defenders early in the fourth quarter, only to somehow escape, pick up a first down, and lead the Birds to another touchdown.

"So long as No. 11 is lined up behind center, coolly dissecting the defense the way you would expect a veteran NFL QB to take control, not some kid from North Dakota State in his second season in the NFL. The Eagles just might be that good. Carson Wentz already is."

The "North Dakota Tough" slogan came up in one of the production meetings the morning of the game, according to the Philadelphia Inquirer newspaper, which wrote a story on how ESPN prepares for a Monday Night Football game. It came one day after ESPN aired a story on Wentz's relationship with Lukas Kusters, a 9-year-old boy battling cancer who befriended Wentz in the weeks before he passed away. The reporting, by ESPN's Tom Rinaldi, was as heart-wrenching as it gets, especially at the point in the story when Rinaldi began to outline a question to Wentz by saying three words: "He was buried ..."

Wentz displayed some raw emotion rarely seen in a professional player in any sport. Wentz teared up, dropped his head with the bill of his "AO1" cap shielding his eyes from the camera and then proceeded to talk about the boy who was put to rest wearing his No. 11 Philadelphia Eagles jersey. The ESPN title to the story was "The Dutch Destroyer," in reference to

Lukas' nickname on the little league football fields in Wilmington, Delaware, a story that had impact around the country.

Especially in North Dakota.

"And you know how everybody feels about Carson in this state," said Jack Maughan, NDSU's senior associate athletic director for development.

A group of boosters put together a package to fly the family to Fargo for the October 11 game between the University of South Dakota and NDSU. They got the first-class treatment. Through a collaborative effort of some local businesses, the family flew in a private jet to Fargo on Friday and spent Saturday making the rounds, from tailgating to being introduced in front of the sold-out stadium of 18,623 fans during a time out in the first half.

The trip first started to get some legs when Craig Whitney, the president and CEO of the Fargo Moorhead West Fargo Chamber of Commerce, watched the story with his wife, Lori, prior to the Eagles and Washington Monday Night game.

"I turned to my wife and said, what a great story it would be if we could arrange the family to come to a Bison home game," Whitney said. "Suit them up in Bison gear and have them have the game-day experience. What you see is what you get with Carson and that's the way Carson is and North Dakota is."

The next morning Whitney got on the horn, texting NDSU President Dean Bresciani and talking with Jon Cole, the general manager of Gateway Chevrolet and a collaborative venture to bring the family to Fargo was off and running.

The NDSU athletic department got in touch with Rebecca Burmeff, Lukas' mother. She had been busy selling "Dutch Destroyer" bracelets for families and organizations fighting childhood cancers. That didn't go unnoticed in Fargo. Gate City Bank purchased as many as were available, about 9,000, and gave them away at their corporate corner in the Fargodome on game day.

"The original goal was for everybody at the game to get one but I think we're exhausting their inventory," Whitney said. "You could only wish we had a bunch more of (Carson Wentz's) in professional sports."

Certainly, Gruden realized Wentz was a rare breed.

Gruden initially took a liking to Wentz a year earlier in his "Gruden's QB Camp" television show, the several-episode look at the best potential quarterbacks for the NFL Draft. "Carson Wentz North Dakota State Bison, welcome to Gruden's QB Camp. It's not the Bison," Gruden said, with an emphasis on the 'S.' "It's the Bizon."

Gruden asked Wentz about NDSU and what kind of player goes to a place like North Dakota State. The reference was obvious with Gruden, pointing to the remote nature of NDSU in the landscape of college football. For starters, with video of bison (the animals) roaming the North Dakota western Badlands in the background, Wentz went with the old athletic department saying of "the strength of the herd is the Bison and the strength of the Bison is the herd."

Gruden made reference to the tradition, which after NDSU defeated James Madison University on January 6, 2018, is at 14 national titles. That included six of the last seven in the Division I Football Championship Subdivision. And a national show with Wentz from his college days couldn't go by much longer without reference to ESPN's "College GameDay" pregame show, which aired in downtown Fargo in the fall of 2013 and 2014.

The crowds packed Broadway and the streets surrounding it. In the opening, the ESPN crew of Kirk Herbstreit, Desmond Howard, Lee Corso, and host Chris Fowler was obviously blown away by the crowd – a sort of subliminal message that I took as the following: How can a hick school near the Canadian border bring this kind of enthusiasm and people to a pregame show? Herbstreit said on the air that day the bar may have been raised with the locations of the show.

Two years later, in his "Gruden's QB Camp" show, Gruden asked Wentz about the video of the "College GameDay" appearance in Fargo.

"I've never seen anything like it," Gruden said. "I thought they were doing a Green Bay Packers game. I mean, look at these people. This is all for their football there."

Gruden asked Wentz why that is, why could this school in the FCS draw that many people?

"There's no professional team," Wentz said. "We're the big show in the state. A lot of local kids like myself go there and it just brings a huge fan base and people love it. It helps when you're winning games. When you're winning, this is what you get."

Wentz blew Gruden out of the water with his advanced knowledge of the game, drawing plays at an NFL level, when he was only a few months removed from his last college game. He finished his NDSU academic career with a 4.0 grade point average and was a three-time recipient of the NCAA's

Elite 89 Award, which goes to the highest GPA in each of the NCAA's championship events. In this case, he won it at the FCS title game.

The kid can also write.

In April of 2016, he wrote a piece for the "The Players' Tribune," an online website devoted to writings of professional players in their own words. The title of Wentz's article was "How We Play Football in North Dakota." I'm not sure if he had a lot of help in the copy-editing process, but the structure of the article was very good.

"You don't get through winters with an average temperature of 12.8° without being a certain kind of tough — the cracked-skin-dried-blood kind of tough.

That toughness comes in handy in a place like North Dakota. You see, up there, jamming your numb fingers against someone's ice-cold helmet happens every practice. Getting decked on the cement-like dirt is just how a play ends.

And here's the thing: I love it.

Because in North Dakota, we don't care for flash or dazzle. That's not our game. We don't do things the fanciest way. We do them the right way.

Going through the draft process, you find yourself answering a lot of the same questions over and over. I get it. This is basically a very long, very public job interview. But the question that seems to come up the most is one that almost makes me laugh at this point:

Carson, coming from North Dakota, are you worried about playing against tougher competition in the NFL?

There's this belief that I'm at some sort of disadvantage coming into the league because of where I'm from. But if you get to know me, you'll understand that being from North Dakota isn't a disadvantage. Not even close. In fact, having been raised in North Dakota is probably one of my greatest strengths.

When I started out in the Bismarck youth football league, I was a running back. Now, I wasn't a shifty, finesse running back. I was an up-the-gut, everyone-knows-where-the-ball-is-going, punch-you-in-the-mouth running back. Since I was a kid, I've had the mentality that if you're going to tackle me ... well, I'm going to make sure it hurts. I was pretty skinny — lanky even — but you can get away with that when you play hard and aren't afraid of contact. And contact was always my favorite part of the game — still is. It was kind of funny, honestly. I was this crazy, string-bean kid trying to truck kids into the end zone. And a lot of the time, I did.

Some of my competitiveness is God-given — but a whole lot of it was developed during weekend wiffle ball games with big bro.

Growing up, everyone was always outside competing in just about every sport you can imagine. If I wasn't the best at a sport I took that as a challenge. I was never scared of putting in the work to get better. And to keep me on my toes, I had the best motivation you could ask for: an older brother who was better than me at just about everything.

When I was a kid, I didn't necessarily dream about winning Super Bowls or national championships. I wanted to beat Zach.

Baseball, football, checkers, number of plates consumed at a buffet — it did not matter what we were doing, everything was a competition. Zach was my benchmark. Knowing he was successful in baseball, football and hockey, and given that he's three years older than me, I knew that if I could match up with him and even sometimes beat him, then I must be pretty darn good myself.

Granted, I didn't beat him a whole lot.

But I never quit trying to replace him as our household's best athlete, even if it meant begging him for rematches constantly. Some of my competitiveness is God-given — but a whole lot of it was developed during weekend wiffle ball games with big bro.

When I got to high school, my focus really turned to football. I always wanted to stay on the field, so I would change positions all the time. One day I would be at corner, another day I'd be returning kicks — wherever I was needed, I played. I saw the field a lot, but as a freshman, I wasn't much to look at. I came in at 5' 8" and about 125 pounds (depending on what I ate for lunch that day). But playing all those different positions as a kid made me grasp the game so much better. The best way to understand the mentality of a safety is to play snaps there. When I eventually hit my growth spurt, they moved me to quarterback, and I stuck.

In North Dakota, people generally choose one of three favorite teams: the Broncos, the Packers or the Vikings.

That preference is usually inherited through your family, but whatever allegiance you do have, it's taken pretty seriously. I grew up a Vikings fan. Jerseys, hats, posters on my wall — all of that. But despite that, I always loved watching Brett Favre. I just admired the way he played football. Nobody ever questioned how serious or competitive he was, and the way he showed off those qualities is what made me love him. The guy would get licked and then get back up, throw a 40-yard bomb and run around the field jumping and laughing like a little kid. He wasn't out there to manage the game. He was a gunslinger. The guy flat out made plays. That's the quarterback that I wanted to be.

Playing in high school taught me a lot, but it also had its fair share of disappointment. Every year, we made it to the semifinals of the state playoffs — and lost. Even worse, three out of the four years we lost to the same team, Fargo South High.

There's no love lost between the cities of Fargo and Bismarck, I can assure you that. Man, we wanted to beat those guys.

My senior year I really thought we had them, but they ended up scoring a touchdown with six seconds left in the game to go ahead by one. That's still the most heartbreaking loss of my life.

In high school, I learned how to lead a team for the first time. And in college, I learned how to win championships.

North Dakota State football is a perfect representation of the grit and work ethic that makes where I'm from a special place.

Our offense might have reminded you a bit of Alabama or Stanford. We were going to start out running the ball, and then we were going to run it again, and then when you think we couldn't possibly do it again, we were going to run some more. And when you're sick of getting dirty with us, we'll get heavy personnel and run with power and move you guys. We love to bring the boom. By the time we ran play-action and went over the top for a touchdown, your defense was just relieved they didn't have to swap paint with us for one more play. Then, the next time we got the ball, we would show you completely different sets. We'd start slinging it around like Baylor. It was tough to defend.

The best way to learn how to win is to be around winners. There wasn't one game at North Dakota State where the entire team did not prepare with the mentality that we're going to win. Even if we were playing a power five school that had us completely outmatched on paper, we expected to win.

Am I worried about whether I can have the same success at the next level? Of course not. I'm excited to show people exactly what I can do.

And we pretty much always did.

The positive results were almost entirely because of the work put in by guys before they ever set foot on the field. Probably 90% or more of the incoming freshmen at NDSU redshirt. And during that year, the staff makes it clear just how important it is for them to develop. We may be an FCS school, but our strength and conditioning program is as rigorous and productive as any other school in the country. And everyone buys into it. We approach it with that distinct North Dakotan mentality. We weren't upset about not playing early, or waking up at 5 a.m. to lift. We were excited about getting bigger and better. Because we knew that when it was our turn, we'd be ready.

By the time I took over the starting quarterback job as a junior, I was fully prepared. And I was done losing in the semifinals. My first year as a starter, we won our FCS playoff semifinal 35–3. My senior year we won in the semifinals 33–7. We won the championship both years, just like we expected.

So am I worried about whether I can have the same success at the next level? Of course not. I'm excited to show people exactly what I can do.

After competing at All-Star games and the combine, I know that I have much more in common with guys who played FBS football than I have differences. Heck, we even beat a few of their teams while I was in college. Like I said before, football is football. At North Dakota State, I was taught to recognize the same zone pressures, blitzes, stunts and twists as the other guys in the draft. Our offense would run the ball with no receivers and then spread it out wide with five guys. We did it all.

The speed will be an adjustment, but it is for everybody, whether you're coming from the SEC or Division III. I'm as ready for it as I can possibly be.

But I still approach the game of football the same way I did when I was a 5' 8" beanstalk flying around the field in Bismarck. The difference now is that I'm 6' 5", 237 pounds, and have been carefully developed into one of the best football prospects in America.

So what do I say to all the people who wonder if I'm ready for the NFL?

I've been getting ready my whole life."

Maybe it's as Bismarck thing. Cara Mund, who graduated one year earlier than Wentz at Bismarck Century High School, was crowned Miss America for 2018 – and then took on the entire pageant organization late in her reign with a letter to other former winners. She was critical of the way she was not allowed to do major interviews and essentially was repeatedly told what to say.

In part, the letter read the Miss American organization "reduced me, marginalized me and essentially erased me in my role as Miss America in subtle and not-so-subtle ways on a daily basis."

That's not the way life worked growing up in Bismarck.

***

Keenan Hodenfield was prepared for Bison football his whole life. You want grit? Take the 2013 walk-on from Ray, N.D., and the son of former Bison player and coach Shane Hodenfield, who has four national title rings. For starters, it couldn't have been easy to follow your father's footsteps, much less a kid who hardly saw the field in his five years with the program. Moreover, he overcame some obstacles that would have shut most players down.

During practice in spring football in 2016, Hodenfield went up for a ball and came down wrong on his foot. Really wrong. His cleats stuck in the turf while his body continued to twist. The result was something no one wanted to see — and nobody on the team did, either.

Tight end Jeff Illies said he saw the replay on tape. And?

"You don't want to know," Illies said. "Let's just say that it was pretty gruesome."

The impact wasn't the half of it. Hodenfield, a senior safety, while lying on the turf, took matters in his own hands for some reason and adjusted his dislocated ankle back into place. That's not "North Dakota tough," that's North Dakota really, really tough.

"I didn't want to wait," he said.

How he did it nobody really knows. He had already waited long enough. This was Hodenfield's fourth spring football. He faced a fifth year of being a walk-on, grinding through workouts and practices without much playing time to show for it. The year before, a broken foot kept him out of practice.

The rehabilitation from the ankle injury took the rest of spring, all of the ensuing summer and a good chunk of the August fall camp. Toward the end of August, right around the time school started, head coach Chris Klieman stopped Hodenfield as he was leaving the Bison locker room in the lower level of the Fargodome and heading to an adjacent team meeting room.

"Keenan, I have to talk to you a second," Klieman said.

Hodenfield stopped.

"We're going to take care of you this year," Klieman said.

Hodenfield's immediate reaction was something on the lines of, "What?"

"Yeah, we're going to put you on full-ride scholarship," Klieman said.

Hodenfield said he was speechless, didn't know what to say or how to react.

"I was shocked," he said.

In this day and age of a non-scholarship player getting a full ride via some sort of clever announcement where the video goes public if not viral, Klieman prefers the more personal, behind-the-scenes, one-on-one touch. The reporter in me had to practically drag it out of him.

"I couldn't thank him enough, it meant a lot," Hodenfield said. "It says a lot about his character. I mean, he said I really deserved it but I didn't know since I hadn't played a whole lot. It's something that he does and it shows he really cares about us."

The 5-foot-11, 182-pound Hodenfield walked on from the 9-man football town of Ray, a player Klieman said did all the right things on and off the field. After the ankle injury that spring, Klieman said he sat down with Hodenfield and asked him if he wanted to continue with the program. There was no hesitation on the other end.

"I started this and I'm going to finish this," Hodenfield said.

"And that made me feel good," Klieman said. "He earned everything he's gotten."

At some point after the practice following the full ride notice, Hodenfield called home to tell his parents, Shane and Stephanie. His mother is an NDSU graduate. In all, five relatives are NDSU graduates.

When Shane answered, Keenan told him he had some news. Shane had heard that line all too often in the last couple of years and only assumed something not good, like another injury. Or maybe the kid finally had enough.

"No, it's good news this time," Keenan said.

Keenan told him the news Klieman had just delivered.

"I dang near cried thinking about the whole deal and realized that he did have an impact on the program, maybe not so much playing but with the other things that he'd done," Shane said.

Shane Hodenfield was a Bison defensive back from 1977-80. He was an assistant on NDSU title teams in 1985, '86, '88 and '90 before leaving coaching in 1995. At the rural family home northwest of Ray sit eight rings with Shane's four and Keenan's four from 2013, '14, '15 and '17.

The rings are bigger and gaudier these days but they mean the same. NDSU won 14 national titles in its football history before the 2018 season began and the Hodenfields have been a part of more than 50 percent of them.

During high school, Keenan told his dad he wanted to follow his footsteps to NDSU; there was no sugar-coating it with either father or son. It was going to be a long road. Both knew it. The Division I level was a different animal than the Division II competition that Shane played against. But Shane said he had a message above and beyond playing time.

"The lifelong experiences will outweigh anything else and I think that's basically what happened," Shane said.

That experience ended in Frisco with the national title win over James Madison University, a game in which Keenan did not play. It was probably OK to the kid since he lived the title dream with his teammates.

Just like his dad.

"I'm always trying to be like my dad, not necessarily comparing myself to him, but to follow in his footsteps, although taking my own path in doing so," Keenan said. "I love being part of this place, this team. I can't ever think about not being a part of it. It goes fast. It's been tough and there have been bumps in the road but, yeah, it's been completely worth it. It's tough but everyone has it tough if they've gone all five years."

The story tugged at a lot of people, especially folks from western North Dakota. Bob Stanek wrote me a word of thanks with the following description: "Having grown up in North Dakota and spent a lifetime (42 years) in the US Army, the North Dakota Tough helped save my life a few times."

It's 2018 and North Dakotans have never had it so good. The state is in the midst of prosperity that it had never seen. The oil boom returned, only in manageable moderation, unlike the out-of-control scene around 2012 and 2013.

"What makes North Dakota so great – we live in this awful place of long winters, high winds, isolated, a set of dynamics that led to the prairie populist movement," said Bismarck resident Clay Jenkinson, a scholar, talk show host and author of nine books. "How do you overcome a commodity-producing state? How do you overcome the isolation of being in a cold, remote spot? That made us really tough."

The average North Dakotan, he said, can weld, can frame a garage, can dig a sewage pit or a drain field, and are resourceful because they've had to do it all themselves.

"The average male is an extraordinary skilled person," Jenkinson said. "This toughness is really part of the North Dakota character, but I think it's changing pretty fast."

Now, I've lived in this state for 54 years and I'm not average. I can't weld, I can't frame a house and I would have no clue why anybody would need a sewage pit.

In a sense, because there are more of me out there than ever before, the state is at a crossroads of sorts, and it may not all be positive. The principle cities of Fargo and Bismarck are growing, perhaps at a rate too fast. The older generation is moving out of the countryside to the more populated areas because of the better health care.

"I'm trying to figure out what it is about us," Jenkinson said. "Is it because we're Norwegians? Is it because we have been so isolated that we've had to look into ourselves? I don't know. But I know this: before the boom, North

Dakotans were a lot nicer than they are now. Now people are edgy because you don't know who you're meeting in the grocery store anymore. The degrees of separation are much greater on average. My concern is why would anyone live in North Dakota? If you were person X and you were shopping around for a place to live, you would never choose North Dakota because you think of the Grand Tetons or you want a climate like Sante Fe or Los Angeles. No one chooses North Dakota as a destination, so there must be something here that compensates for all the problems. What is it? I think it's a certain quality of character, a certain gumption and resourcefulness and the capacity to put up cheerfully with some disagreeable elements. That came from our past."

The ideal place to live if you're a true North Dakotan, Jenkinson says, are in towns like Mott, Harvey, Cooperstown, or New Rockford. In those towns, you can still find the kid who goes to school for eight hours, works for six hours, does chores for another couple or so, doesn't complain about it and sleeps for a few hours. Then gets up and does it all over again.

And doesn't complain about it. Fargo, the state's largest city, is no longer a North Dakota city. It's a midwestern city.

"Whenever I go to smaller towns, that's where you meet the woman who organizes a lecture series, drives the school bus, is the student congress organizer for the school and she's working on the county history," Jenkinson said. "It's way more than one individual would do in Bismarck or Fargo or Jamestown. It cuts both ways. It's like Sinclair Lewis' 'Main Street': It's confining and claustrophobic and everybody wants to know your business and there's some small-town repressiveness. On the other end of the spectrum, there's where you don't need to get volunteers to help with the wheat harvest. They all just turn up."

That's not happening anymore. That's why organizations exist like Farm Rescue, an army of organized volunteers that come to the aide of farmers in need. Jenkinson sometimes wonders what happened to the North Dakota he knew growing up as a kid. It perhaps is getting too much of a suburban mentality.

"Maybe we want to be Maple Grove, Minnesota," he said. "Maybe we don't want to be that old North Dakota anymore. I always think, it's not for me to try to lock us into an agrarian view of life. People have turned their back on that view of life. I just don't know what matters to people anymore, but I don't think you can maintain the best qualities of North Dakota if we cease to be somehow connected to agriculture, small towns and the land. But I'm in the minority on that. I think most North Dakotans think, hey, good times are here. We have full employment. Whatever happens in the boom or bust cycle, we have a lot of carbon and the world wants it. And by the way it's all out there somewhere, I don't have to think about any of the downside of it. And if you were to ask people about it, I don't think they would have much to say about the problems."

There have been boom times on the athletic front, built with people in the lead roles like Carson Wentz, Roger Maris, Jim Kleinsasser, Virgil Hill, Phil Hansen, and Phil Jackson. But there is so much more that most people don't know about.

And that's what you have here.

These are stories that you either forgot or don't know about.

II. The Kid on the Horse

The day started without an alarm clock. Well, at least one that plugs into a wall outlet. It was a Timex, one of those wind-up ones whose ring made Dave Osborn jump out of bed like he was taking on a linebacker. Damn near scared him every time the bell wailed. There was no electricity in those days in the Osborn country house. No running water. No indoor plumbing. No television. No sprinkler system in the lawn. No X-box. No three-stall garages. No golf courses nearby. No sidewalk out front. No garbage trucks to pick up your refuge. No dishwasher. No washing machines. No dryer. No wondering what wattage of light bulbs to buy. No Menards 10 minutes away. No anything 10 minutes away.

No pretty much anything.

Well, that's not true. But they had each other. They had their family. These days, Dave Osborn, one of the greatest running backs in the history of the Minnesota Vikings and a player who had his number retired by the University of North Dakota, lives in a very nice rambler in a very nice section of Lakeville, Minnesota. He has two double-stall garages, which is four more stalls than he had growing up. The suburban route to get to his house has that gentle windiness to it, like a lot of modern developments. The roads all have names to them that are not Main, Broadway, or First Street. They are either names of prominent people or important-sounding words.

They are so un-Dave.

At least the Dave who grew up on a farm near Cando, N.D. He was maybe a 10- or 11-year-old when that loud Timex alarm clock ring would get him up for another day on the farm. He headed to school, about three miles by road or 1½ miles cross-country by horse. That was the preferred route, if not the necessary route. When Dave drove to school, he got on his horse and the horse drove him to school. In the winter? No problem. He would put on a parka of some type, one or two pairs of long underwear, get on his ride, put his head by the horse's mane to help stay warm and away they went.

The horse knew the trail, needing little navigation by the rider. The country school was located five miles west and five miles south of Cando, which on a map is located about as middle-of-nowhere as one can get in North America. It's 2,015 miles to Rockport, Maine, which is near the gateway to the Atlantic Ocean. Puget Sound and Seattle is 1,338 miles to the west. Flin Flon, Manitoba, is 800 miles to the north and that's just a fraction to get to the Arctic Sea. One would have to drive for days to get to the Caribbean to the south. It's not the Geographical Center of North America, which Rugby, N.D., still claims; but many people believe because of global warming and the melting of the polar ice cap that the true center is in Robinson, located 98 miles south.

Solid brick construction made the school rather new by country standards.

The school was rather new by country standards, and it was Dave Osborn's center of education. Dave would stable his horse in a barn stocked with hay and head into the school room.

"We didn't know anything different," he said. "The horse knew where to go, you just let him go. He might go a little slower going out to school but coming home he would be wide open because the horse wanted to get home."

Dave attended the very small-populated school from first through eighth grade. By the time he was in eighth grade, there were only five students remaining and three of them were in his class. The next year, with just two students left, the school closed for good.

"It was beautiful, probably one of the prettiest country schools you'll ever see," said Kathie Carlson, Dave's younger sister by eight years. "It was a light brick building with hardwood floors on the inside. It was like when the school closed, the teacher walked out and closed the door, but for years afterward we would go into the school and the black boards were still there; the books and papers were still there. It just closed."

It was not an easy life, but the Osborns didn't know any different. Without electricity, light came via kerosene lanterns.

"You just turn the dial … it's what you had," Dave said.

Water came from a well in the yard, and to get it out of the ground one had to pump the handle. It wasn't a problem in the summer, but in the winter the cattle needed water – and so did the Osborns. Water was brought into the house to wash clothes, dishes, and to drink. Without refrigeration, food was mostly canned and stored in a cellar. Every morning and night, Pearl Osborn, the mother of the house, would milk the 10 cows by hand, take it and pour it into a separator that produced skim milk in one bucket and cream in another. The milk would go to the calves and pigs and the cream was put into a five-gallon pail. Once a week the family would go into Cando to the creamery to sell it.

"You would probably get about $8 to $10 for it," Dave said. "That was about how much groceries cost per week, about $8 to $10."

The family didn't need to buy a whole lot. On the farm, they had their own livestock that they butchered and cooked. They had chickens for eggs. They raised potatoes and grew vegetables.

The telephone with a battery pack was something out of an old movie, with several neighbors hooked on the same line. Each house had its distinct ring. For the Osborns, this was three shorts followed by a long, which if translated into writing would go something like rrrr rrrrr rrrr rrrrrrrrrrrrrrrrrr.

A party line system meant anybody could listen to anybody.

"So, on the phone you would hear 'click, click' and that was other people picking up the phone," Dave said. "You didn't want to say anything on the phone that you didn't want to be heard."

A breakthrough came after Dave's 10th birthday when the family finally got electricity. They were prepared, having already bought a refrigerator.

Winters were something else, however. At times, it bordered on survival when a storm would hit and render the rural farmers homebound. To clear a road, the dads of the neighboring households gathered around 9 a.m. and headed for town. If there was a drift, they would shovel it out and move on to the next one. No such thing as a snowplow existed in Towner County in the 1940s and '50s.

First things first, however. Cars had to be started. Nobody had garages. In some instances, dads placed heated charcoal under the oil pan of a car to get the vehicle going because the oil in the engines was so heavy.

"Then you would get a team of horses and pull the car down the road to get the car running because the battery was too cold," Dave said. "You would get the cars running, the neighbors would all go together single file to town, get groceries and things that had to be done, and then everybody would head home at the same time in case of bad roads. Everybody had to help each other out. That was the normal routine back in those days. You tell my grandkids this stuff and they almost don't believe you. They think you're making this stuff up because it seems so far-fetched. This stuff seemed like it couldn't happen, but it did. It's just the way it was. We were 25 miles from the Canadian border, we were up there where they didn't have a lot of highways."

The biggest town was Devils Lake, located 36 miles to the south. As a kid, Dave remembers driving there only once or twice a year, and it was a big deal when they did.

"Now people drive from Cando to Devils Lake every day," he said. "That was a trip in our day."

Farm life eventually turned to a life in law enforcement for the Osborns after his father, Bud, was elected county sheriff. The family moved into the living quarters in the basement of the courthouse in Cando, "a situation where it was almost like the Andy Griffith Show," Kathie said. "We lived in the basement. The jail was upstairs. There were a couple bars in one jail that were missing and Dave would go up there and have a little fun with the person that was incarcerated. He would offer to give them haircuts and do different things."

***

I first encountered the legend of Dave Osborn thanks to my father, Ed Kolpack, who as the Sports Editor of The Forum newspaper would often cover Minnesota Vikings home games in the 1970s. Dad would take his three boys to games and let us roam the stadium while he worked in the press box. I was a very small boy, in those days and probably too young to have my brother Dave, four years older, be the guardian of sorts. But it was a different time when we didn't worry about abductions and getting lost.

I remember some iconic games, like the Drew Pearson miracle Hail Mary catch in an NFC Divisional Playoff game in 1975. I was 11 years old. During the game the referee was hit with a whiskey bottle thrown by one of the fans. I don't remember that. I remember being cold, but not giving a rip. I remember my mom despising Cowboys head coach Tom Landry, to the point she couldn't even watch a game on TV with him on the sideline.

I don't remember a whole lot of No. 41 running the ball other than the lasting image of Dave Osborn and Bill Brown in the backfield, I reconnected with his persona in mid-April of 2018 in Grand Forks. Osborn was the featured guest of a Farmer's Union event at the UND alumni center.

He was 75 years old and one would never know it. A niece from Cando, standing a bit in the distance, marveled at how he does some sort of activity every day. He had fire, man, and he had presence. He's a great idol, not so much for football, but in how to age with grace and a sense of purpose. He was in shape, with only a couple artificial knees and simple age preventing him from going over to old Memorial Stadium to run a few drills and pop a few linebackers.

One man from Cando brought a large cardboard advertisement that he kept in his garage for many years, an example of one of the few times pro athletes got into the marketing game of some sort in those years. "QuicKick," was billed as a "super energy action drink,' an early version of Gator-Aid or Powerade. Osborn held a ball in his left hand like a running back with his leg up as if he just completed a kicking motion. Perhaps a kicker would have been a more appropriate spokesman, but that was the effect the marketing folks for Osborn wanted at the time. The poster was signed "Dave Osborn" and at 75 years old, he was asked to sign it again.

The signatures were identical, down to the loop through the "D" and the "O."

Before the event, he stopped by his old fraternity, Sigma Alpha Epsilon, to check out the house, where he lived in college. He's a legendary figure with the football program, the only player to have his number retired. He signed autographs, posed for pictures, reunited with old teammates and talked with UND head football coach Bubba Schweigert for at least a couple of hours. Then, with Beverly, his wife of 54 years, the couple headed to Cando that night.

Cando is home.

Dave and Beverly went to school together, she is one year younger.

Amazingly, he hardly played football growing up. In the country school until eighth grade, there was no team. He hadn't even seen a game until his freshman year of high school at Cando.

"You're a country boy, a farm kid, do you want to come out for football?" the coach asked.

"Yeah, I'll give football a shot," Dave replied.

Osborn had no clue what position he could play. All he knew was that he was one of the bigger kids in his grade and that he was fast. In the country school at "play days" he was always winning races. The coach put him at tight end in preseason practices, but a physical examination before the first game put his career in jeopardy before it started. Discovery of a heart murmur forced him to sit out his freshman season.

He tried out again as a sophomore, and this time his physical produced better news. The heart murmur was better, and he could play; but he was told to take it easy. Whatever that meant. He immediately reached the

Cando starting lineup as a cornerback and tight end. About halfway through the season another obstacle hit him. He broke his collarbone when he tried tackling a bigger running back from Lakota.

"So now going into my junior year, I'd hardly played yet," Osborn said.

There would be more to that story. He was switched to running back his junior season, but a big snowstorm toward the end of the year canceled the remaining games.

"I get into my senior season and I've probably played five or six games," Dave said.

That would be five or six games in his young life; not a resume of a college prospect much less one with professional aspirations. His big break came in the final game of his high school career when the Cubs played at Cavalier. One of the referees was a major from the Grand Forks Air Force Base and another was the head men's track and field coach from the University of North Dakota, Frank Allen "Zaz" Zazula. He knew football because he was an assistant coach for the Sioux from 1946-59 as well as the track and cross country head coach from 1956-82.

Osborn was on his game that night, running hard and looking like a bigger boy among boys. Zazula took notice and after the game, he and the major went up to Dave and asked him about his future college plans.

"I don't know," Osborn replied.

He explained to them he was thinking about maybe going to Jamestown College, a small private school in North Dakota. However, Zazula and the major took note of their firsthand observation of this running back from Cando and reported back to their superiors. Within a week, Dave Osborn had an appointment with a recruiter from the Air Force Academy in Colorado Springs, Colorado, and a full football scholarship at UND.

One week. That's all it took.

"I came from the boonies," Dave said.

All of this, and the kid in all reality only played one full season of football in his junior high and high school career. How ironic. The one season that he played all of the scheduled games, his senior year, and in the final game somebody took notice. What if there had been different referees than Zaz Zazula or the major from the Air Force?

"So, it's a good story," Dave said.

At that point, Dave Osborn had yet to ever watch a professional football game on television. There was no TV at the farm. Yet, he was starting to get to know the game. He was Cando's biggest player his senior year at 185 pounds, and also the fastest. Kids just weren't that big back then – the Cubs' defensive ends weighed about 150 pounds.

"I was pretty fast, I would get around the end, turn the corner and some of those cornerbacks – I would just run over them," Dave said. "One hundred and eighty-five pounds was a good-sized guy in my day. Kids didn't lift weights like they do today. I was 6-feet tall and I think I was the biggest guy on the basketball team. In a town like Cando, most of your athletes played every sport. You had to, there were not enough people. In the fall it was football, then right to basketball, and then right to baseball and track at the same time. In baseball, you would practice with the team and then run over and do a couple of starts on the track team."

In Dave's senior class of 32, only eight were boys, and all eight played at least one sport.

And only one of the eight headed to Grand Forks on a football scholarship. Thanks to a referee.

His UND career paralleled his high school days in terms of playing time. The NCAA didn't allow freshmen to play varsity ball back then, so Osborn was on the Sioux freshman team. He doesn't remember many games, maybe three against Minnesota-Duluth, Bemidji State and Minnesota-Crookston frosh teams. And even with that there were so many players that playing time was tough to come by.

At one point, Kathie said her sister Judy, two years older than Dave, recalled one day when Dave called home and said he didn't want to stay at UND and wanted to come back to help farm. So, he came home.

"Dad turned around and drove him back to Grand Forks to college," Kathie said.

His sophomore season was spent as a backup running back, so far down the depth chart that he didn't make the travel squad. Again, the old rules were not in his favor. Teams were not allowed to substitute freely, so the more two-way players a team had, the better. Still, Osborn hung in there and dressed for home games, eventually seeing the field in the second to the last game of the season.

"I carried the ball twice, I think, and both were a couple of long runs and I scored a touchdown," he said. "All of a sudden, they were like, where did this guy come from?"

Dave Osborn started the last game of his sophomore season. And that was a sign of things to come.

His total games played to date at that point at UND including high school? Certainly, fewer than 20 and most likely around 17. He had yet to even letter with the Sioux.

A farm kid, he started to make hay his junior and senior seasons at UND. He scored four touchdowns in his first start and became the team's leading rusher both years. In the 1963 season opener, he had 12 carries for 202 yards in a game against Minnesota-Duluth, averaging 16.8 yards per carry. The Sioux went 6-3 that year, 4-2 in the North Central Conference, including a 21-7 win over NDSU. They were even better his senior year going 8-1, beating NDSU for the Nickel Trophy 20-13, and were 5-1 in the conference.

In his Lakeville home, Dave has several UND treasures including a game-worn No. 41 jersey. It's rather simple in design, a green jersey with white numbers and no UND or Sioux lettering. It's hanging on a hook along with his old college track spikes.

In 1963, Osborn finished with 92 carries for 613 yards and five touchdowns. He had one catch for eight yards. He was a little better in his senior season getting 118 carries for 631 yards and 10 touchdowns. They made more use of him in the passing game with seven receptions for 159 yards and one touchdown. Perhaps he shined the most on the punt team where he had five returns for 112 yards, an average of 22.4 yards. His longest return was 50 yards. He made the all-NCC team in 1964.

Still, he wasn't a slam-dunk professional prospect. Osborn, in fact, doesn't remember a single scout watching him play. But, somehow, somebody got word about the kid from Cando, North Dakota, who made a splash in his final two years of college. The Minnesota Vikings were willing to give him a shot.

At the NFL Draft in November, the Vikings made him a 13th-round draft choice in the age when there were 20 rounds.

"I had no idea I was going to be drafted," he said.

A slight problem arose in immediately signing with the team, however. Before he left for the Twin Cities to visit the team, Zazula the track coach, said whatever you do don't sign a contract because that will make you ineligible for the spring track and field season. The sprinter Osborn was one of the top point-getters for the Sioux. Remember, Zazula was the guy who got Osborn a college scholarship so Osborn felt some sense of indebtedness.

The Vikings, however, didn't want their draft picks running track. But Osborn figured he could stall himself for some time before signing a contract. He got ready to head from his hotel in Minneapolis to the Minneapolis-St. Paul airport for a 5:30 p.m. departure.

"Then a guy comes to my hotel room and says, seriously Dave, we just got a call from the airport and your flight was canceled," Osborn said. "We can't get you on until a 9 a.m. flight tomorrow morning. As it turned out, they were stalling me."

The pro team won the stalling game. These days, all professional prospects have an agent of some type to handle contractual matters. Osborn had to figure it out himself.

"I ended up signing a contract that night or I might still be in the hotel room," he said.

***

Training camp for the Minnesota Vikings in 1965 was held in Bemidji, Minnesota, on the campus of Bemidji State University. It was not a pleasant place for a rookie trying to make an NFL roster. Dave Osborn came from a small school that in all reality most of the players from Division I major college schools had never heard of. About the only NFL player of note from North Dakota at that point that anybody in the 1960s knew about was kicker Steve Myhra. He played high school football in Wahpeton, attended UND and became a 12th-round draft choice of the Baltimore Colts in 1956 as an offensive guard or linebacker. He emerged as a kicker for the Colts in his second year in the league.

Myhra, by the way, played a major role in what was affectionately known as "The Greatest Game Ever Played." The 1958 NFL Championship game took place at Yankee Stadium between the Colts and New York Giants. The Baltimore quarterback was Johnny Unitas. The Giants' big-play receiver was Frank Gifford. Myhra became a star when kicked a 20-yard field goal with seven seconds left in regulation sending the game into overtime. Baltimore won 23-17 in the first NFL playoff game to go into sudden-death OT.

With so few NFL players from Osborn's neck of the woods, he rated his chances of making the Vikings as not good. In fact, he figured just hanging around for a little while before getting cut would help his chances in landing a better coaching job, an occupation suiting his life path.

Training camp started right after the July 4th holiday. The head coach for Minnesota was Norm Van Brocklin, an old school guy who believed in talking tough and working players to the bone. He yelled and shouted. Early in camp, Osborn sensed the coach's style played in his favor.

Van Brocklin, an interesting character, who after leading the Philadelphia Eagles to the 1960 NFL championship felt he was in line to take over the Eagles' head coaching job. A year later, after his belief that the Eagles went back on their agreement, he took the same position with the Vikings expansion team. In the revolving door style of camp, Osborn observed no player was safe from getting cut.

"There were like 70 rookies, every day they would cut 10 and bring another 10 in," he said. "There was constant turnover. I didn't know what to expect competing with these other guys from bigger conferences. Then I realized I wasn't just here to try and get a better coaching job, but that I thought I could make this team. I'm just as good as these guys from the bigger schools. Van Brocklin liked hard-nosed guys and I'm the type of guy who would run through a brick wall and then run through another brick wall. So, I hung in there."

He hung in there so well he made the team.

"I might not have had enough talent at the time to make a lot of teams and those teams wouldn't have waited for me," Dave said. "But Van Brocklin saw something in me and said, hey, this farm kid is tough. Let's hang with him and that's what he did."

Osborn spent his rookie season returning kickoffs and punts. It was a tough depth chart to crack since the Vikings had Tommy Mason, their first pick as the No. 1 player taken in the 1961 draft. He was a pretty consistent producer rushing for 740, 763, 691 and 591 yards from 1962-65. But in 1966, Osborn's second year in the pros, Mason hurt his knee in the seventh game. At the time, Osborn saw himself as the fourth string running back.

On the sideline, the players stood as far away from Van Brocklin as they could, mainly because they were afraid of him. The second string running back couldn't be immediately found, which was followed by Van Brocklin shouting the following word:

"Osborn!"

Dave wondered why Van Brocklin was calling his name. But he ran up to the coach anyway. Van Brocklin put his arm around him. He looked Osborn in the eye.

"Get in there and see what you can fuck up," Van Brocklin said.

The coach shoved the player on the field.

"I was half stumbling getting on the field," Osborn said. "I tell people, 10 years later, I was still in there. All of a sudden, he shoved me on the field and I must have done something right. He liked me. But, boy, everybody was scared of the guy."

That was Van Brocklin's last year as the head Viking coach. The new head man, Bud Grant, was as opposite in demeanor as a coach could be compared to Van Brocklin. Osborn thought he died and went to heaven when thinking about the difference in the two.

In Osborn, Grant recognized an honest guy who could be trusted. So did general manager Jim Finks, with whom Osborn had a trusting relationship. Before starting his third NFL season, the first with Grant as head coach, Finks called Osborn into his office to discuss the contract that season. In those days, players operated on one-year deals.

Osborn made $12,000 in his second year and was hoping to get a $3,000 raise this time around. But he didn't ask Finks, instead signing the contract without a money figure and with the following stipulation: "Whatever you think I'm worth, just write the figure in the blank."

"I told a couple of my friends and they thought I was crazy doing something like that," Osborn said.

Days went on in training camp, and Osborn hadn't heard anything from Finks. A player can't play in a game without a signed deal, so two days before the first preseason game, Finks finally called Osborn back into his office.

"Dave, I've figured out what you're worth," he told him, "so I have your contract filled out."

Osborn was sweating. Finks handed him the contract, but the running back didn't look at it. He folded it up and put it in his back pocket. Finks didn't let him leave, instead asking him to open it.

"I want to see what you think," he said.

Osborn opened it. Then he stared at it. The one-year deal called for $30,000. He would have settled for the $3,000 raise at $15,000.

"Will that work?" Finks asked.

"That will work," Osborn replied.

From that day, that's how Osborn and Finks did business every year. Osborn would sign a blank contract at some point in the summer and Finks would fill in the numbers.

"He was always fair to me," Osborn said. "The year I hurt my knee and I missed part of the season, he gave me a $1,000 raise but the other years, I just told him, Jim, all I want is to be paid for the work. Back in those days, everything was a secret. You signed your contract and you didn't tell anybody what you were making. They didn't want anybody to know what you were making."

His sister Kathie knew, and she remembers thinking her brother was making a lot of cash playing football.

"As I look back now, I guess he really wasn't," she said. "He used to say, he did it because he liked to play football and it's not all about money and things. He is probably the nicest person you'll ever want to meet."

Osborn started all 14 games in 1967, rushing for 972 yards, which would be his career high. He finished his 11-year Viking career with 4,320 yards and being selected to the Pro Bowl once in 1970. He was a three-time All-Pro who spent his final season in 1975 with the Green Bay Packers. Not many people remember that, albeit he had a limited role with the Packers that year.

In the basement of his Lakeville home, he still has a couple Green Bay items.

Dave and Beverly Osborn still own a house in Cando. They bought a place next door to where Beverly grew up after her parents moved into a senior living center in Cando. They would visit once a month and needing a place to stay, they found the house for a cheap price because of its poor condition. Restoration took work, like stripping old lead paint, but they made it to a nice place.

It's mostly a hunting shack these days.

But it's home. And instead of riding a horse to get around town, he has a nice car. Times have changed; his attitude hasn't. He's still the gritty kid on the horse.

III. Native Sons of Sakakawea

The 1977 NFL Draft at the Roosevelt Hotel in New York City was certainly not like the modern-day, made-for-TV spectacle that it is these days. The two-day, 12-round non-event featured rather notable picks in the first round but after that people probably didn't pay much attention. In Minot, N.D., Randy Hedberg went to work as a student teacher the morning of the second day of the draft, like any other day that spring semester at the Magic City Campus.

Hedberg had completed a stellar career as the Minot State quarterback, but there would be no post-season all-star game, no NFL Combine or no Pro Day to run the 40-yard dash, bench press 225 pounds as many times as he could, and no one to test your vertical and long jumps. There was nothing like that.

Hedberg left his apartment that morning, helped teach the physical education classes, and came back to his place after school. His roommate greeted him with a message from Tampa Bay Buccaneers head coach John McKay and a phone number. Hedberg returned the call and McKay relayed the news to the quarterback that the Bucs drafted him in the eighth round. He was the 196th player taken overall.

During a somewhat productive, somewhat strange, and yet not real busy two days for Tampa Bay, which had the first overall selection, they took USC running back Ricky Bell. The Bucs took USC linebacker Dave Lewis with the first pick in the second round and Alabama defensive end Charley Hannah to start the third round. Tampa would not pick again until the first pick of the eighth round, thanks to various trades and moves. In the order of colleges of their first four picks, they went with USC, USC, Alabama, and Minot State. After taking players from Boston College, Arizona State, and Florida, the Bucs chose the small college route again in North Dakota, taking North Dakota State cornerback Chuck Rodgers in the 11th round.

Hedberg was oblivious to all of this on that day. There was no ESPN, no national radio coverage and for the most part no real way of getting immediate information on all that happened at the Roosevelt Hotel. Just a conversation with McKay.

"We'll get you down here in May and teach you as much as we can," McKay told him.

Thus, the professional career started for a kid from Parshall, North Dakota, a small town in the northwest portion of the state that consists of seven streets to the north of Central Avenue and three avenues to the south. It sits on the north end of the Fort Berthold Reservation that has been subject to the plusses and minuses of the oil booms over the years and on the edge of the formation of Lake Sakakawea.

If Addison Hedberg, Randy's father, were alive today, he could tell stories of towns disappearing after the construction of the Garrison Dam was completed in 1953. A student at Minot Model High School, he could tell you of a basketball game at the small town of Shell Village, where there was a hot stove in the middle of the basketball court the players had to navigate around. He saw the disappearance of communities like Elbowoods and Sanish whose remains sit dormant under the waters of the Sakakawea. In all, nine "underwater ghost towns" lie under the big lake, but the water did not consume Addison's wheat farm four miles southwest of Parshall adjacent to the Missouri River.

***

I've always been intrigued by Elbowoods. What was the high school like? What kind of businesses were in town? Was there more than one bar on Main Street? What did it feel like to be a long-time resident only to be told your town is going to be underwater in six months so you better pack up and leave? What was it like to see the flood waters that would eventually become a permanent lake creep toward your town, ever so slowly? Knowledgeable boaters on the lake today will note that whatever is left of the town, probably just some foundations since the structures were cleared out with the dam construction, is about 60 to 90 feet underwater near Elbowoods Bay.

The town has some basketball history to it, too. The school was officially declared the 1942 North Dakota Class B state champion almost 60 years after it finished runnerup to Lakota – a 32-31 loss that must have been as heartbreaking as it gets. For the longest time, "no champion" was listed next to 1942 on the NDHSAA champions list. Lakota was found guilty of using an ineligible player. This infraction of playing a player who was too old took decades for a resolution for Elbowoods.

Nobody knows what happened to the 1942 state title trophy. Conventional lore says somebody from Elbowoods took it not long after Lakota gave up the title for the rules infraction and the trophy is now somewhere on the bottom of Lake Sakakawea. Lowell Peterson cleared some things up when he wrote a letter to the editor at The Forum in 2016:

"We were told that the Lakota team was awarded the trophy for beating Elbowoods in the final championship game. It was later learned that the superintendent of the Lakota school, B.F. Stevens, was informed that Lakota had played a student who was not eligible because of the age requirement. Mr. Stevens investigated and found that it was true. He informed the North Dakota High School Activities Association of this and Lakota returned the trophy, but it was not awarded to Elbowoods for some reason. Elbowoods appealed that decision two times. After the second appeal, the trophy was awarded to Elbowoods at a ceremony at New Town."

Why did it take the NDHSAA so long to formally recognize Elbowoods? There's a lot more to the story than just a cool name for a town. It's got athletic history. Man, does it have history.

From 1942-52, until the town got flooded out, the Elbowoods Warriors made the state basketball tournament six times. The Warriors had athletes. Man, they had athletes.

When linebacker Esley Thorton intercepted a pass in the 2014 FCS national title game against Illinois State that sealed the championship for North Dakota State, it was a victory for Elbowoods, also. Thorton has relatives dating back to the Elbowoods' era of basketball excellence. His grandfather, Esley Thorton Sr., was a Warrior.

"It's something I've heard about since I was a kid at family gatherings," Thorton said.

Thorton isn't the only one. Mark Fox, the chairman of the Three Affiliated Tribes, said many of the good Native American athletes of today have bloodlines reaching back to players on those good Elbowoods teams. NDSU women's track and field sprinter Lexi Woods, who won a Summit League Indoor title in the 200 meters, is Fox's adopted daughter. She grew up in Parshall, a four-time champ in the 400 meters at the Class B state track meet. As time goes on, remembering Elbowoods gets harder and harder for the younger generations.

Just ask Marilyn Hudson, who was part of the last graduating class at Elbowoods in 1953. She was 17 years old at the time.

"We always had good athletes at Elbowoods," she said.

That included Esley Thorton Sr., who back then was known as Esley Fox. Esley and Marilyn were classmates at a relatively new school built in 1936. She said Esley lived in the dormitory at the school, which she said was the place to be.

"I lived on a ranch a mile away and I was always envious of the kids at the dorm, there was more social activity than those of us who were stuck in the boondocks," Marilyn said. "Esley played football, basketball, he did everything. He was a very good athlete. But by the time we got in high school, everybody was planning to move and relocating somewhere else, so there wasn't as much emphasis placed on sports as there had been earlier."

The relocations split the Elbowoods athletes to a variety of towns. Some went to White Shield, some went to Parshall, some to Mandaree, and some to New Town. The Elbowoods class of '53 consisted of 21 students – 14 boys and 7 girls. But with the school being erased by a lake, there is no town to return to for a high school reunion. One all-school reunion in the early 1990s was held in New Town, but that's been about it.

"There's not too many of us left," said Marilyn, at 81 years old. "Your question is a good question: how long will the memory of Elbowoods live? Some young people who have been interested have visualized it, I think they regard it as some sort of Camelot or something. It was a beautiful place, but the living conditions were difficult. Everyone had to work hard."

Everyone remembers the '42 Warriors as the first mostly-Native American team to reach the state tournament in North Dakota high school history. The first-round pairings were as follows: Fargo Sacred Heart Academy vs. Richardton Assumption Abbey, New England St. Mary's vs. Elbowoods, Minot St. Leo's vs. Lakota and Benson County Aggies of Maddock against Alamo. Interesting. One of the criticisms of the Class B world in this century is the advantages of the private schools in larger cities playing in the smaller class. See Fargo Oak Grove, Minot Ryan, Dickinson Trinity and Shiloh Christian from Bismarck. Seems the issue is many decades old. Fargo Sacred Heart Academy, by the way, is now the modern Fargo Shanley. And, in a testament to the era of the 1940s, Sacred Heart was considered a longshot after beating favored Portland in the regional final. Yes, Portland, which is now one-fourth of Mayville-Portland-Clifford-Galesburg.

Nevertheless, the tournament presented new ground for the kids from Elbowoods, who had all of nine players, with seven native to the land. They played a style of ball, fast, that was uncommon to those days and it piqued the interest of fans in the region. Keep in mind, basketball in the '30s and '40s was mostly set shots and set plays.

"Behind-the-back passes, fancy dribbling," said Fox, whose father and uncle played on the team. "There wasn't even standing room. Everyone wanted to see what kind of ball they were playing."

They packed the little Elbowoods gym that had a heater near the sideline, partially in play. Word has it that John Rabbit Head figured out a play to use the radiator as a spring board toward the hoop. Elbowoods was different in that it had a dormitory for kids to live in while going to school, so they didn't have to travel so far from their home on the Fort Berthold Reservation.

"That was fairly new and a unique thing," Fox said.

Sadly, all nine members of the '42 team have passed away, but the stories cannot die. And the story of how the dam displaced a tribe cannot die, because it wasn't easy. The hardest part for Fox: when the tribe had to dig up the graves of their deceased and move them to higher ground. For a spiritual people, that was brutal.

People for decades assumed that for 60 years when no champion was declared for 1942 that it was because of World War II. It's an easy assumption. The headlines in The Fargo Forum the week of the '42 state tournament centered on naval battles in the Pacific. One read, in huge font, "ALLIES BATTER JAP BASES, 23 SHIPS SUNK." Or "ALLIES FIGHTING FIERCELY ON JAVA." Meanwhile, on the inside pages, a Class B basketball tournament was being fought and there weren't many words to the stories.

I would argue the lack of recognition of Elbowoods' title involves some disingenuous folks in the North Dakota High School Activities Association, who way back in the day refused to acknowledge a Native American champion. Elbowoods, by the way, held Rabbit Head out of the title game against Lakota because he turned 20 years old that day and therefore was ineligible. The Warriors played by the rules – and it took 60 years for them to be rewarded for it.

"Politics for what they are," Fox said. "A lot of teams complained that we had close games with Lakota, too, and it was unfair to give it just to Elbowoods. St. Leo's complained the most. But Elbowoods was a great team. Of those nine players, the seven Indians on the team voluntarily entered into World War II and became veterans. The two non-tribal players continued to farm."

Fox is a veteran of the U.S. Marine Corps and has a law degree from the University of North Dakota. His father played the title game on a "badly sprained ankle," he said. Sidney Fox fouled out before the third quarter was over, and so the depth got real thin. Elbowoods led the entire game until 35 seconds remained when Lakota got the advantage with a few free throws. Elbowoods came back with a hoop to regain the lead, but Lakota won the game on a couple more free throws.

"It still put Elbowoods on the map," Fox said. "Everybody was celebrating this Indian team that made it."

Legendary basketball coach Dale Brown, as the story was told to folks back in the day, watched that title game at the old Minot Auditorium. The game was sold out and he couldn't get in, so he used a little creativity climbing the shutters on the outside of the building and watched the game from a corner vantage point. He was in sixth grade.

Within a couple of months, officials discovered that Lakota used an ineligible player. It was revealed by accident when the ineligible player registered for the draft and his age became public knowledge, Fox said.

Fox approached the NDHSAA board and asked it to reverse the '42 decision in 2002. It wasn't unanimous, but ultimately Elbowoods was given its place in history. Listen to his voice, and the pain of his ancestors having to leave their town and watch it go under water still seems fresh. There was a big price to pay for Lake Sakakawea and the biggest cost wasn't the dam; it was the natives being forced out of their homeland.

"People say the building of the dam was the most devastating thing to our nation," Fox said. "It drove us up to dry, arid lands, in land where we couldn't grow crops but we were forced up there. We were very self-sufficient before that, growing corn and beans. At one time we were an original trade center. There were two in North America and we were one of them. Driving us north caused great poverty to our people. We weren't dependent on the federal government; we had our own mill, cows, and a hospital. The only thing more traumatic was a smallpox epidemic in the 1830s where we lost 80 percent of our people."

They didn't lose the Thorton family. Esley has a cherished photo, an "iconic" photo as he calls it, of his great grandfather James Hall as one of seven gentlemen hovering over the signing of the 1948 Garrison Dam Agreement. All seven have a serious look to them, and one wonders if all parties agreed. Whatever the case, it was the end of Elbowoods.

But Esley's family tradition lives on.

"Elbowoods was always described to me as a community and land that was rich in resources and joy to many," he said. "The devastation to those people is well depicted in the picture of the signing of the 1948 Garrison Dam agreement. For that community and those athletes to be recognized to this day after everything they went through is great, especially since I have family that went through those difficult times and competed athletically for Elbowoods. The athletic tradition and competitive mentality of my family members from the Fort Berthold Indian Reservation and Elbowoods is something that was passed down to my dad, and ultimately to me. I am proud of my Native American heritage and proud to have descended from people with such rich athletic traditions.

***

The Hedbergs have a cabin on Deep Water Bay on Lake Sakakawea, which is straight south of Parshall. Go another three miles straight south on the lake and you would be right on top of what used to be Elbowoods.

"We're as close to Elbowoods as anybody most of the summer," Rick Hedberg said. "We drive over the top of it with our pontoon."

The Hedbergs knew all about the Native American life, employing several Native Americans to work the farm when Randy was growing up. The family got to know some of them quite well.

"Some really dedicated workers who helped us on the farm," Rick said. "That was a neat experience growing up on a reservation. Obviously, we were a white family but the relationships we built continue into today. We don't have a lot of family there anymore – we sold most of the farm land and rent some of that land out – but I wouldn't trade it for the world. It was a great place to grow up, with the values that you develop and the mentors that you have. It was a really neat thing."

During harvest, young Randy would get up at 5 a.m. and head over to the school for 6 a.m. football practice. Farm towns commonly practiced football in the early morning, especially during harvest. After football, it was off to school all day and then Randy would get in the car and head back to the farm. He would combine until the sun went down, go home – and do it all over again.

Addison was more efficient at the harvest than most, a result of his trade as a custom combiner. Before starting a family, he would start in Texas and work his way north working the fields of the middle section of the country until ending up in North Dakota.

"We made it OK," Randy said. "There would be ups and downs because of the market of grain but dad did a lot of different things."

Addison was a mechanic who could fix almost anything. As a pilot he would land his plane on a gravel road by the farm and park the plane in the yard instead of keeping it at the local airport. The second oldest of his sons, Randy, meanwhile, could pilot any sport he tried. And he was good at all of them.

The 1970s were glory days for Parshall athletics. The Braves went undefeated during Hedberg's senior year, but in those days that was it. The North Dakota High School Activities Association playoff system started two years after he left high school, so if Parshall was indeed the best small school football team in the state, nobody will ever know. They played 11-man football with just 18 players on the roster in the bigger-school Northwest Conference.

The field in Parshall wasn't big. The Friday night lights didn't have much wattage to them. An electrical wire that connected the concession stand crossed the field of play.

"If you threw a fade in the end zone, the wire might come down," Hedberg said. "That actually happened. I hit the wire."

The Braves were a throwing team with good athletes and a few big linemen. In basketball, the Braves won their first 27 games and reached the title game in the North Dakota Class B tournament, before losing to Hillsboro.

"When you come back for all-school reunions, they always talk about those '70s teams and a lot of those kids went on to college football," Rick Hedberg said. "That's the neat thing about a small town. You're always welcome to go back and the stories always seem to get better."

Rick Hedberg, 11 years younger than Randy, quarterbacked Parshall to the 1983 9-man state title, a 16-12 win over Cooperstown. There were five kids in the Hedberg family: Gary, Randy, DeeEllen, Brent and Rick. All talented in their own right; the most special of them was Brent. Born with Down's syndrome and 10 years younger than Randy, Randy left the house by the time Brent got to the growing-up years.

"He's pretty important to us," Randy said.

Randy may have been the NFL player, but Brent was an athlete himself. He participated in the beginning years of the North Dakota Special Olympics, which was founded in the state in 1972 by Roger Kerns. Doris Hedberg, the kids' mother, insisted that Brent get involved in the program.

"He spent many years following us around so obviously he wanted to participate on his own," Rick said.

Now in his 50s, Brent remains involved, coaching a Special Olympics basketball team in Minot. He's spent a life in the mainstream, something that Doris was bound and determined to happen. Brent was born in 1964, and it was common for special needs kids to be institutionalized and removed from normal home life in North Dakota.

"My mom didn't want that to happen," Rick said, "so she made sure he was involved in everything we did. He trailed along to a lot of games, and he still does that. That's a big part of our family."

Many kids growing up in northwest North Dakota looked up to Randy Hedberg as the star quarterback and basketball player who got drafted by the NFL. The family? In a sense, they look up to Brent.

"He puts us in perspective," Rick said. "Brent always brought us back down to reality and added a lot to our family gatherings. He balanced us out, you could say in a good way."

***

One of the first players Randy Hedberg talked to when he took the assistant coaching position at North Dakota State in January of 2014 was quarterback Carson Wentz. In Hedberg, Wentz saw a coach who had been through the rigors of football at all levels, and a quarterback mentor who not only knew his stuff but walked the talk. The mutual respect was immediate. Wentz ascended to the second pick in the 2016 NFL Draft and had a shiny first couple of years in the NFL.

It was virtually opposite of the start of Hedberg's pro career.

Hedberg joined Tampa Bay, a team going through the expansion blues and a team that set an NFL record for most consecutive losses going 0-14 in its first year in 1976. The streak reached 26 games in Hedberg's rookie year. He started camp as the fourth-string quarterback, but a series of team injuries gave him the starting job in the final preseason game. He led the Bucs to a 14-0 upset victory over the Baltimore Colts giving fans hope. Some wore T-shirts titled "RH Positive, a Bucs Transfusion" along with his picture. Others had buttons that read "Why Not Minot?" High hopes despite going 10 of 25 for 148 yards and one touchdown. His teammates gave him the game ball and started giving him nicknames in earshot of reporters, like "Randy Iceberg" or the "Lonesome Polecat." Why the latter one? "Because he's from way up there in North Dakota and he seems like he's involved with everybody, yet he's so distant," running back Anthony Davis told the Associated Press.

He became a national story, getting his shot after veteran quarterbacks Mike Boryla and Gary Huff suffered knee injuries. Boryla's was a season-ender and Huff's a few weeks. The other quarterback in camp was second-year guy Parnell Dickinson from Mississippi Valley State.

Still, years later, Hedberg said he was skeptical.

"I knew I was moving up the depth chart but I didn't know I was going to make the team until the last preseason game," he said. "To be honest, I played too early, I wasn't ready to play with my background. Not like Carson was. I could have used some learning."

Hedberg's statistics reflected that. The Bucs went 0-4 with him as a starter. He threw 90 passes with no touchdowns and 10 interceptions and had a quarterback rating of 0.0. He also played behind perhaps the worst collection of offensive linemen a team could put together. He was sacked 15 times, including one blind-side hit by Mike Butler of the Green Bay Packers that left him with a concussion.

The shot sent him to the sidelines in the first half but not out of the game. Not only was the NFL Draft in the dark ages, so was concussion protocol. Hedberg went back into the game – and afterward right to the hospital, where he spent the night "not remembering any part of the game," he said.

There's a photo out there somewhere taken from an end zone angle of Randy throwing a Hail Mary pass at the end of the second quarter with no time left on the clock. Rick remembers it well because he was at the game as a junior high kid.

"You see him throwing it and you know he's half cuckoo," Rick said. "They said in the huddle that some of his teammates said he made no sense, they knew he had a concussion. But back in that day, they didn't worry about those things. I remember going up to the hospital and he asked us seven or eight times if we won the game. No, you lost another one we kept saying."

Randy was back at practice the following week, trying to figure out how not to get whacked.

"That was somewhat my issue, I probably didn't get rid of the ball quick enough," Hedberg said. "We weren't very good. We had a young team and you have to have some consistency on the offensive line. We had a bunch of guys on the offensive line who were re-treads."

Why John McKay felt the need to insert a kid from Minot State into the starting lineup could go down as one of the all-time bad coaching decisions in Tampa Bay history, if not NFL history.

Hedberg missed a few games with the concussion and never did get back to his brief icon status.

He spent the 1978 season on the injured reserve list with arm problems and was traded in the offseason to the Oakland Raiders for an undisclosed amount of cash. It was going to be tough just to make the team, with the Raiders having veteran quarterbacks Kenny Stabler and Mike Rae and a young Jim Plunkett. Released by the Raiders, he had a chance after that to play in the Canadian Football League. By November, he returned to Minot State, accepting a position as an assistant football coach and admissions counselor.

"I came back to Minot, that's what I was comfortable with," Hedberg said. "I was thinking there would be more security in coaching than playing – and that probably isn't true."

Football wasn't over. He remained in touch with the Packers after his release from the Raiders, and in January of 1980, a year out of the game, Green Bay signed him. By July, he reported to the Packers' training camp. Released by the end of July, he returned to Minot State as an assistant coach. This time, coaching was here to stay.

Hedberg was a rare multi-sport athlete in college playing football, basketball, and baseball, earning four letters in each. He probably could have played a higher level of football, certainly Division II, but chose Minot State so he could play more than one sport. He threw for over 5,700 yards in his college career with 49 touchdowns. He was a starting forward for three years on the basketball team leading the team in scoring his sophomore and junior years. As a pitcher on the baseball team, his best year was going 5-3 in 1975.

Eventually, he did something almost rarer – become a head coach in all three sports in the same season. He was named the Minot State head football coach in 1981, essentially switching positions with Bert Lindholm, who stayed on as an assistant football coach and head track and field coach. Coaching more than one sport was common in those days in the small college game, with head coaches in one sport also being assistants in another. In 1985, Hedberg ran the football program like he always did and was also an assistant basketball coach.

"We would finish playing in November and then I would recruit in November and December," he said. "Then I would start with basketball practice in early January."

This season would be different. Halfway through the basketball season, right around the time Hedberg finished his football recruiting, head basketball coach Ken Becker was fired, and needing somebody to fill in, the school turned to Hedberg. The Beavers went 7-9 in Hedberg's lone stint as a head college basketball coach. Becker had been the head baseball coach, so Hedberg did that job, too.

***

In early January in 2015, Hedberg was no longer a head football coach and assistant basketball coach. Or a baseball coach for that matter. He's a Division I assistant for North Dakota State and the Bison are in the FCS championship game against Illinois State. He entered his fourth decade in the game as the quarterbacks coach for NDSU. There were some stellar teams in those years, from the University of North Dakota to Southern Illinois.

On the day before the title game, he reflected on something he thought he would never do: coach in a national championship game.

"No question about it, I appreciate it," Hedberg said. "I appreciate the guys I work with, the staff and this opportunity. You don't get a chance to play for a national championship very often, and that's something pretty special."

Hedberg was familiar with the Missouri Valley Football Conference having coached at SIU, where the Salukis reached the FCS quarterfinals in 2009. But that's as far as he got in the Division I playoffs.

"He's been coaching for what, 30 years, and this is his first time ever?" said NDSU running back John Crockett. "People don't understand, we've been spoiled. Bison fans have been spoiled. The state of North Dakota has been spoiled. It never really happens like this. This is really a great thing that is happening. Win, lose, or draw, people have to understand this has been an amazing run."

Hedberg understood. He left SIU a year prior to join first-year head coach Chris Klieman's staff at NDSU. He wanted to return to the state. His state. He was the head coach at Minot State from 1982-89 and an assistant at the University of North Dakota from 1996-98.

"I think all of these coaches are enjoying this," Carson Wentz said. "It was a little bit of a difficult road to get here this year, there were a lot of doubters and those type of things, so it's been a lot of fun for everyone involved."

Hedberg and Wentz were linked as coach-player on a one-to-one basis probably more than any other assistant-to-player on the team. In a lot of ways, they seem alike, such as in stature — both have ideal quarterback height — and in mentality. Both take a calm, cool approach to football.

"Carson elevates the other three quarterbacks in the room because of his work ethic," Hedberg said. "That's one thing I noticed and mentioned to Coach Klieman in the spring: Our quarterbacks work hard, and Carson led the charge. When you have a starting quarterback or a starting receiver or whomever leading the charge, you expect good things."

Wentz texted Klieman at 6:15 Sunday morning – the morning after the team returned from the 2013 title game in Frisco. Wentz wanted to meet the team's new quarterbacks coach. It was the culmination of an undefeated season, perhaps the best team in FCS history, and it was the end of a tormented month when Bohl announced he was leaving for Wyoming, yet stayed on as the Bison head coach. It was pretty well known that Klieman was going to hire Hedberg, with Klieman banking on the veteran Hedberg to take Wentz to the next level. Brock Jensen had just finished his career as the all-time winningest quarterback in FCS history and now it was Wentz's turn.

Hedberg and Wentz talked for about an hour that morning before Wentz went home for the remainder of semester break. They talked about fundamentals and leadership.

"Carson is a very intelligent guy," Hedberg said later that day.

Almost a year later, the two were in Frisco. Hedberg said earlier that week that one of the things he was most looking forward to in Frisco was the Bison's Friday practice where former players gather around the team at the conclusion of the open workout. Klieman continued the tradition that former head coach Craig Bohl started with the 2011 title game. Hedberg could rip off the names of Bison legendary figures like Ron Erhardt with the best of them and, as usual, there were several players from the 1960s and 1970s at the Friday practice.

"I've heard from Coach Klieman and other coaches that this is important and special," Hedberg said. "The tradition — I go back to being a North Dakota native and those guys from way back when the tradition got started here. I have connections to most of those coaching staffs as they went through. There's a great tradition of coaches."

A tradition that Hedberg experienced first-hand starting in the 2014 NDSU season. By the end of the 2017 season, he had three national title rings.

And Elbowoods has its trophy. At least in spirit. As for Hedberg? Those late Friday afternoons in Frisco talking with the Bison alums were precious. His career so prolific in so many ways in the state of North Dakota. He even spent a few months at Minot State with legendary state high school star Steve Blehm.

IV. Legend of Steve Blehm

Navigating the great outdoors is a gift for Steve Blehm and those who hunt or fish with him could vouch that there is nobody better. He's the first one to spot the deer, off in some brush where the common man needs binoculars to spot. Or he can detect the wings of a bird well before anybody else can. When he tells fellow hunters to get their guns ready, they know Steve saw something that they didn't.

The eyes. His eyes. They aren't the pupils of Superman, but then again, nobody can be real sure. Walk into his garage/man cave/shed at his house on the rolling hills outskirts of Staunton, Virginia, and on the wall are wildlife trophies everywhere, most shot by either himself or his brother, David Blehm.

The antlers of elk, deer, and antelope are like wallpaper. Those animals probably didn't stand a chance once they got into the visionary scope of Steve, mostly because of those eyes. He's a visionary ace because he hasn't been able to hear since the age of 1, the probable result of medicine given to him when he was sick. Cheryl, his sister, was given the same medication and also has hearing loss.

It was not for the faint of heart when his mother, Irene, found out about his hearing loss. She sensed something was different with her baby, although there were people who didn't believe her. She took Steve to the doctor, and in the exam room the doctor snapped his fingers on each side of Steve's head.

"Yep," the doctor said, "he's deaf."

That story is told by Sarah Blehm, Steve's youngest daughter, who used the word "callous" when describing the cold mannerism of the doctor.

Yep, he's deaf.

But after spending a day at the Blehm home on the beautiful 10-acre spread in the Shenandoah Valley, a visitor walks away thinking he's the one with the disability. It takes 5½ hours just to mow it, with the drive in something akin to driving into Augusta National Golf Club only without the Butler Cabin and the golf course. When the family first moved in they were the only house in the area. Now there are neighbors, albeit still more than a shouting distance away. The back yard is wooded, with Steve sometimes taking his bow in there to go hunting. It's technically in the city limits, so only a bow is allowed, but any hunting is good hunting for the legendary basketball player from the North Dakota School for the Deaf.

Oh, did we forget to mention that?

So did he – to his three daughters Vera, Maddie, and Sarah. They never found out about the 47.3 points per game he scored in 1971, or his appearance in Sports Illustrated's "Faces in the Crowd" weekly collection of unique feats across the country, until they were almost teenagers. The article read: "Steve Blehm, 19, a senior at the North Dakota School for the Deaf, scored 3,589 points during his four-year basketball career, setting a state single-game record of 85. Blehm averaged 61 points per game in tournament play this season."

The daughters discovered his basketball legend almost by accident. A sportswriter at the local Staunton newspaper who graduated with Vera in high school in Staunton got wind of it. He wrote a story about the local post office worker who happened to score 85 points in one game.

"We were like, 'What you talking about?'" Sarah said. "He said your dad is a big deal in the basketball world. We're like, 'What?'"

Not long after that, Sports Illustrated came out with its 50 greatest athletes in all 50 states, with Blehm landing at No. 22 on the list. That's when it became official with the family: OK, he is a big deal.

The reason for the secrecy is humility. Be humble. He got that from his father, Milton, who while in high school won five state championships – two in basketball, one in football, one in baseball, and one in track and field. Steve didn't find out about all of those accomplishments until after his own high school career.

"I think it's best," Steve said. "You encourage your kids to do their best and learn about you later. Motivate them, and they don't have to live up to any kind of expectations."

The humbleness was so pronounced in him that he didn't let Sarah or the other two daughters know of some scrapbook items until I showed up at his ranch in early June of 2018. They were stored somewhere, all these years, without the kids having a clue. Sarah's eyes lit every few minutes with each passing article in a scrapbook that the kids never knew existed. The stories and articles were numerous, many written by former Devils Lake Journal sportswriter Mike Belmore. I'm sure "Boomer," as we knew him in the sportswriter world, saw how Blehm operated. Fans were given a scorecard at the School for the Deaf's games, with 15 "2s" signifying field goals and 10 circles to fill in for free throws to keep track of each player's points. At the bottom was another line that read "Extra line for Steve Blehm fans" followed by 15 more "2s" and 10 more circles. There were many times when that extra line came in handy.

Those eyes.

The ones that can spot a deer before anybody else. As a deaf basketball player, his eyes were the reason he was able to score at will. Nobody could tell him a defender was coming up from behind, so he was always looking, peripheral vision at its best. The awareness of players around him was at an elevated level at all times. In a sense, his eyes were also his ears.

Steve Blehm was not the best high school basketball player the state of North Dakota produced, and, in all probability perhaps not in the top five or 10. The best include Phil Jackson from Williston, who of course went on to a legendary career at the University of North Dakota and later the NBA. Scott Guldseth from Edinburg signed at LSU before transferring to the UND. Les Jepsen from Bowbells played at the University of Iowa, was a second round NBA draft choice and finished his career in the CBA. The state's all-time leading scorer, A.J. Jacobson from Fargo Shanley, went to Division I North Dakota State and played in an NCAA tournament. Blehm went to Minot State for a year and then transferred to Gallaudet University in Washington, D.C.

No, he was not the best player by any means.

But he is the greatest.

National sports historian Doug Huff lists the top 10 single-season scoring averages in the history of high school basketball in the United States as of the end of the 2017 season. His list was documented on Maxpreps.com's assessment of the top 10 scorers:

    1.   54.0. Bobbie Joe Douglas, Marion, Louisiana, 1980: Douglas set the national record for scoring average in a season by scoring 2,052 points in 38 games at Marion, a Class C-sized school in northeastern Louisiana. Douglas had a high game of 93 points and finished with 4,070 points in his career. Douglas went on to play at Northeast Louisiana University, but he did not match his high-scoring ways from high school.

    2.   53.7. Ervin Stepp, Phelps, Kentucky, 1980: The Stepp name can be found throughout the state record book in Kentucky. Ervin's brothers Jim and Joe each led the state in scoring during the 1970s while Ervin led the nation in scoring as a junior with 47.2 points per game. Ironically, Stepp did not lead the nation when he averaged 53.7 points during his senior year in 1980 (see No. 1 Bobbie Joe Douglas).

Stepp had a career high of 75 points in one game and played college basketball at Eastern Kentucky.

3. 52.4. Johnny Benjamin, Central Florida Academy, Orlando, Florida, 1988. Benjamin had a troubled high school and post-high school career, but he was unstoppable his senior year at Central Florida Academy when he averaged 52.4 points per game. Benjamin played his sophomore year at CFA before transferring to Jones (Orlando, Florida) as a junior.

4. 50.9: Bennie Fuller, Arkansas School for the Deaf, Little Rock, Arkansas. According to Bob Heist in a story written for the News Journal in 2012, Fuller is the only deaf basketball player to ever score over 100 points in a game. He did so on Jan. 19, 1971, thanks to a 38-point flurry in the fourth quarter. Fuller set the national scoring record for season average that year with 50.9 points per game and he finished his career with 4,896 career points.

5. 50.4. Kent Hyde, Onida, South Dakota, 1954. The first player to ever average over 50 points per game, Hyde set the record in 1954 with 1,411 points in 28 games while leading Onida to a Class B state championship. A 6-foot-5 center, Hyde reportedly had 42 offers coming out of high school but chose to play at South Dakota State. Drafted by the St. Louis Hawks, Hyde's basketball career ended due to a back injury.

6. 49.8. Steve Farquhar, Calvary Baptist, Lakewood, New Jersey, 1985. A 6-foot-2 guard who played college basketball at Liberty, Farquhar scored 1,494 points in 30 games for the tiny New Jersey school. His 37.5 ppg average for a career ranks third in national history according to the National Federation of State High School Associations record book.

7. 49.6. Bjorn Broman, Lakeview Christian Academy, Duluth, Minnesota, 2015. It was the highest average since Johnny Benjamin in '88.

8. 47.7. Tom McMillen, Mansfield, Pennsylvania, 1970. McMillen concluded his high school career in 1970 and was hailed as one of the greatest high school basketball players ever. He attended the University of Maryland and earned a silver medal in the 1972 Olympics. He also became a Rhodes Scholar and played 13 years in the NBA before beginning a career as a United States Congressman.

9. 47.4. Ochiel Swaby, North Miami, Florida, 1991. The national scoring leader as a senior in high school, Swaby played college ball at the University of Miami and Central Florida and had a brief stint with the Charlotte Hornets in the NBA.

10. 47.3. Steve Blehm, School for the Deaf, Devils Lake, North Dakota, 1971. Blehm set his record during his sophomore season, when his lowest scoring game of the season was a 32-point outing. Blehm also holds the state record with 85 points in one game.

"He kept life pretty exciting at our house for years," said Irene Blehm, now living in Loveland, Colorado. "He had a lot of publicity, which was for sure. He was a very good kid, never gave us any problems. He gave us a lot of fun problems."

***

The Blehm family grew up in Bismarck, N.D., moving into a new development at 1429 22nd Street South. Milton and Irene had three children: David, Steve and Cheryl. Raising deaf children certainly had its share of challenges and moments they look back at now with a chuckle.

Like the time when Steve went for a two- or three-mile run in Bismarck at night because it was hot outside. A Bismarck police officer, who was looking for a reported peeping tom in the area around the same time, thought it seemed suspicious that this kid was running – so he yelled for Steve to stop. Obviously, the boy couldn't hear the officer, so he kept on running.

"We don't know why, maybe he thought Steve was running from something," Irene said. "He finally caught up to him and pulled Steve back – and it just shocked him."

They checked his tennis shoes to see if they matched footprints found outside of a window. Finally, the mistake was realized and the officer came to the house to apologize to the family, saying he didn't know the boy was deaf.

"It was a funny issue at the time," Irene said. "Things like that would happen."

Milton loved the outdoors, a hobby that he passed on to his two boys. They would take their Lund boat and drive 70 miles south to Fort Yates, North Dakota, camp along the Missouri River and fish in one of the most scenic areas of the state. When young Steve wasn't in school at the Devils

Lake School for the Deaf, or shooting baskets in the driveway of his home, he hunted or fished. He endlessly shot baskets, often playing the game "Around the World," where the shooter picks spots from one corner, out to the top of the key and over to the other corner. He cannot advance unless he makes the shot. Steve would not quit until he went "Around the World" twice without missing.

"Every time dad talks about North Dakota, there's this huge nostalgia," Sarah said.

School was another matter. The family tried the Bismarck Public School system for Steve for one year, but it didn't work to their satisfaction. One teacher simply refused to teach Steve.

"He couldn't handle it, you almost have to have a special teacher," Irene said.

Milton and Irene faced the difficult decision to send him to Devils Lake and live in the dorm. Milton was on the road a lot working for an insurance company, so he was able to visit Steve more often than Irene. It wasn't easy seeing their son off to an out-of-town school at such a young age.

"That was a big, big day for us to do it," Irene said, "but it was a good one because he did so well. Bismarck was quite a ride, especially in the winter time. We would bring him back on weekends when we could. It was quite a jaunt when the weather was bad."

Steve remembers going away to school being tough on his parents. They knew the exact mileage from door to door: 189 miles. Steve lived in a large dorm room with 8 to 10 other students. Sarah, while communicating via sign language with her father, laughed and wondered how anybody got to sleep with so many vibrant boys in one room. The School for the Deaf offered something hard for deaf kids to get in the public-school system – a social life of communicating with other kids. The importance of socialization and having others with whom to communicate is a factor often overlooked. It's not healthy being in one's world all the time.

"The public-school system still has a long way to go," Sarah said. "I do think it's getting better. Technology is helping. I think you'll see apps where you'll be able to interpret on the phone. There's been a lot of advancement but there are still kids who are isolated."

She questions if allotted funding reaches the deaf kids in the public system. She saw at an early age the meaning of socialization between deaf kids when at 10 years old she went with her family to a North Dakota

School for the Deaf reunion. She remembers being bored, but she also remembers her father having a grand time with old friends.

"They don't get that all the time," Sarah said.

Facetime technology on a smartphone has been a godsend to Steve and his daughters, giving them the ability to sign through the video system. Steve says the education of the deaf student is an on-going adaptation and although strides have been made over the years, more need to be made. I couldn't agree more. In an hour at a restaurant in Staunton, I realized the hurdles that exist if Sarah wasn't along to interpret for her father.

"People sometimes get nervous," Steve said. "They don't know how to respond. I am here to educate people until the day I die."

Steve was a quiet kid in high school and wasn't into dating girls. Coach Henry Brenner says Blehm was usually the first one to practice and the last one to leave. About the only time he gave Brenner trouble was right away in seventh grade when he and another student missed basketball practice to go hunting.

"I was furious," Henry said. "They had to run, run, run, and then he started crying. Other than that, we got along fine. I had no problems with him."

The only other issue occurred when he was senior and the Bulldogs had just lost to Edmore in a regular season tournament. Steve went down to the basement of the gym after the game, followed by his father Milton, and the kid threw a temper tantrum.

"He just lost it," Brenner said. "His father had to calm him down. Mr. Blehm told me to sit him down the next game against Crary. I sat him down the first period."

The Bulldogs went on to beat Crary.

Established in 1890, the North Dakota School for the Deaf has a long history. Currently, it has a comprehensive academic program for students in kindergarten through 8th grade with high school students attending Devils Lake High School. The NDSD offers sign language services to the public school. The original three-story brick structure built in 1892 was torn down in 1975.

The extracurricular background is proud and meaningful. The school has three North Dakota state championships, winning both the 1975 Class B Track and Field indoor and outdoor titles and the 1976 indoor championship thanks to sprinter Drexel Lawson, a one-man scoring machine. The head coach, Dwight Rafferty, went on to coach the gold medal-winning United States team in the Pan Am Olympian Games for the Deaf in Venezuela. A prized graduate is Phyllis Frelich from the 1962 class, who won a Tony Award for her performance in the play "Children of a Lesser God." She was the first deaf actor or actress to win a Tony.

The gymnasium, which was built in 1953, is used for recreational purposes today. Steve Blehm running the floors was a thing of beauty. That 85-point game on Jan. 27, 1971? It could have been 100. Against Hampden at the Ramsey County Tournament, the game ended with the School for the Deaf winning 122-22. Sitting in his living room in Staunton, Steve said his Bulldogs had just six players because other players were being saved for a junior varsity tournament. It became apparent to the team that the goal was to beat the current state record at the time of 71 points held by Gordon Baumgartner of Oriska. The North Dakota Class A record of 69 points was set earlier that season by Bob Eaglestaff of Fort Yates.

"The fans and the teachers wanted me to keep him in to break the record," Brenner said recently. "It really wasn't my idea. They kept saying, keep him in, keep him in."

Blehm beat the 71 somewhere in the third quarter and Brenner took him out in what was assumed for the rest of the game. Problem was, a North Dakota Deaf player fouled out, and Steve remembers Brenner asking the referees if the Bulldogs could continue with four players on the floor. The refs said no, and Blehm went back into the game.

Steve wasn't sure how much he played in the fourth quarter, but he is certain he didn't play the entire eight minutes. Asked if he could have scored 100 that game, Steve stayed silent, with a hint of a grin. His humble nature kicked in.

The answer was yes.

"If there were 3-pointers back then, yes," Brenner said. "He had good timing. Just an all-around great player. He was extremely talented, coachable, and smart. He could shoot from any angle from 1 foot to 22 feet."

Brenner took some criticism for that 85 points from the Hampden folks. They accused him of running up the score. Later that spring at the Ramsey County track meet, Brenner said the Hampden coach got some revenge by disqualifying Steve in an event saying something to the effect that he went over a line in a long jump. Or something like that.

Interesting side note to that state-record performance: Blehm didn't play the following game against Churchs Ferry because Churchs Ferry (a town that was later bought out by the government because of the rising Devils Lake) refused to play if Blehm played. The Bulldogs cooperated and Blehm spent that game working the concession stand. Fans wondered: "What is Steve doing in the concession stand?" News of his scoring outbursts were drawing more fans than usual, many coming just to watch him play.

"Churchs Ferry was short of players, some of them were injured," Brenner said. "Churchs Ferry appreciated us not playing Steve."

Broadcaster Lee Halvorson, who described many of Blehm's games for KDLR-AM radio in Devils Lake, recalls the School for the Deaf having just seven or eight players.

"Henry Brenner is just a wonderful, wonderful guy," Halvorson said. "He could have taken him out of the game earlier but the other guys were not basketball players. They were just guys who put on a uniform. They had to have some semblance of a team out there. As the game went on, everybody knew it was going to be the all-time record."

Halvorson was dumbfounded at the thought of Blehm having the 3-point line in that game. He said the Bulldogs' offense was rather simple: the other four players would hang out on the perimeter and Blehm would run around them like they were a picket fence until he found an opening.

"And a lot of those shots came outside the perimeter," Halvorson said. "Had they had the 3-point line, I would say 40 percent of his shots came outside of 3-point range. The reason I say that is because at the School for the Deaf that year, he didn't have a lot of good teammates. That didn't happen until he was a senior. He was so gifted of a basketball player. He was never cocky or arrogant or anything like that. Just a good kid. He was pure. He was just pure."

A typical conversation between Halvorson and coaches from the area were like the one he had with Lakota head coach Duane Schwab. Blehm had 42 against Lakota two weeks prior when Schwab came on Halvorson's pre-game show.

"What do you have to do to beat the School for the Deaf?" Halvorson asked.

"The key is Steve Blehm, if we can hold him to 30 or less, we can win," Schwab replied.

Blehm scored 52 and the Bulldogs won.

Afterward, Halvorson ran into Schwab.

"We did a heck of a job defensively, didn't we?" Schwab joked.

Halvorson is a North Dakota Hall of Fame broadcaster who worked the trade for 43 years. That 85-point game is among the top four of games he'll never forget. The other three were a Williston State regional basketball game, Devils Lake's Doyle Heisler scoring 44 points against defensive-minded, Dick Vinger-coached Grand Forks Central, and the 1977 eight overtime state hockey championship game between Grand Forks Red River and Grand Forks Central that ended in a 1-1 tie.

Steve Blehm is in good company.

Meanwhile, Milton and Irene commuted from Bismarck as best they could. In Milton's case, as a traveling businessman, he was a rock star of a parent attending 90 of Steve's 95 career games. One of the game's he missed: the 85-point game against the Hampden Honkers.

***

The best seat in the house for Blehm's prep career was Brenner, who retired in 1992 after 36 years with the North Dakota School for the Deaf. Odds meant nothing to Henry. He attended a school for the deaf in his native Rhode Island before enrolling in a public high school in Woonsocket, Rhode Island, in the late 1940s. At that time awareness of the hearing impaired wasn't what it is now. He was an all-state football and basketball player. He was a deaf role model to kids like Steve, who saw that overcoming a disability is possible.

At the University of Rhode Island, Brenner was an all-Yankee Conference offensive guard in football. He was 5-foot-9 and 185 pounds. The Philadelphia Eagles showed interest, most likely as a defensive back.

He and his wife, Jo-Ann, are spending their retirement years at a twin home in south Fargo. It's easy to spot Henry's vehicle – his license plate reads "URI" for his allegiance to his college alma mater. He has mementos from Blehm's playing days, like handwritten statistics from Steve's years on varsity. Henry wanted to bring Steve up to varsity as an eighth-grader but was denied by his school administration. As a freshman in 1968-69, Blehm averaged 35.8 points and 15.4 rebounds per game. After his 47.3 average as a sophomore, he averaged 37.2 points as a junior and 43.8 as a senior. His field goal percentage went up every year from 43 percent to 48 percent to 49 percent to 50 percent.

As testament to having better teammates around him as the years went on, he attempted 944 field goals as a sophomore and 810 as a senior. In 94 career games, he made 1,516 field goals in 3,188 attempts with an accuracy of 48 percent. He made 827 of 1,152 free throws for 72 percent, finished with 3,859 points for a career average of 41.1 points per game.

Twenty-six years ago, I interviewed the Brenners for a story in The Forum newspaper at their home in Devils Lake shortly before his 1992 retirement dinner. He had an enthusiasm and quiet sarcasm about him that made one feel welcome in just a few minutes. At the time, the couple who met at the University of Rhode Island, had been married 36 years. They raised their three sons, Mark, Terry, and Tim in Devils Lake. Mark's first year at Devils Lake St. Mary's High School remains a popular family story.

His first varsity game was against the North Dakota School for the Deaf – with his father on the other bench.

"My coach didn't indicate to me that I was going to play varsity that night," Mark said. "I was assuming I would play junior varsity and watch the varsity game from the bench. All of a sudden, the coach calls my number and told me it was my time to report in. I remember looking over at my dad on the other bench and he was rubbing his eyes, really playing it off. Later in the game, they had called a time out and I was good at sign language. He was telling his team what they were going to do and I stepped out of our huddle and said, 'They're going to run a 2-2-1 press.' So, I started telling my teammates what they were going to do. Then dad looked at me and said, 'Oh brother.' Then he got all of his kids standing up on chairs around him and he was down in the middle of the huddle signing."

That story brought laughter to Henry and Jo-Ann, who always cheered for her kids whenever they played Henry's team. She turned to her husband after my question and said in a combination of voice (Henry could read lips) and sign language: "Because they had only four years. You had 36."

In those 36 years, Henry Brenner told me the Blehm years were one of his favorites.

"He had talent but he also had a great work ethic," Henry said.

It was also one of his biggest disappointments, Mark said, when the School for the Deaf lost in the region championship game to Fessenden. The Bulldogs were 66-24 in Blehm's career, but never got to the big North Dakota Class B show. It was the closest the School for the Deaf ever got to the state tournament and was tough to swallow because the team wasn't at full strength. One player missed the title game with a sprained ankle and another played with mononucleosis.

Fessenden had standout player Rocky Fleming, who was assigned to guard Blehm. Fessenden head coach Bill Fruhwirth told Lee Halvorson that if Fleming could hold Blehm to 35 points or less, his team had a good chance to go to state. Blehm had 41, but his less-than-full-strength teammates couldn't pick up the slack.

At the time of his graduation, Blehm held three national high school records: highest career average (41.1 ppg in 90 games), highest average as a sophomore (47.3), and highest average as a freshman (35.8).

Times were golden for all involved. Brenner lost his hearing at 9 months old. It never slowed him down. He loved football growing up and loved coaching the sport in Devils Lake. He said when the School for the Deaf dropped football in 1970, "it broke my heart." Steve Blehm was a freshman at the time, and most likely a promising prospect as a defensive back on defense and a running back and wide receiver on offense. After football was dropped, he picked up cross country, where he finished 13th in the state meet his senior year.

"I could have pushed it more," he said.

Steve Blehm enrolled at Gallaudet University; ironically, the university's football team invented the huddle. Like Henry gathering his players around him so his son Mark couldn't steal the sign language, the same scenario applied to a player named Paul Hubbard in the early 1890s. Hubbard gathered his teammates around him so he could shield his signing from the opposing team.

At Gallaudet, Steve left as the school's seventh all-time leading scorer. For all the points in both high school and college, consider this: he did it without the 3-point line, a player who was sharp with the 20- to 22-foot jump shot. Furthermore, he was the best player on the United States basketball team that won a gold medal in the 1977 World Games for the Deaf. He was the only deaf athlete in Sports Illustrated's 50 greatest sports figures in any state.

To get a perspective on his career total of 3,930 points, second place on the all-time list in North Dakota high school history belongs to Ron Waggoner of New Town, who scored 2,714 points in the early 1960s. That's a difference of 1,216 points, which makes it seemingly an unbreakable record. He's the Wilt Chamberlain of high school standards in his home state. Chamberlain once scored 100 points in an NBA game in 1962; the next closest since then is 81.

***

Not everything in Steve's life was as euphoric as the Sports Illustrated publicity or catching the perfect walleye. He's had heartaches, too.

"Our life has had some ups and downs," Irene said. "Life goes on, but you never know what turn it's going to take."

Sitting in his Staunton living room, Steve was going through his post-high school timeline, with a brief stint at Minot State before transferring to Gallaudet. Minot State wasn't a good experience; and Steve didn't want to go into it in detail, although he said "I don't" regret the decision." It appears the school, which was touted to have one of the best special education programs around, didn't follow through on that promise. There were the always-present problems of communication, both with fellow students and coaches. Hardly anybody knew sign language so navigating around as a deaf student in a hearing world was hard. Brenner said University of North Dakota head coach Dave Gunther offered Blehm a one-year scholarship out of high school, but Steve wanted four years so he chose Minot.

That fall, Minot State was playing a pre-season scrimmage against another school in nearby Leeds, N.D. Blehm did not play in the game despite a following of teachers and fans from the School for the Deaf being on hand.

"One of the teachers was so upset about it that he went to see (Minot State head coach) Wes Luther in the second half," Brenner said. "Steve got frustrated. So we just said why don't you go to Gallaudet?"

Steve had two choices in mind: the National Technical Institute for the Deaf in Rochester, New York, or Gallaudet in Washington, D.C.

He chose Gallaudet, even though he would have to sit out a year because of NCAA transfer rules. It was an up and down career. He was the team's most valuable player in two of the years but didn't play a whole lot his senior year. Still, it was a great choice, for just one reason:

"That's where I met my wife," he said.

A few seconds later, he broke down. So did Sarah, who reached for a couple of tissues for the tears. I told her to get three.

"He's taken some shots," Sarah said.

His wife, Linda Blehm, died unexpectedly after being sick with the flu for about a week in March of 2017. She went to the hospital twice within several days and appeared to be feeling better. After an autopsy, the belief is she became septic from the flu and passed away due to an aneurism. Her death came after Steve's father Milton passed away at age 89. In 2011, his brother David, a Fargo doctor, took his own life at age 59, a tragedy that motivated his widow, Julie Blehm, to do something about suicide prevention.

She spoke out about the pressures of doctors and the rate of physician suicide in a 2015 story in The Forum, in which she talked about the importance of doctors not only taking care of people but themselves as well. She became active in the North Dakota American Foundation for Suicide Prevention chapter.

When Steve arrived at Hector International Airport for the funeral, he and Julie had a conversation on the reality of it all.

"Julie, it had to be an accident," he said.

She replied that it wasn't an accident.

"It has been very, very tough on him," Julie said. "Every time he sees me he says his older brother is gone. He loved hunting with David and he really looked up to David. In grade school, David was his protector. Steve being deaf and having trouble learning to speak, he was teased a lot. I think David was the person who stood up for him. When David was at UND, he would drive across the state to see Steve play."

Linda, who was born deaf, was about to retire from teaching at the Virginia School for the Deaf and Blind in Staunton, a beautiful campus located not far from their home. One of the buildings was a hospital back in the Civil War and Sarah fondly recalls stories from her mother of ghosts on the top floor. It may have been another way of her mom telling the kids not to go up there because there was no adult supervision.

Linda was an idol to the deaf community in Staunton. The library for the School for the Deaf is named after her. Like Steve, she was humble; not making a big deal out of all she did for the school and the community.

Staunton, population about 25,000, is full of those historic buildings, most of which are well maintained. The downtown has history oozing every 10 feet, with places like Stonewall Jackson Hotel, the birthplace and presidential library of Woodrow Wilson, and the American Shakespeare Center. It's a great place to raise a family. It's a perfect place for a love story of a deaf kid from North Dakota meeting a deaf girl at Gallaudet.

"They had an incredibly close relationship when you saw them together," Julie said.

Julie's favorite story about Linda is touching. Linda grew up with sign language as the sole ability to communicate while Steve learned to speak.

When they first got cell phones for the first time Linda could instantly write something to her husband.

"She told me, 'I loved it when I was able to text,'" Julie said. "'Now I can tell Steve I love him.'"

Linda was the planner and organizer of the family. If they were thinking of a trip, she was the one who put it together. Since Linda died, the three daughters have been helping with life in general on the property.

"That family is very, very close," Julie said. "Just very close and very kind and considerate of each other."

These days, Steve maintains his job at the post office, where he's had a mail route for years. He has the town's largest route with 890 customers, with most of those now being delivered in a vehicle. Everybody in Staunton knows him. There was a time when he went to the door of a house to obtain a signature when the person answering was blind. She couldn't see him trying to tell her he was deaf. But they made it work. They found a way.

There is talk of retirement but the post office has been so good to him over the years. In Bismarck, while working at the post office in high school, he met fellow high school basketball players Tom Petrik and Mark Swanson, who were two of the state's best. Steve has an article of the North Dakota all-state team, with Petrik, Swanson, and Blehm on the first team. At his home in his living room, he pointed at the two players and smiled. They were his friends.

He hopes to return to Devils Lake, a town that gave him so many memories. He's read about all the flooding of the lake over the years, wondering if he would even recognize the area. He knows all about the great fishing, and wants to test his expertise in the big lake.

That big lake has been destructive since the days of Steve Blehm. The entire town of Churchs Ferry, located just west of Devils Lake, was bought out by the Federal Emergency Management Agency, also known as FEMA. All but six residents took the offer. Driving on Highway 2 going west out of Devils Lake one senses the low elevation. Reeds growing out of sloughs are more common than solid ground. There's still a sign for Churchs Ferry, but not much else. The sight of lifeless trees dead from wading in standing water too long is common.

The lake began to rise in 1993, a summer when it rose 5½ feet. Over the next several years, homes by the lake were inundated or destroyed and, in those days, in order to collect a FEMA buyout, a structure had to sit in water for at least 90 days. By that time, it was most likely destroyed anyway.

"Imagine the trauma and hardship and heartache it caused the home owner," said Jeff Frith, the manager of the Devils Lake Basin Authority. "You would lose your home and then watch them light it on fire and burn it."

For every foot the lake went up, it consumed 10,000 acres of land. Land owners wanting to hold on to their land in hopes of the water receding one day still had to pay property taxes. Counties reduced the payment, sometimes lowering it from $900 or $1,000 a quarter to around $35, but that put a burden on the county budgets. Miles of county and township roads were lost. U.S. Highway 281 that ran directly through the town of Minnewaukan had to be rerouted two miles to the west, cutting off a valuable lifeline to the town.

Before the lake started to rise, the highway was eight miles from Minnewaukan. It reached the point where the waters threatened the local high school, so federal and local dollars built a new school. In all, the rising lake cost around $2 billion in infrastructure protection, roads, dams, railroads, bridges, and the buyout of homes. Those who fish the lake will tell you one of the hottest spots are the old ditches next to underwater county highways. By the summer of 2018, the lake came down five feet from the 2011 record high; and because of that farmers were able to regain 52,000 acres of land. Those farmsteads that were flooded? Some are still there. Vacant and damaged. In 2011 alone, 700 structures, mostly rural farmsteads, were inundated with water.

"On a farm, you're looking at, what, 20 buildings?" Frith said. "Ten grain bins, a couple of shops, a barn and maybe a garage. What do you move? Where do you start? It was very difficult for a lot of agricultural producers."

Frith, like a lot of Devils Lake residents, embraces the days of Steve Blehm. When I mentioned his name, his first words were, "What if he had the 3-point line back then?"

Steve continued to play basketball at local Staunton gyms twice a week until he was 58, when his knees just told him that was enough. Just like his family, he never told fellow players in Staunton about his prominent high school years.

He would probably rather talk about the big elk or moose he's landed. Certainly, hunting and fishing will always be in the cards. Asked what he was or is better at: hunting, fishing, or basketball? Steve paused to think about it.

"That's a good question," he said. "I can't pick one."

V. Small Town Ball

It's a teaser question that makes a veteran North Dakota resident think. What are the six towns in the state that have only three letters?

Young adults making their way in the 1960s would name Zap. It wasn't Woodstock, but a "Zip to Zap" party was organized by college students in the spring of 1969 at North Dakota State -- the genesis an article in the school newspaper that gained steam to require the National Guard called in to restore order. The kids, an estimated 2,000 to 3,000 of them, drank the town bar out of alcohol and became moody and destructive in the aftermath.

There's Ray, the hometown of NDSU football player Keenan Hodenfield. Max is located between Bismarck and Minot. Jud had a population of 72 in the last census. Orr looks more like a large farm than a town, but so be it. It's a town. Zap. Ray. Max. Jud. Orr. And that brings us to Ayr.

Of those six towns, it's hard for any of the first five to top Ayr from a historical perspective. The town was home to the greatest girls basketball dynasty this state will probably ever see. When it comes to winning streaks, no school will touch the Rifles teams from 1937-42. In 1942, the march to the title game by the Elbowoods boys' basketball team was overshadowed in the headlines by the girls from Ayr. Six games into the 1943 season, the girls' team had its 109-game winning streak come to an end against Gardner.

Yes, 109 straight.

Ironically, the head coach at Gardner was the head coach at Ayr when the streak started – Jack Lynch. And, ironically, the 100th win was against Gardner in the 1942 North Cass County basketball tournament. In the modern day, Cass Valley North High School now consists of the five communities of Arthur, Hunter, Gardner, Argusville, and Grandin.

The Ayr teams in the '30s played in what was called the North Dakota High School League, not to be confused with the modern-day North Dakota High School Activities Association, which does not recognize the Ayr "consolidated league" titles. Two players, Lucille Moen and Doris Boyd, were on teams that won all 109 games.

A Forum story in 1942 reported the girls were "sensations" in their first state tournament. They were both in junior high.

"They wind up their careers this season, with their scoring records almost equal over a five-year period," according to the Forum story. It reached a point where the girls' teams wanted to play in the boys' league.

The streak began in the first state title in 1938 with 27 wins in a row. The 1939 team went 19-0. The 1940 team went 20-0 to run the streak to 66 straight. A 17-0 season in 1941 made it 83 in a row. By the time the streak reached 100 straight, the Rifles outscored their opposition 4,409-1,087, an average margin of 44.1-10.9. Prehistoric basketball by modern-day standards, Ayr played by the same rules as the other teams and beat them routinely 44-11. Perhaps these days that would be 88-22. It's all relative. In their day, the Ayr girls were as dominating a dynasty as any this state has seen.

Who were Lucille Moen and Doris Boyd?

The Boyds and Moens were quite the athletic families. Lila Boyd, Doris' older sister, played on Ayr's first state title team in 1938 and later coached state title teams in 1944 and 1946. A pioneer in the game, she also coached the Ayr boy's teams from 1943-44 and 1946-47. "The boys begged her to coach and Lila says they promised to listen and do everything she said," said a passage in the Ayr yearbook. "Only Lila and the boys know who listened to whom."

Lila was a go-getter. After the father of the Boyd girls died in 1947, she took over the farm until retiring to Fargo in 1986. She died in 2010 at Bethany Retirement Living in Fargo.

It's interesting where the path of searching for people can take one. I set on a quest of finding Doris Boyd, only to realize she died in 1989. From there, it was a question of finding family members, namely her husband Vernon Wang. The starting point was the entire country; Vernon could have been anywhere. Through a search engine, I found a couple of addresses in north Moorhead, and knocked on both doors, to no avail.

One house, on 11th Street North in Moorhead, looked promising with a metal "W" on the side screen door, presumably the first initial of the last name. More on that house later. Seeing the last name Wang and knowing there was a Cody Wang from Moorhead High and Concordia who was a pretty good football player, I private-messaged Cody on Facebook to see if he was related to Vernon. Initially, he wasn't sure but sent word a few days later saying an aunt knew about him. Vernon lived at Rosewood Retirement Living in north Fargo, less than 10 minutes from my house. Starting with a search of the entire U.S.A, I ended up at a place I drive by almost daily.

Vernon Wang was 96 years old when I stopped to talk to him. He was true to his generation – the Greatest Generation. They prefer not to talk about themselves. They did heroic things in World War II and didn't ask for any special treatment upon return. Neither did Doris, evidently, talk about her accomplishments. Although she didn't go to a war, she was still an epic part of 109 straight victories. In all the years she and Vernon were married, not much was said about the great basketball streak. They were all about living their lives.

Doris went to a "hairdressing academy" after high school. Think about that. In those days, there was no option of playing college women's basketball because there was no college women's basketball as we know it today. She worked at the hair salon at the old deLendrecie's department store in downtown Fargo. That closed in 1972 and Doris eventually opened her own shop in the basement of their home at 11th Street in north Moorhead. The entrance was at the side door with the metal "W" on it.

"She did that for many years," said Waldo Hilde, Vernon's nephew. "She was very pleasant but died young. She would do anything for you."

But she never talked about her basketball records. Doris Boyd was the Lynette Mund of her day. Lucille Moen was the Nadine Schmidt of her day. Lila Boyd was the Tanya Fischer of her day. Mund, Schmidt, and Fisher were stars on NDSU national championship teams in the 1990s. Because those Ayr players were so good before their time, they left high school without ever losing a game and never got a chance to prove it at the next level. Instead, Lila Boyd ran a farm by herself, with the only basketball in her life being the memories of winning almost every game she played.

And that was probably OK with Doris and Vernon, too, because they lived the next seven decades not caring about high school basketball. If there were photos of Doris in high school around the house, Vernon doesn't remember where they were or if they even existed.

"That's what I heard, she was a good player," Vernon said. "But I didn't know too much about basketball myself. Never got to high school or anything or did I play much. She was kind of quiet."

They were married in 1948 and never had children. Vernon was born and raised in Ulen, Minn., but never finished high school. He was a garage mechanic at several places in Fargo and Moorhead. They made several trips back to Ayr when Doris' folks were still living there on a moderate-sized farm consisting mostly of crops and cows. Even the parents didn't bring up basketball.

"They didn't have much to say about it," Vernon said, with a chuckle. "I know they had quite a record."

They had quite the dynasty.

The first title came in 1938 and was played in front of a packed gymnasium in Buffalo. Legendary Forum sportswriter Eugene Fitzgerald covered the game and wrote a story that you wouldn't find in today's world, both in the way it was worded and the sexist nature of it. Part of the story read:

"Ayr's kid team shuffled out of Buffalo with the first North Dakota Consolidated high school league girls basketball championship tonight.

The tiny Cass County community, with a pair of 12-year-old eighth graders leading the scoring attack, mustered the courage they needed in the all-Cass county final. The score was 24 to 19.

Amenia's feminine stars faced their neighboring rival in the final only after surviving two tough encounters. But the only team in the tournament coached by a woman, battled courageously, twice pulled in front threateningly, but could not match the accuracy of Lucille Moen and Doris Boyd, the eighth-grade sharpshooters, who in a dozen years have learned more than a lot of aspirants to cage stardom learn about making a basketball whip through the net.

Amenia's tall back court trio did a splendid job of minimizing the accuracy of this twin tallying combination, but it crashed the scorebook for 22 points, 13 of which were contributed by the Boyd half. She scored six field goals and a free throw.

A throng which crammed every inch of available space and even jammed into the corners of the playing area, saw Ayr jump off in front. Ayr took a 19-18 lead in the first minute of the final quarter and was never behind (sic) thereafter. It remained close until Boyd shoved in a field goal three minutes before the game ended, and then banged in another with 1½ minutes remaining to clinch the decision."

Ayr beat Cleveland 43-27 in the 1939 title game. Amenia offered some resistance in the 1940 championship, but Ayr prevailed 18-12. The 1941 title game wasn't much of a game, with Ayr defeating Norwich 50-16. That game was also memorable in that about 500 people spent the night in the basketball arena because of a snowstorm. With Boyd and Moen now seniors, nobody came close to Ayr in the 1941-42 school year, with the fifth straight title being a 61-11 win over Buffalo. The game was aired by KVOC-AM in Valley City, the first-ever girls basketball game in North Dakota to be broadcast on radio. The announcer was Bill Weaver, who went on to a legendary TV career most notably at WDAY in Fargo. Weaver saw Boyd and Moen finish their careers scoring over 1,400 career points.

They were part of a great run of athletes.

"They were strong kids," said Collette Folstad, whose mother Sylvia Benzmiller played on the first-ever Ayr girls basketball team in 1929. "I knew those ladies later on, but they were strong and all just wonderful people."

They were also tall. There were a couple of 6-foot players on those title teams, like Lucille Moen. Lila Boyd could take the ball from one end of the court and hook pass it to the other end. Like most of the players, they were farm girls and, in their case, they had a basketball hoop in the hayloft of their barn. The routine was simple: help dad with the chores, sweep the hay out of the way, hope the dust wasn't too bad and shoot baskets.

Asked why they were so good, Folstad paused for a few moments while staring at a team photo from a scrapbook.

"When I look at them, I remember the stories and all the things they did," she said. "They were really skilled is what I figured out. My mom was highly skilled, people talk about her all the time. They were also funny. I didn't know them but I feel like I know them. They were so much fun. But very athletic. They were tall and a lot of them were sleek and quick."

Some said the Ayr girls played like boys, because they were farm girls who played against their brothers in pick-up ball. Farm girls like the Boyds and Moens, who combined made up eight players in the dynasty years – Anna, Lila, Doris and Charlene Boyd and Lucille, Mildred, Bernice and Betty Moen.

"They were neighbors and they were always playing, either at home or during noon hour at the school," said teammate Betty Lentz Eckert, in a 1989 Forum story. It was six-player basketball back in those days, with each team having three guards in the defensive end and three forwards in the offensive end, none of whom were allowed to cross the center line. Rival teams would say the Ayr girls would go to class with a basketball in one hand and a pencil in the other, with some of those teams saying they left out the pencil. That was a joke, I think.

After the winning streak ended and not defending a state title in 1942-43, Ayr came back to win its sixth state championship in seven years taking the 1944 title game 49-40 over Gardner. With the star player now Charlene Boyd, Doris' sister, who averaged over 20 points a game, Ayr made it seven championships in eight years in 1945 beating Bordulac 37-35, a game that was played in Carrington. At that point, Ayr had won 192 of its previous 197 games in a 10-year span.

A lack of girls forced the school to not field a team from 1947-51. A lack of space to play and a lack of coaches also contributed. There was another reason, too, according to a published report: "In 1950, there were enough girls to again have a team, but at this time there was a heightened popular belief that strenuous exercise was harmful physically for the female, and there was a lack of administrative support. In 1952, there were 13 girls with their parents who persisted until they were granted permission to organize a team."

That included Collette (Buhr) Folstad.

Now 79 years old and sitting in a coffee shop in north Fargo in the spring of 2018, she's still amazed that society was that discriminating. It was a world where rules were written by men and controlled by men. Growing up, Collette never knew that world because she was working the farm at a young age. She did everything but seed, and that included driving a combine, driving truck, cultivating corn and plowing fields. She said her father opted not to hire "some old guy" to run a combine because "Colly" could do it better than anybody.

But when the girls were done with high school basketball, they were done. There was no option to play in college.

"I didn't know that, I was devastated," Collette said. "They would say, 'Oh no, it's too hard on you to play.' I slid into bases in steal cleats since I was 15, plowed, worked, and milked cows and you're telling me it's too hard? It was the times, what do you do?"

Collette went on to a standout career in coaching and teaching at Concordia College and NDSU. She became the first-ever women's head coach at NDSU in 1966-67. The Bison went 0-2. NDSU went 8-2, 5-4 and 9-1 in the next three seasons before she went on to something else. Nine years later, the Bison hired Amy Ruley, whose run of success will forever be legendary in college women's basketball. During the title years, Folstad was part of the official scorers' staff and that perhaps brought her a satisfaction she never envisioned after finishing high school and seeing no opportunities to play in college.

She watched NDSU win a national championship. In women's basketball.

"It was truly a dream of mine when I could sit at the NDSU scoring table and watch them play national championship games," she said. "It was an honor to be able to do that."

Collette said the Ayr girls basketball alumni have always wondered how good the girls could have been in college. She thinks Lila Boyd was every bit the athlete of Mund, Fischer, or Schmidt. You have to wonder: What if Lila Boyd graduated in 2017 instead of the 1940s? Would she have been a Division I recruit who got her school paid for along with the NCAA cost of attendance stipend? Would her cell phone be constantly busy from text messages from college recruiters? Would she have committed to a university basketball program after her junior year of high school? How would a college strength and conditioning program hone an already powerful athlete? Think about a pair of Ayr 6-footers in the 1940s, who in this day and age would probably be equivalent to 6-5 kids who can run and jump.

"They had a work ethic, they stuck together like glue," Folstad said.

Instead, most of the girls went back to the farm or started a life without basketball somewhere else. It's a sad thought. Very sad.

The Ayr school closed in 1969. About all that's left to the town is a large, modern elevator, the post office and Rosie's Cafe. Only three avenues remain: Main, Fourth and Fifth avenues. There are three streets: First, Second and Third. Only Main is paved. The first one-room school house built in 1894 is still there, restored by Keith Johnson in 1976 and looking in good shape. Ayr at one time was a thriving community with three grocery stores, two livery stables, two meat markets, a blacksmith shop, a pool hall and bowling alley, a bank, hardware store, hotel, barber shop, machine dealer, potato house and city hall. Fire claimed several buildings and others disappeared as the population dwindled.

"Ayr was a unique community," Folstad said. "We were very attuned to what was going on in the outside world. They dressed in the latest fashions. Whenever they put something on, whether it was a baby shower or a community program, it was always done to perfection, just like you would do if it were high class. We were raised by a village; it was a tight-knit community. Basketball was a thing that brought them together. They were so proud of that and we still are."

***

The rural communities have been good to the state's athletic teams, too, like the NDSU women's basketball juggernaut of the 1990s. Most of the players came from smaller communities in Minnesota and North Dakota and formed one of the greatest dynasties in NCAA women's basketball history. The Bison won four NCAA Division II titles in five years, at times playing in front of sold-out crowds of around 6,000 at the Bison Sports Arena.

The Bison women of the '90s were built with kids who didn't grow up driving BMWs. Some of them drove gravel country roads with an old vehicle. And practicing the game of basketball? Ah, a little cold weather never hurt anybody. The gym is closed? No problem. Grab a shovel and clear the driveway. Then shoot baskets until your hands are numb. If it keeps snowing, keep shoveling. The will and perseverance of those girls made for captivating stories from that era and much was written about it.

"I would wear my gloves and shoot around," said Rachael Otto, echoing a story that was all too common with the Bison women's basketball team.

Otto, from New Rockford, N.D., and her teammates didn't need gloves the week she spoke to a Forum reporter. NDSU was getting ready to host the NCAA Division II Elite Eight tournament in the warm confines of the Bison Sports Arena. In the storied history of Bison women's basketball, a definite tradition within a tradition was so evident: The small towns were good to the Bison.

"That's not to say the kids from bigger communities don't have a good work ethic," Ruley said. "But in general, we found the kids from smaller communities really enjoyed their basketball in the absence of other things to do. They dedicated a lot more time to it so I think they spent a lot more time in the off-season at camps and working on their game."

Otto, for one, was a picture of dedication. "She was constantly playing whether it was winter or summer," said Deb Burgad, Otto's coach at New Rockford.

The run of excellence probably started with Pat (Smykowski) Jacobson from Lidgerwood, N.D., at the time in the 1990s a town with a population of 1,838. Her farm had a Cayuga, N.D. address. To say she attracted a lot of attention in her high school and college reign is a massive understatement.

"People not only from Lidgerwood would watch her play but from other towns as well," Mund said. "I went to watch her play and I thought if she can do it, I can do it, too."

Mund practiced on a hoop in a hayloft. If the weather got cold, she said, she would put on mittens. She finished her Bison career as the 12th all-time leading scorer. Second-place Janice Woods was from Fosston, Minn. Third-place Lori Knetter was from Lakota, N.D. Fifth-place Darci Steere was from Windom, Minn. Then there was Schmidt, next on the scoring chart. She was from tiny Braddock, N.D.

"I remember I took about a 10-mile stretch of gravel road where I thought it was a hunter's paradise," Ruley said of her recruiting trip to try and sign Schmidt. "I saw more pheasant than I did people. I was driving up and down everywhere, the hills, the gravel road."

Schmidt eventually signed with NDSU. Four years later, she had two national championship rings and was instrumental in the start of NDSU's run of titles. Small-town players ending up in a Bison uniform got to be contagious. And never was that displayed more than in NDSU's summer camp. Players and ex-players work as coaches. For instance, when Fischer was in junior high and high school, she idolized Schmidt.

"When I was a sophomore, Nadine was my (summer camp) coach," Fischer said. "She's a small-town North Dakota girl and she got to that next step. I thought if she could do it, I could do it."

Fischer went on to become North Dakota's all-time high school career scoring leader at Bowman High School, located in the southwest corner of the state. That mark was broken in 2016 by another small-town girl, Rylee Nudell of Buffalo, N.D., and Maple Valley High School.

Fischer was from the peace and serenity of the Badlands. The Larry and Loreen Fischer ranch had a Rhame address but was 10 miles from that town and 23 miles from the nearest movie theater, which is in Bowman. Like Otto and Mund, Fischer didn't let the weather interfere with basketball. She practiced endlessly on a court next to the barn.

"Rain or snow, it didn't matter," she said. "I played all the time against my brothers. I would pretend I was different players. My total dream was to play college basketball."

Her dream didn't wander nation-wide. The closest Division I school to Rhame was Wyoming, but the Bison had the inside track. Ruley called that the best of both worlds. An athlete could play in front of big crowds, something that wasn't prevalent in Division I, yet could do it within driving distance of home. The Bison set the all-time Division II attendance record of 7,543 in a 1996 game against the University of North Dakota, breaking their own record of 7,302 set the previous year against the Sioux.

***

The best chance for a great winning streak is in small-town ball simply because of the odds. Less-populated schools have a tougher time putting together a competitive team, much less a juggernaut. But every once in a blue moon, it happens. In the mid-1950s, not long after the Ayr girls put together their juggernaut, a town that is a blip on the radar on Highway 66 north of Devils Lake, close to the Canadian border, found a basketball dynasty that nobody could ever have predicted.

Alsen.

In the 2010 census, the population was 35. In keeping the legend alive, one of the best stories out there was written by Greg DeVillers of the Grand Forks Herald, who visited the old school in 2007. His report was spot-on, a journalist who went to the scene of the greatness and wrote something from the heart:

"ALSEN, N.D. - The hallways of the one-story, cement-block school here are dark, dusty and musty. More than two decades have passed since students roamed the hallways between classes. In the gymnasium, the backboards, the score clock, the two rows of bleachers that lined both sidelines are gone. The space is now rented by a beekeeper for equipment storage.

Small and declining enrollments resulted in Alsen closing its school in 1980. Yet this school still holds the record for the biggest winning streak in North Dakota high school basketball. It was 50 years ago, at the start of the 1956-57 season, that the Alsen Broncos began a run that would include two straight 34-0 seasons, back-to-back Class C state championships and a winning streak that would reach 79 before it was halted.

'It was pretty exciting to be a part of it at the time, something unusual,' said Gil Herbel, a starter on the two state championship teams (who also was) a state legislator from Grafton. 'Now, you savor the opportunities we had to be a part of those teams. It's amazing when you talk to people. There are very few places I go to in the state, when people find out who I am and where I'm from, where they don't ask if I was on those teams.'

The school's enrollment reflected its record-setting basketball team. It was small.

There was never as many as 40 students in high school during its three-season run of wins. And that basketball success came with a roster that didn't have anybody taller than 6 feet; most of the players were shorter than that. Speed and skill overcame lack of stature. It was a team that played ahead of its time with its running style and pressing, in-your-face, man-to-man defense. Alsen outscored opponents by a 70-40 average margin during its first title season. In the second title run, the Broncos scored an average of 79 points while allowing 47 a game.

Small Town Ball

'We played fast,' said Don 'Skip' Spenst, a starter on the two championship teams. 'We had to compensate for what we gave up in height. We were all pretty good athletes. That was a main ingredient. We went for everything (on defense), double-teaming, stealing the ball, intercepting passes. We were the only team I remember then that played pressing, man-to-man defense. Every other team would sit back in zones. We never had a play (on offense), not that I can remember. We'd come off screens and rolls. And we loved to run and gun. We didn't mess around.'

Spenst, Gil Herbel, Dennis Schmiess, Paul Glock and Ken Towers were regulars on the 34-0 team in '56-57. They were veterans coming off a 23-2 season in 1955-56. They opened the 1956-57 season with a 64-44 win against Clyde and the streak was on. After Glock and Towers graduated in the spring of 1957, Ray Herbel, Mark Kreklau and Alvin Klein got starting time on the team that repeated as undefeated state champion. It was a group that grew up on the basketball court together.

'There wasn't anything else for us to do,' Gil Herbel said. 'We didn't have snowmobiles. Nobody had cars. There were no video games. Most of us didn't have TVs in our homes. I was a junior in high school when we got our first TV. You played ball. It was the thing to do. We'd play morning, afternoon and night. And we all loved it.'

Details of most of the games in the streak are vague to the Broncos. But two wins - and two baskets - stand out. The first was against Oriska in the quarterfinals of the 1956-57 season, in a Monday game in Jamestown. Two Gordon Baumgartner free throws gave Oriska a 55-54 lead with six seconds left in overtime. The ensuing inbounds pass went to Gil Herbel, who dribbled to midcourt and threw up a desperation shot that was short of the rim. But Klein caught the ball with his back to the basket and threw an awkward shot up over his head - and made the winning basket, his only field goal of the game, as time expired.

'I just threw it in,' Klein says. 'Sometimes you have to have some luck.'

Alsen beat Fort Totten 62-50 behind Towers' 19 points in the semifinals, then beat Taylor 65-56 in the title game as Glock scored 30 points, Towers 16 and Spenst 11. In the 1957-58 state tournament, Alsen opened with a 65-51 win against Fullerton, with Gil Herbel getting 19 points and Spenst 16. Alsen won a shootout in the semifinals, 87-74 over Tower City behind 29 points from Spenst and 25 from Gil Herbel. But in the final against Fort Totten, Alsen led only twice. The first was at 2-0. The last was at the final 50-49 score. Spenst scored the tying and winning points when the right-hander hit a left-handed hook shot with 1:04 left. Spenst had 13 of his team-high 18 points in the second half to spark a comeback.

'No question, those were the defining moments in the streak,' Gil Herbel said. 'If Alvin wasn't in the right place at the right time for that rebound basket, we wouldn't have had the streak. Nobody would be talking about us. And winning state a second *straight time really is a significant thing. Skip was a money player, one of the best pure shooters of our time.'*

Alsen won its first 11 games to start the 1958-59 season. But the streak was halted Jan. 20, 1959. Langdon topped the Broncos 64-47 in a foul-plagued game in the first round of the Cavalier County tournament. Duane Verk's 19 points set the pace for Langdon.

'I think we all felt some pressure,' Ray Herbel said. 'Everybody expected us to win. And when you win that many games in a row, everybody is gunning for you. Nobody wanted to be on the team that finally got beat. It was sad, disappointing.'

But, he added, 'You do feel a little relief.'

Unlike the girls from Ayr, the boys from Alsen had life after basketball. Of the 19 players on the Alsen three-year dynasty run, seven played college basketball. Five went on to coach basketball in North Dakota with Ken Towers being the signature guy leading Grand Forks Red River to the 1969 Class A state championship.

Towers went on to be an owner of the Italian Moon restaurant in Grand Forks. What happened to the state title trophies from Alsen? They can't be found in town. As DeVillers wrote, "At the Moon, in a place of prominence above the buffet table, the state championship trophies sit with a picture of the '56-57 team placed between them. There's also a plaque listing the 19 players, as well as coaches Sam Kreklau and Bob Morehouse, who were with the team in the streak."

Long live the Broncos.

VI. Farm Tough

Winters on the farm in North Dakota are black and white. The snow is white, or a shade darker if wind-blown soil gets mixed in. Country roads are black top, or at least a shade of gray if the surface is older. Grain bins are gray. Farm houses are white; rarely a bright color. Old barns are red, but they're becoming an extinct species and the new ones – metal structures that can be put up in seemingly a week – are neutral in color. Leafless trees appear as stark branches on the flat horizon. If there are pine trees in the Red River Valley, the soil-rich area in eastern North Dakota, they're well hidden. Occasional green street signs intersect county or gravel roads, the only color found on the route from the small town of Harwood, N.D., just north of Fargo, to the Dane and Kris Larsen farm west of Harwood.

Oh, and there's Prosper, N.D., the really, really small town that greets visitors with the following sign: "Prosper: Next 4 exits." There are four streets off of Highway 22 in Prosper, the closest town to the Larsen's place, a family farm that traces its origin to 1932. It consists of 3,200 acres of corn and soybeans. In early March of 2018, a spring blizzard blew through the area leaving a fresh coat of white powder. Such weather would close 80 percent of the country and paralyze cities with thousands of people. When it happens near Prosper, Collin Larsen hops in a very large tractor with a plow and has some fun clearing roads.

Everything is big in the country. The vehicles. The equipment. The land. Even the family dog, a Great Dane so big its appearance could scare horses. He's calm, though, friendly and shy, with a demeanor that doesn't match his size. Collin Larsen is 28 years old; or 12 years removed from a horrific accident that would send most people into a downward spiral of pity.

Sept. 24, 2006. Sunday afternoon. The family returned from church and Collin planned to attend a confirmation party of a close friend and farming neighbor, Brandon Rust. He rode his motorcycle to the Rust farm, but they had yet to return from church. He decided to ride around the countryside, cruising down a road that had corn on one side and soybeans on the other. The concern in approaching an intersection was the corn, its height made seeing traffic coming from another direction difficult. Collin was on the corn side. A green Ford Expedition was on the soybean side.

Collin thinks the color of the car blended into the soybeans. If he had been driving his motorcycle in the drab colors of a black and white winter, this wouldn't have been an issue. The green car would have stuck out like a sore green thumb. The driver of the car had his cruise set on 58 miles per hour, which is about the speed limit. Collin on his motorcycle was going about 40.

"I blew the yield sign, it was completely my fault," he said.

The car and Collin collided; the grill of the car sending him flying into the ditch. He remembers at that moment thinking, "This isn't going to be good." It was surprising, in retrospect, the car didn't run him over. He was wearing a helmet. He was wearing leather boots. The theory is the boots prevented his foot from being totally severed.

"Even with a helmet, it's nothing less than a miracle I didn't die," Collin said. "There's no reason I should be alive."

Meanwhile, Dane and Kris, Collin's parents, were repairing a fence on the farm when they heard the medical helicopter from MeritCare Hospital in Fargo flying over their land.

"My instant thought has always been somebody's life, somebody's priorities, just got changed today," Dane said. "We hear that quite often. You feel bad when you hear that stuff because it's rarely good."

This time, the sounds of the helicopter blades were because of their son. A short while later, they were walking horses into the barn when a pickup rushed into their driveway. At that point Kris realized the helicopter was there to pick up Collin.

At MeritCare, doctors quickly figured out Collin's lower right leg needed more medical attention than they could offer. His leg below the knee was ripped open. His Achilles tendon was severed and the bones in the foot and ankle were crushed. He was transported to Hector International Airport in north Fargo and life-flighted by the medical King Air airplane to the St. Paul Downtown Airport, which handles private aviation in the area. In and out of drugs, Collin told either the nurse or pilot during the flight he needed to check on his soybeans. Once landed, Collin was admitted to Hennepin County Medical Center; and because he was 16 years old, he was placed in the pediatric center. Over the course of the next month Collin endured a series of eight surgeries aimed at trying to re-establish blood flow to his foot. At times he could wiggle his toes, and he figured that was a good sign. The smell told him it wasn't going well.

"It just kept getting worse," Collin said. "It smelled like death. It's like walking down into the basement and there's a dead mouse down there."

On the weekend of Oct. 11, Central Cass High School assistant football coach and head wrestling coach Travis Lemar drove to the Twin Cities to visit Larsen. They had a bond that stemmed from working out against each other in wrestling, since both weighed about the same. In small North Dakota towns, it's usually tough for the upper-weight wrestlers to find practice partners. In this case the head coach Lemar filled the bill for Collin.

Lemar coached the Friday night football game. On Saturday, he was in Collin's hospital room when doctors broke the news to the family that saving the leg may not be an option. In the hospital hallway Lemar sees Kris, who told him the gravity of the situation.

"You go in there thinking, 'What can I do to make this kid's day and it turns into a let's-try-to-get-through-this-life-altering decision,'" Lemar said.

They talked. They joked. They talked some more. Then Lemar laid it on the line for his student-football player-wrestler-friend.

"Let's talk," Lemar said.

"What do you mean?" Collin replied.

"You know what I mean," Travis countered.

They both knew a decision was imminent on taking the leg.

Lemar remembers thinking how young Collin was part of a mature decision. Lemar showed him the example of Anthony Robles, who was born with one leg and making his way up in the national youth wrestling circuit. Robles went on to become the 2011 NCAA Division I wrestling champion at Arizona State. They talked about what life could be like with a prosthetic. They talked about wrestling. They talked about getting back on the mat and how that could be done.

"I'm willing to do the work if you are," Lemar said. "I'll contact who I can contact on what you can do in wrestling with a prosthetic or without it; what the rules are and what kind of game plan you need."

The conversation went on for hours. Dane and Kris had those conversations over the course of their stay, but with Lemar, it was an afternoon to remember just with the emotional intensity of it all.

"He decided, let's take the leg so I can live as normal of a life as I can as a teenager and after high school," Lemar said years later. "That decision alone was so difficult."

On Oct. 11, doctors performed the procedure to cut off his leg just below the right knee. Reality hit, but help was almost immediate. Another gentleman who had the same procedure came into Collin's hospital room and showed him what he could do with his prosthetic. He told him that he was able to do pretty much most things he could do before the amputation. A little depressed after the operation, Collin gained hope that success was possible.

On his way to at least getting out of the hospital for short periods of time, Collin hoped to attend the North Dakota State - University of Minnesota football game at the Metrodome on Oct. 21. He told doctors if he was healthy enough to go to the game, then he could go home. Doctors rejected the plan, but he watched the game, a 10-9 Gophers win that went down to the final seconds, from his hospital room. Collin knew football. At the time of the mishap, he was having a very good season with the Central Cass Squirrels as a running back and middle linebacker, probably averaging around 100 yards per game carrying the football.

The Friday before the accident, he played his best game at running back. The Squirrels were at Lisbon, a game the Broncos won, but Larsen played lights out. He rushed for over 100 yards against a good team and led the team in tackles. Just a sophomore, at around 200 pounds, he was already showing college potential.

Comparisons were made to running back Andrew Grothmann from Hillsboro, N.D., who went on to an outstanding career at NDSU. Larsen and Grothmann had similar makeup: both were farm kids; both were big, strong, and fast; and both were good wrestlers. Grothmann won back-to-back Class B state wrestling titles at 189 pounds, the last in 2009. Central Cass was never a football power. With the sophomore Larsen, their rare college prospect on his way to a standout career, team success was looked to improve.

"He moved like Grothmann when Grothmann was a tailback at Hillsboro," Lemar said. "I said it back then and I'll say it now. Andrew Grothmann was a great Bison football player, a great wrestler and I've known Andrew for a long time. But if there was a healthy Collin Larsen, no one would have heard of Andrew. He was that talented of a football player. He loved the Bison and there is no doubt in my mind he would have gone there to play football."

Five weeks after the accident and one week after the Bison-Gopher game, Collin headed home with no lower right leg, and his athletic career looking to be over with no more dreams of being the next great Bison fullback.

***

For the next three months, Collin got around on crutches because specialists would not fit him with a prosthetic leg. The swelling needed to subside. He never ruled out athletics at any point after the entire accident, but his immediate want was to get his license to drive a car back. His right foot, after all, is the one used to push the gas pedal. Two things had to happen: he had to get off painkillers before taking his driver's test and he had to get his prosthetic leg.

He never felt like he was abusing pain medication, but man, the leg hurt. He decided to go cold turkey and stopped taking all pain pills. The withdrawal symptoms became noticeable in school when he was sitting in Mrs. Grommesh's home economics class sweating profusely. Then he felt cold.

"You feeling OK?" the teacher asked Collin.

"I feel fine," he replied, lying through his teeth.

Grommesh told Collin she figured his condition was because of the medication withdrawal, something that blindsided him.

As for the leg, that was an early Christmas present for the family. The Shriner's Hospital for Children, like it's done for so many kids over the years, took care of all expenses with the leg, for which the family will forever be thankful. The first one was fitted on Dec. 23. His first steps, aided by a crutch, were painful. They came on Christmas Day.

"I remember my mom being pretty emotional," Collin said. "It was a Christmas gift; he's walking again. I didn't really feel that way because I had bigger and better things I was going to try to do."

Like wrestling again.

Like what?

There was no wait-until-next-year for Collin. He researched other amputee athletes and how they were able to compete in athletics. He returned to practice. On the first day, while the other wrestlers were running around the practice room warming up, Collin couldn't run. Lemar had another idea. While they warmed up, Larsen was to do pushups and situps.

"I was back with my friends," Larsen said. "It was a good feeling. I had no expectations of being good."

Lemar was blessed with good assistants who could handle the lower and middle weights. It afforded Lemar more time to work with Larsen on how to wrestle as an amputee and the first order of business was to come up with a different strategy. They found video of other wrestlers with one leg and how they competed. It didn't happen overnight, but Larsen and Lemar orchestrated a game plan.

"The hardest thing for me was seeing a kid you knew whose future was so bright and have that taken away and still willing to come in almost as if nothing had ever happened and still work at it," Lemar said. "It was like he had two good legs."

Their game plan called for Collin to be quick off the whistle. He started on one knee, which put him close to the opponent's legs, so at the whistle he had to usually go for an ankle. The object was to go for the pin because the inability to drive with both of his feet made scoring points over the course of three periods a hard task. Larsen had to learn how to control his opponent's hips and apply pressure with his one good leg.

On Jan. 9, about three and a half months after the accident, Central Cass hosted its first home dual of the season against Lisbon, a perennial power in North Dakota small-school wrestling. Collin Larsen, who was down to 166 pounds during his hospital stay at Hennepin Medical Center, was in the starting lineup at 215 pounds against Lisbon's Chris Smith. About 500 people packed the Central Cass gymnasium, and everybody knew why most fans were there. As each match got closer to the 215-pound clash, the anticipation grew. Fans from both schools stood when Larsen took the mat, a moment so loud that nobody could hear the public-address announcer.

"There were a lot of us that teared up," said Lisbon athletic director Joe Howell. "One of my friends said to me, 'I wouldn't mind seeing our kid lose.'"

Larsen couldn't wrestle with his prosthetic, so he hopped out to the center mat and had to wrestle constantly from the "down" position. He was undersized weighing around 190 for the 215-pound match. Moreover, another consequence of the accident was a collapsed lung, which left him with just partial use of it. The byproduct made getting in wrestling shape that much harder. What he did have was a strong upper body thanks to the use of crutches for three months.

Larsen wrestled Smith in the past, and they were acquaintances. Smith had a couple of takedowns in the first period; and, in retrospect, Collin said Smith probably took it easy on him. Over the course of his final three seasons of high school wrestling he never really sensed that happen. Smith pinned him in the second period. Yet, Lemar remembers thinking his one-legged protégé just wrestled one of the best wrestlers in the state and did OK. Despite getting pinned, there was hope he could make this work.

"I was exhausted," Collin said. "I was so exhausted I couldn't put my leg on. People say you're either in football shape or wrestling shape, and I knew I had a lot of cardiovascular work if I was ever going to do anything. So, we went from there."

To get in shape, he summoned the use of an elliptical machine, one that has low impact on the legs yet has resistance for the heart. The wrestling got better. He wasn't winning, but he figured at times it was better than a forfeit for the team. Then came a tournament later in the season, ironically, in Lisbon.

He faced a wrestler from Ellendale-Edgeley who Larsen figured wasn't very good at basketball and wanted to try another sport. The score was close, but early in the third period Larsen, trailing 7-4, uttered the following phrase in his head: "You can do this." He wrapped his opponent in a half-Nelson and pinned him. It felt like the equivalent of a state title.

Travis Lemar will admit several matches brought him to tears. Watching the struggle of a once-prominent college prospect go through the pain and struggles of starting over again and not giving up.

That tournament match was one of them.

"It was probably more emotional for me because I was his wrestling partner for all those days at practice, when things were not going good," Lemar said. "It will always hold a special place for me."

***

Playing football for the Bison was no longer an option. But that didn't mean playing football wasn't an option. If he could wrestle, Collin thought, he could play football and that is precisely what he put his mind to before starting his junior year at Central Cass.

The Squirrels didn't have a lot of players, so the players that played usually had to play both offense and defense. Larsen was the running back and middle linebacker – and playing both on a prosthetic was going to be a challenge.

"I was still trying to figure out my leg configuration, to do the best I could at football," he said.

When Larsen started sweating in the heat of games or practice, the padding on the prosthetic would slip. He won't forget his last carry, a play called 32 fullback trap against rival Kindred. Larsen took a handoff with a wide-open hole in front of him, but the padding didn't hold up. He went down right at the line of scrimmage. At that point he made a decision, no more trying to play running back.

He played middle linebacker his junior and senior seasons. He led the team in tackles both years. The senior year was somewhat of a heartbreaker, however, with the Squirrels threatening to make the Class B state playoffs for the first time in several years.

Life was going well for Larsen, who had a girlfriend and was named the school's homecoming king. The team had to beat Fargo Oak Grove by six points or more in the last game of the season to make the playoffs. It didn't happen, and there's nothing to sooth Larsen's memory on one good leg or not.

I love Farm Tough kids. I covered them all the time in all the years of writing about Bison football. Pick almost any year in any successful sport at NDSU and one can see the small-town influence. Take Bison football in the 2017 FCS national title game in Frisco, Texas.

***

One particular weekend in January 2017, nobody was home in the communities of Drake, Anamoose, and Balfour.

Wendy Volson tells why.

Everybody was in Frisco.

"Don't go and rob us now, nobody is there," she joked to a reporter.

Wendy is the mother of Bison offensive linemen Tanner Volson and Cordell Volson. She and her husband Ralph were part of a traveling party of several vehicles that made the trip to watch the Bison take on James Madison University. The Volson van, a white 12-passenger beauty the family bought in 2016 because of football, was hard to miss with "The Thunder Rolls" decals on the side. The back had a graphical photo of both Volson players with the following caption: "Small Town Big Dreams." It was designed by Midwest Graphic & Signs in Anamoose.

"It's the coolest thing ever to follow the Bison around," Wendy said. "I'm kind of a hands-on mom so I wasn't going to miss their games."

There were interesting trips that season, like the middle-of-the-night drives to Indiana State and Illinois State. Sleep wasn't an option. They arrived in Terre Haute, Indiana, at 5 a.m. Saturday and stayed up the rest of the day for the game. That was a trip when Wendy drove through Wisconsin in a heavy rainstorm and 50 mph winds.

"The windshield wipers couldn't keep up," she said.

It was hard to keep up with the number of family and friends in Frisco. The count was at least 50. Any lights left on in Drake, Anamoose, or Balfour were on a timer. The Volsons are from Balfour, population 27, which is located six miles west of Drake. The joke is Balfour is a suburb of the other two towns, with Drake having a population of 283 and Anamoose 253. Wendy will never forget the day Tanner first told her he wanted to play at NDSU.

"I want to play D1 ball," he said.

"You want to play D1 football?" she replied.

"Yep, I'm going to play in Fargo," Tanner said.

"You are, huh?" Wendy said.

His insistence impressed her. "It was his dream and he made it," she said.

The recruitment of the 6-6, 299-pound Cordell, who is two years younger than Tanner, was different. The University of Wyoming, with former NDSU head coach Craig Bohl, had Cordell down for a visit. The University of North Dakota made a nice offer, Wendy said.

"Actually, we did have a couple doubts," she said. "We were out with Craig Bohl, of course, out there visiting and hanging out. Then we went to UND and Bubba (Schweigert) offered him pretty good, so it was kind of tough. It was a long hard decision for Cordell."

The decision to go to NDSU made for quite the Drake, Anamoose, and Balfour party on that Friday in Frisco. It wasn't hard to find the group. Around 200 jerseys with either No. 74, No. 67 (the players' numbers), or both were made.

One of my favorite descriptions of Farm Tough was written by Los Angeles Times writer Earl Gustkey, who came to Fargo in 1990 to do a story on Bison All-American defensive end Phil Hansen. Sometimes, getting a different viewpoint on the state from a big-city guy makes for the realization of the rural beauty we take for granted. Gustkey's first few paragraphs were words of genius:

"Fields of golden sunflowers, dense stands of corn, thousands of acres of waving wheat lie beneath the hot summer sun. Fields of dreams, in North Dakota.

Straight, lightly traveled rural highways crisscross the endless flat farmland. The country road rolls through one farm town after another, past an occasional country cemetery, where tilted headstones mark the dreams of other times. Hawks cruise lazily over freshly plowed fields awaiting the late hay crop, looking for mice and insects.

The Hansen farm lies eight miles south of Oakes, population 1,742, in southeastern North Dakota. Here, Allen Hansen, 50, raises corn, sunflowers, cattle, sheep, oats, millet and football players. The Hansens own 1,000 acres of farmland and lease another 3,000. Hansen's No. 2 son, Phil, is an All-American senior defensive tackle up at Fargo, 120 miles away, at North Dakota State University. His No. 3 son, Steve, is a promising freshman linebacker at North Dakota State, America's best NCAA Division II football program. Oldest son John, who didn't play football, works the family farm with his father.

Hansen is showing a reporter around his farm, explaining the economics of family farming and the necessary work ethic.

"All three of my boys spent every day of their summers in fields like this one," he said, pointing to a 65-acre field, recently shorn of its wheat. "And when I say days, I mean sunup to sundown. Football is the perfect sport for my sons, because it requires a lot of work and preparation. Growing up here . . . heck, that's all my boys know, hard work."

Hard work is a common theme every year in fall camp at NDSU when a freshman from the farm shows up for practice. The players get up around 6 a.m. for practice, which for a farm kid is like sleeping in. I once asked NDSU head coach Chris Klieman who he thought was the toughest kid on his 2017 team. He refused to do it.

"We have a lot of tough kids," he said.

The question came the week after Jon Gruden made the North Dakota Tough phrase trendy. Not long after that an old newspaper article from the Waterloo-Cedar Falls Courier surfaced, thanks to the Twitter account of Courier sportswriter Jim Nelson. It carried the following description: "Sometimes you find gems on microfilm. This one is from 1984."

It was a game story between local high schools Waterloo Columbus and Waterloo West. Toward the end was a tidbit on the Columbus quarterback—Chris Klieman.

"Klieman suffered bruised ribs in the first half and missed a series of plays, but returned to action after his ribs were taped," the story said.

Bruised ribs do not feel good. They can literally hurt with every breath. And it's not like that thin, white athletic tape provides much protection. Sneezing, coughing or getting out of a chair can be a house of pain.

"Bruised ribs are tough," said Scott Woken, NDSU's assistant director of athletics for internal operations and a wily veteran of sports medicine. "You could just as well fracture them, that's what it feels like. With a fracture, obviously, an X-ray or picture will show the crack. Truly bruised ribs are just as painful, with so many muscle and cartilage connections. Every time you breathe, the ribs actually move."

Klieman didn't remember much about the game, mainly because it was his junior season and most of his memories are from his senior year. Put it this way: Nobody would want to play against Northern Iowa, Klieman's alma mater, with pain in the rib cage. Those are two teams that annually try to crush each other.

The competitiveness of the matchup was nothing new to Klieman, an assistant at UNI in 2008 when the NDSU-UNI series was renewed at the Division I FCS level.

Waterloo West, by the way, won that 1984 rivalry game 18-15 behind quarterback Courtney Messingham, NDSU's offensive coordinator in the 2017 season. Messingham signed a letter of intent at UNI and Klieman joined him a year later. Messingham was the better high school quarterback. But there's no known written evidence of Messingham playing with a bruised rib.

Collin Larsen would play with a bruised rib.

***

Those close to Larsen say not once did he ask for special favors. There wasn't a time, Collin said, when he took the mat with the feeling his opponent felt sorry for him. If that were the case, he probably would have forfeited on the spot. On the flipside, nobody recalls anybody from another school making fun or light of his situation. Nobody remembers any jokes, finger pointing, or bullying.

"He never wanted to be a charity case," Lemar said. "He never used his leg as an excuse for anything. Never."

Collin wondered how he was going to help around the farm without two healthy legs. He wanted to prove he could do anything he used to be able to do, and that included more than athletics. He wondered about the basics of getting up into a large tractor or combine. He worried about getting his license back, something that he eventually did, albeit it took a couple of tries.

"How would I be able to plant, harvest, and spray?" he asked.

That's the nature of farmers in this part of the world. There are times, however, when they need help and can't do the job. When Collin was in the Twin Cities hospital and his parents spent most of their time there, the farm didn't care. It still needed daily work, which in this case came from Roger Larsen, Dane Larsen's first cousin. Other help came from friends from church, with Roger coordinating the entire help operation.

It's a small world, North Dakota. I've known Roger Larsen for years as the co-pilot of our company plane at Forum Communications. We traveled the country covering NDSU football games, spending a lot of time in private aviation centers and hotel lobbies. Roger was the guy in the 2011 FCS national title game in Frisco who upon arrival on Wednesday before the Saturday game watched the Bison practice across the street from his third-floor hotel room with binoculars looking through the window. Bison equipment manager Brian Gordon noticed and went storming into the hotel, thinking it could be somebody from Sam Houston State, NDSU's title-game opponent. Roger was bored after we landed earlier that morning and was looking for something to do. All involved laugh about it now.

Anyway, Roger is a caring man and I wasn't surprised to learn he helped with the Collin Larsen case. Roger grew up on a farm; his father Ralph Larsen operated 950 acres north of West Fargo. That's the thing about farming, Roger said; it's rare a farmer comes in from the outside and starts from scratch. They almost always are born into it. Ralph bought his land in 1957 and like anybody else had to deal with issues over the years. The 1975 summer flood that left their house surrounded by sand bags. Their land was a virtual lake. The only way to get in and out was by a tractor navigating through about two feet of water.

"It was assumed you were going to follow your dad's footsteps," Roger said. "You have to like it. Even today. I'm over 70 years old and can't do the work I used to but I enjoy getting out there and looking at things. My wife can't figure out why I watch the weather so much. My income or what I do now is not affected by weather, but it's in your blood. You're watching the weather. You're watching for hail. It's still there. It doesn't go away."

Weather is dangerous. Winter is dangerous. One can die in minutes from exposure when it's 30 below and a stiff wind. As a kid, Ralph's best friend was killed by lightning, hit while driving an old John Deere tractor with a loader on it. Thankfully, five to six neighboring farmers came to the aid of the family and finished off the crop.

Roger quit farming for a position with the National Guard until retiring in 2002. He returned to farming with Dane's operation, a fortunate stroke of luck for the family that he did. When Collin had his accident, Dane turned to his cousin for help. They had just finished putting steel siding on the barn when the crisis hit.

"I remember the picture," Roger said. "Collin was standing on top of the barn. That was three days before the accident. When that happened, his dad called me up and said you're going to have to jump in and take over. It wasn't a big deal because I farmed most of my life."

The one problem for Roger was that he had never harvested corn, so he went through a quick self-education. Harvest involves many details like lining up truck drivers and figuring out the fertilizer situation. The biggest problem that fall was inexperienced truck drivers and the worry they knew what they were doing. It was a daily grind from around 7 a.m. until 10 at night. During harvest, farmers start early and go as long as they can without dropping from exhaustion.

The Larsen family had people willing to help. These days, in the age of bigger farms and fewer neighbors in the country, that's not always the case. For those people, there is a godsend.

It's called Farm Rescue.

The organization has been a savior to farmers in the Midwest. Examples are everywhere. When Roger Larsen was young, he remembers neighbors switching back and forth for help without money switching hands. For instance, if one farmer got help from a friend for three days last year, the friend returned the favor for three days this year.

"Those kinds of days are gone," Roger said. "Things are so hectic and everybody is trying to get things done so quickly. It's more of a single-farm operation now."

In the summer of 2017, Gary Marks of Ypsilanti, N.D., fractured the vertebrae in his neck in an auto accident, leaving him unable to handle his 2,800-acre operation. The crew that came to his aid, all retired John Deere employees, brought their expertise to the Marks farm and helped him out. It was the second time Marks had to call on Farm Rescue; six years earlier he broke his leg and had to seek help.

A year earlier, 44-year-old Jason Sandvik, who farms northwest of Williston, suffered a heart attack that laid him up for a few weeks during planting season. In the timing of farming this is about as unfortunate as it gets. The cavalry from Farm Rescue was soon busy planting his 800 acres with durum wheat.

Tanner Millang, a farmer from Bottineau, was the field operations manager for Farm Rescue on the project.

"As a farmer, you're putting so much on the line, you're basing your investment on six inches of topsoil and the hope that it rains," Millang told the Williston Herald newspaper. "If you miss one year you could go bankrupt. North Dakota is a great state, especially the farmers."

In 2013 alone, Farm Rescue helped 50 farm families for reasons that spanned from paralysis, broken bones, cancer and natural disasters. How did it all start?

Trace it to one 30-minute drive by Bill Gross.

He's the engine that founded Farm Rescue.

Gross grew up on a farm near Cleveland, N.D., and attended aeronautical school at the University of North Dakota. He flew the world, at times making long trips over oceans. In one instance, he was in the cockpit of a Boeing 747 working for UPS when he and his co-pilot got into a lengthy conversation on what they wanted to do when they retired.

"I'm going to be a random good Samaritan," Gross told his co-pilot. "I'm going to get on a big John Deere tractor, start out in the western part of the state of North Dakota and drive across the state. I'm going to pull in somewhere where a farmer looks like he's having a tough time or has run-down equipment. He'll wonder, 'Who is this guy?' I'll put fuel in and plant a few hundred acres."

Then he'll leave. Hence, the random good Samaritan.

Awhile later, Gross was in Seattle having dinner with his old college roommate, Kevin Mateer, who asked his friend what he planned on doing when he retired. Gross relayed essentially the same story he had flying the 747 at 40,000 feet, telling Mateer about his love of farming and ranching and giving back.

"I just have a couple of questions," Mateer said, in a serious tone to Bill. "Why wait until you retire? You don't know what tomorrow will bring."

"I don't know," Gross said. "I just thought I would do it when I retire. I never thought of doing it now."

The second question?

"Instead of randomly helping people," Mateer said, "Why randomly? Were there people who were injured or ill on the farm when you grew up?"

"Yes, there were," Gross replied.

When dinner was done, Gross got in his car for the 30-minute drive back to his home. It turned out to be a historic 30 minutes for Farm Rescue.

"A lot of times, any one of us do our best thinking behind the windshield," he said. "You start to think about things."

He started thinking about "why not now?" A lot of people come up with ideas but then think about reasons not to follow through with them. It's a process that could take all of 60 seconds. A great idea? Bam. Gone.

"You can come up with a million reasons why it won't work," Gross said. "In those 60 seconds, you can dismiss it and it will be gone forever."

Not this time. Not in those 30 minutes. He thought about other kids who came from farm backgrounds have thought about the same thing – helping other farmers. There can be volunteers out there, he thought to himself. He thought about an organization that has to be run differently, an entity that needs to find funding from different sources. And the media? They would want to cover a story like this. It's a good story. It's a human-interest story. And the volunteers will get rewarded for the feeling of helping other people, he thought to himself.

Thirty minutes later, he arrived home.

Gross didn't have the name "Farm Rescue" on his mind yet. He went to his computer and started surfing the Internet. He searched domain names, because in this day and age it has to have some World Wide Web association to it. He typed "rescuing farms." He typed "saving farms." He typed "farm rescue" and it showed the domain was available. "That's what we're doing," he thought to himself.

Farm Rescue.

The next quest was figuring out the non-profit sector of Farm Rescue. Gross did it himself, bypassing hiring an attorney by researching all the steps. He filed paperwork with the IRS, which approved the venture. Next on the list was securing sponsorships, with RDO Equipment Co. being the first on board. He solicited the help of a couple of seed companies. There were five volunteers that first year in 2006, one tractor and one planter.

The first case was near Lefor, N.D., to help Matt and Laura Biel, at the time parents of two small children. Matt lost his hand in an auger accident. Then it was on to a Richardton, N.D., farm, where a farmer lost his arm. Another case involved a man who suffered brain damage after getting rolled over by a horse. The crew moved to near Cando, N.D., when a farmer, sleeping in a tent, had a tree fall on him during a lightning storm. Another farmer that year near Kensal, N.D., needed help after being partially blinded.

True to Gross' theory in his 30-minute drive, the news media started reporting the feel-good stories. In the ensuing two years, the national media picked up on it. CNN named Gross a "CNN Hero." Farm Rescue became a viable project with more volunteers and more sponsors hopping on board. The volunteers were not just from North Dakota, either, but from virtually every state. As of early 2018, the Farm Rescue data base counted over 1,000 volunteers.

"It mushroomed," Gross said. "This thing called Farm Rescue just mushroomed. I did not foresee the amount of success. I thought maybe we could help a few farmers and ranchers in North Dakota."

The organization spawned into other helping entities for farmers. In 2017, areas of North Dakota were hit hard by severe drought, with hay for livestock being sparse. Farm Rescue commenced "Operation Haylift," with the idea coming from a 1949 assistance program that used helicopters to drop bales of hay to cattle caught in the snow because of a blizzard. Donations of hay came from everywhere -- Michigan, Wisconsin, and Iowa. How would it be feasible to deliver the hay? It was $4 to $6 per mile to truck it. In came Farm Rescue, which offered to either haul the hay for free or give some sort of fuel reimbursement based on the size of the herd.

In 2017 alone, Farm Rescue helped 127 farm and ranch families, with the footprint extending into eastern Montana, South Dakota, Minnesota, Nebraska and Iowa. And it all started because one pilot wanted to be a random good Samaritan and a college friend encouraging him to start a non-profit organization to provide an avenue of goodness. Gross loves those three words – avenue of goodness. If he were to describe Farm Rescue in a handful of words or less, that would be it. He's proud his non-profit is true to those words, operating with a small staff and no paid executives. Based in Horace, N.D., it has one administrative assistant, one fundraiser, one marketing person and one operations director. A board of directors consisting of five members, people who know the farming business, guide the organization.

Questions of help never cease. One day, Gross asked himself, what about the families and their life after Farm Rescue leaves? That thought grew into the Farm Rescue Foundation which provides assistance to help farmers or ranchers in their everyday lives. If a farmer was paralyzed from the waist down, it's all good to harvest his crop, but what about the following year? Farm Rescue Foundation is a separate non-profit from Farm Rescue that provides equipment so farmers and ranchers can maintain their livelihood. It helped the family of Larry and Rosalind Leier of Hague, N.D., with a "track" wheelchair for their son to help him maneuver around the farm. A regular wheelchair with wheels isn't productive around a farm, but one with tracks can navigate the most uneven terrains. There are other wheelchairs that help lift farmers up into their combines or tractors.

"This is the silent side people don't see a lot," Gross said.

Gross went to a high school, Cleveland, that is now silent. The school closed after his junior year with his classmates going to either nearby Medina or Jamestown high schools to finish their senior year. Gross got his high school diploma through correspondence while staying on the farm. He took his tests in Medina.

In essence, that's why Farm Rescue is needed. The neighbors aren't there anymore to help. Families that used to have five kids now have one or two. No longer are the kids around to help out. The smaller farms have disappeared.

Farm families requiring help need that avenue of goodness. Gross saw the demographics of rural America changing and he saw them changing quickly. When the Cleveland school closed, the town gas station and grocery store went away. About all that's left is the elevator and post office.

It's probably about as big as Prosper.

Remember Prosper, the town with four exits and four streets?

Doug Simunic, top, managed the F-M RedHawks for 22 years. The writer catching up with Steve Blehm, left, at his rural home in Staunton, Va., and Brad Gjermundson at his ranch near Marshall, N.D.

Dave Osborn, top left, at his home in Lakeville, Minn. Bill Sorensen, top right, spends his summers in Medora, N.D. Dick Johnson was an outfielder for the 1958 Drayton Legion baseball team that reached the final 12 in the country.

VII. Cowboy Tough

Driving through the town of Marshall, N.D., population one inhabited house and one church, the piece of art emerges like a big white tail deer roaming the ditch of Highway 8. It's a large metal statue of a man on a bucking horse, athletic as can be to not get thrown onto some dirt arena floor. A scoria rock throw later, take a left on the red scoria road named Rodeo Road West and head west to the ranch of Brad Gjermundson. Drive almost four wavy, hilly miles to the compound that has been home to Brad and his wife Jackie and their children, Kane, Jori, and Hali for almost 30 years. They bought it as newly-married young adults, not certain if it would work out financially.

"At the time it seemed like we were living in the middle of nowhere, but it's really not," Jackie said.

To a city kid, it is the middle of nowhere. The size and scope are enormous, especially for any city inhabitant who regularly doesn't see such beautiful country. It takes 20 minutes to mow my lawn in north Fargo. The Gjermundson ranch consists of 2,800 acres that they maintain and another 4,000 that they lease. Nobody has measured how many miles of scoria (red gravel) roads meander through it, but a runner could finish a marathon with several miles of road to spare.

The Knife River slices through the middle, a calming large stream that cut its swath in the land through the years. The views from bluffs above the river are picturesque. There's history to it. Jackie has found buffalo skeletons near the river bottom, the probable result of a buffalo jump – the practice usually done by Native Americans centuries ago to chase buffalo over the cliff to hunt and kill them. Don't underestimate the nostalgic, calming river, however. It gets nasty, like in August of 2014 when it changed the Gjermundson house forever.

The family built a new house on higher ground, leaving the old Victorian-shaped home next to the river because of a prior flood. Jackie feared for mold after waters got the best of it, so it was time to do something different. The new place was perfect, with a walkout basement facing south and seemingly safe from the Knife River. After the 10-inch rain in 2014, the waters rose higher than they ever imagined, creeping into the ground floor of the basement. It went higher than the doors of a barn by the old house, a fact marked by a large horizontal line on the structure.

As fast as the waters came in, thankfully they went out just as quick. There were other hazards, like the herd of cattle being funneled across the river not long after the waters had receded. The sandy bottom was mushy, so soft that 12 calves got stuck and were trampled to death by the ones walking behind them.

"That river can be wicked," Brad said, while surveying the lush-looking green valley.

It could be a scene out of a movie, like a couple of shots in Kevin Costner's "Dances with Wolves." When he was competing, and if money wasn't an object, Brad would have a landing strip on his ranch with his own plane and pilot available to hit the open road. Only the Lord knows how many miles he put on in a vehicle or in the air on his way to becoming one of the all-time greatest rodeo cowboys in American history.

He earned it, man. They, his family, earned it.

For all the trophies, paintings, small sculptures, plaques and mementos in the family home, there was sweat and nerve equity many times more everybody put into it. For example, in 1979 when Jackie heard of a plane crash involving four cowboys in a general area where Brad was performing, which put a jolt to Jackie's nerves. To add to the fear, the plane that went down was similar to the one Brad was flying from one rodeo to another. Moreover, one of Brad's rodeo friends from Montana called Jackie and asked if she's heard from Brad. She hadn't. This was before cell phones, so there was no picking up her iPhone and dialing his iPhone to see if he was OK. In a worrisome state of mind, she called the Professional Rodeo Cowboys Association office; somebody on the other end at least told her it wasn't her husband on that plane.

"I hadn't heard from him that day," Jackie said, but the call eased her mind.

The life of a traveling cowboy is brutal, especially in the summer when going from one event to another. Brad was all over the country for many years. In 1982 alone, he performed at 210 rodeos. That year a limitation was put on how many a rider could enter and still count toward the world standings. From 1981 through '84 and into '85, he was rarely home.

A small plane was the way to travel but wasn't always feasible. When possible, a cowboy could knock off rodeos in record fashion. A July 4 one year Brad started at Cody, Wyo., at 1 p.m., flew to Red Lodge, Mont., for a 3 p.m. event and back in the air to Dickinson, N.D., for a 6 p.m. start. The day wasn't over; there was a rodeo in Mobridge, S.D., at 8 p.m. In most cases, the schedule was doable because rodeo arenas oftentimes are c. to an airport. In essence, Brad and a friend or two who did the same schedule to make the air travel affordable would arrive at a rodeo after it had started, ride their event, head back to the airport and take off.

"I don't know if you call it crazy or whatever ... motivated?" Brad said.

Weather was the obstacle. If the plane had to go around a storm or the skies were too stormy, the cowboys would have to forfeit their entry fee and pay a fine generally around $25 if they didn't show up. It wasn't just private planes that offered a hectic travel schedule. One week, Gjermundson was in the Denver airport eight times thanks to the Frontier Airlines hub. The schedule went something like this: Start in Orange County, Calif., fly to Denver, catch a connection to North Platte, Neb., back to Denver, head to Omaha, back to Denver, flew to North Platte again, back to Denver and finally to the home airport in Bismarck.

"You just learn to sleep in a car or sleep in a plane," Brad said. "All you had to take care of was yourself. I did all my own entering of rodeos and all my own reservations."

Duane Daines, a fellow cowboy and travel partner of Brad's for years, will never forget the small plane trip after leaving the Calgary Stampede for St. Paul, Ore. The flight started out fine, but thunderstorms began forming on the horizon. Flying at around 12,000 to 13,000 feet, the thunderheads were too tall to fly over, so the pilot tried to find a break in the clouds.

"We went down through a little hole," Daines said. "Then we started following a river in the valley. I remember thinking this is crazy. You're just trying to make it from one rodeo to another."

Daines was also a pilot who would take his own small plane from one rodeo to another. Starting out as a young adult, he was trying to learn both: be a good saddle bronc rider and a pilot who flew with some measurable amount of safety.

"You're trying to hit a couple rodeos a day," he said. "It's amazing we were able to do that without cell phones, although they started to come around later in our careers. There were a lot of dog days of summer, just a lot of traveling."

Traveling like the time Daines was so in a hurry that he hopped in his plane for a trip to Salt Lake City, Utah. A backup of Delta planes had the airport bottled up, but Daines was able to maneuver into the landing pattern. His plane stopped in front of all the jets on the tarmac, a place where everybody could see the cowboys get out of their plane. They were a muddy group from the rodeo earlier in the day and in Daines' case, he still had his boots and spurs on.

"The next day, they put on my window of the plane flying regulations from 1925 that they found in the gift shop," he said about some practical jokester. "And No. 7 was no flying with spurs on. You just didn't have time. It's all in fun talking about it now but you just wonder how the heck you did it."

That schedule was more doable in the age before the scrutiny of the modern airport security gate. Often, Gjermundson would carry his saddle and spurs on the plane and throw them in a baggage area. Daines remembers one flight to Denver when the cowboys left their saddles in an open space in first class. Nobody cared, and in fact were quite intrigued by it. One time, at North Platte, the rodeo had already started when Brad landed and a friend had arranged a ride for him from the airport to the arena. It happened to be a local police officer who turned on his lights and sped Gjermundson to the competition.

When driving to rodeos, Brad would try and hook up with another rider or two. They did their best to plan a thought-out circuit, avoiding doubling back on a road. It was mile after mile. They took turns driving and sleeping in the vehicle. In the early years, every event counted because it was a chance to make another dollar. Brad's philosophy was simple; if he missed a rodeo, he felt like he was missing a day's work.

In 1981, when he won his first world saddle bronc championship, he was victorious in Houston in a ride that paid him $8,000, a sum that he told the Bismarck Tribune was like "a year's wages." He said he earned about $95,000 the following year.

"When you have a goal of making the national final or being a world champion, you just have to do what you have to do and that's a priority," he said. "It didn't matter the size of the rodeo. But the older I got, there were certain ones I tried to avoid."

As he got older, so did his family. During times of Brad's travel, Jackie stayed home and handled the babies and the house.

"You have to give Jackie a huge part of this," Daines said, "because the champion gets all the accolades but the whole family is what makes it all happen in the rodeo business. It's no different with any rodeo family. I remember seeing the little kids around the arena and now they're the champions. On the other hand, no one is forcing you to do it. If you don't like it, then you have to change it."

Jackie and the kids would stay close to the house thinking Brad was going to call home at a certain bubble of time. There were times that wasn't possible, like when the traveling cowboys would get to a hotel at 2 or 3 in the morning. While on the road, the only time Brad could call was when he found a pay phone during a stop. Jackie never really was concerned about Brad trying to stay on a bucking horse and getting thrown off without hurting himself; the worrisome part was between the rodeos. And just getting there.

"Just the driving, that kind of thing, you learn to trust God a lot," she said. "It was hard for us. You want him to do well but yet we were home on the ranch and we, of course, wanted him here, too."

The family got help, from Brad's father, brother, uncle, or the neighbors. In 1986, the family got assistance when Brad was homebound – the result of a broken leg that wasn't pretty.

It happened at a July rodeo in Glasgow, Mont., when the horse turned backwards in the chute, came out backwards, and hit Brad. The break was bad enough that Brad took a charter flight from Billings, Mont., to Fargo where he went under the care of noted orthopedic surgeon, Mark Askew. He was hospitalized for a week. Jackie and Kane drove to Fargo.

Perhaps the worst injury came 10 years later when Gjermundson tore a bicep tendon near the elbow, the probable result of wear and tear over the years. The injury was so severe that a Bismarck hospital wouldn't treat it, instead they sent Brad to a medical center in Minneapolis. But, all things considered, Gjermundson survived a dangerous occupation in pretty good shape.

Not everybody did.

Daines was 36 years old and competing in a rodeo in Armstrong, British Columbia, in the mid-1990s when a horse named Blue Boy pinned him in the back of the chute against the metal rails. A broken back left him paralyzed below the waist.

The first cowboy to visit him in the hospital in Vancouver was Brad Gjermundson. There's a unique culture within professional cowboys; they compete hard against each other in the arena but are best friends and confidants away from it. That explains how they travel so well together and how they endure the intense road trips.

"He was right there with me," Daines said. "I had a spinal cord injury; it was a fluky deal. The horse just lost his footing and came up over me. But I feel fortunate I had all that rodeo training. This is a new chapter in my life. It's good to have good friends and that's what you get in rodeo. I remember the good ol' days. Our families are a big part of the rodeo business, that's your support group. I had to reach back to everything I had. You don't think about it, it's just how you persevered in the rodeo business. Like I said, this is a new chapter. Good friends, that's what it's all about. Brad is a good bronc rider but an even better person."

The chapter on Gjermundson's physical rodeo talent would read great balance and quickness and the ability to anticipate the bucking movement of a horse. He wasn't big at 5-foot-5 and around 140 to 150 pounds during competition; but rodeo isn't about the biggest guy, either. It's a mindset, knowing every horse at every event will be different and having the anticipation to handle each one. Daines said his friend was a fierce competitor in the arena who just wanted it more than others. He said Brad had the heart to go with the talent.

"When you got on a better horse, you were more aggressive," Gjermundson said. "A good horse is an easier ride than a mediocre horse because of the timing, and most of the time they kick harder. The opportunity is way better on the good horses, but you still have to do it. If you're not laying it on the line, you're going to get bucked off. A guy who doesn't get bucked off doesn't win very much. It's like the guy who takes 23 shots in a game in basketball vs. the guy who takes two – percentage wise you're not going to score. I don't know if it was an adrenalin rush but I was always ready."

Fearful? Maybe. The fear of not getting out of the chute just right.

"I felt like horses could sense you were fearful or scared," he said. "I was very fortunate to not ever get hurt in the chute. I've had horses flip over but I got out of there and didn't get hurt."

The family is testament that toughness can be hereditary.

Brad is the son of Stanley and Sharon Gjermundson, lifelong ranchers who built the house in Marshall in 1970 and raised their five children: Tammy, Brad, Lyle, Casey, and Connie. All got involved in ranching and rodeo, with Brad going the farthest of the bunch.

"They grew up with, and rode horses every day when they were kids," said Stanley, prior to accepting the Rodeo/Rancher Award in 2008 in Dunn County. It's given to a recipient who symbolizes a western way of life.

All three of Brad and Jackie's kids got involved in rodeo. At the ranch, they fenced off an area perfect for practice. The family rented bucking horses from a man across the highway. Kane competed at Central

Wyoming College in Riverton, Wyo., Jori went to Dickinson State, and Hali competed for the club team at North Dakota State. They had their successes with Kane and Hali riding professionally and; of course, in a sport where confrontation is probable, they had their injuries.

Kane was competing in a professional saddle bronc competition in Colorado when he got bucked off with his foot stuck in the stirrup. The result was a twisted fracture sending him to a hospital in Parker, Col., for 10 days. He also had a pulmonary embolism in his lungs.

"I always worried way more about Kane than I did Brad," Jackie said. "He's had more accidents. He broke his elbow once, his shoulder blade. Brad always hoped his kids didn't feel like they had to ride broncs because he did, even though all of our kids were in rodeos since they were real small. They loved rodeo, but if they didn't want to do that, we would have been OK with that, too."

In 2007 when Hali, a junior at Richardton-Taylor High School, competed in goat tying on the first day of the North Dakota High School Finals Rodeo. She tore the ACL in her knee, although that didn't stop her from competing.

Sportswriter Dustin Monke of the Dickinson Press newspaper wrote the story of Hali "slapping some tape and a brace on" and continuing for the next two days without really knowing the seriousness of the injury. No matter. She won her second straight girls all-around title despite the ACL injury.

"It was torn all the way," she told Monke.

She reinjured the knee during the basketball season of her senior year, yet trucked on to win three straight rodeo all-around state titles. The goat tying event of her junior year was shelved because it was too tough on her one leg.

"Though the knee still bothers her," Monke wrote, "it hasn't shown in her performances."

Just like it didn't show in her father's performances. When Gjermundson was inducted into the North Dakota Cowboy Hall of Fame in 2009, he had some major league company. Nominees included former Gov. Art Link and Marquis de Mores, the founder of Medora. Even Ronald Reagan wrote him a personal letter dated January 16, 1986. It read:

Dear Mr. Gjermundson:

Congratulations on your championship win at the National Finals Rodeo. Nothing captures the spirit of American ingenuity like these events. The courage and determination

which made this nation grow are to be found in great abundance in the men and women who compete in our rodeos. I commend your enthusiasm and your achievements.
Nancy joins me in wishing you continued success and happiness.
Sincerely,
Ronald Reagan

Three years earlier, the Gjermundsons were invited by the Reagans to a "Barbecue at the White House," after a Professional Rodeo Cowboy Association event at the Capital Centre.

The final tally of accomplishments read like this: North Dakota High School Rodeo Association saddle bronc titles in 1976 and 1977 and the all-around title in 1977; National Intercollegiate Rodeo Association region title at Dickinson State in 1978 and NIRA national champ in 1980. From there, he turned pro and captured Rookie of the Year honors in his initial PRCA year in 1980.

He won four PRCA saddle bronc world championships starting the following year in 1981 and then ripped off three straight from 1983-85. He was inducted into the North Dakota Cowboy Hall of Fame in 1990 and the North Dakota Sports Hall of Fame and the Pro Rodeo Hall of Fame in 1995. He retired in 1999.

Though retired, he still competes occasionally in steer roping. On her phone, Jackie has some fine highlights of Brad still able to do it at age 59. He's relatively healthy for a guy who took so many spills on a bucking horse, about the only regular medical attention an occasional chiropractic visit. He was never one to take many pain relievers saying when you compete almost on a daily basis and using the same muscles, they get conditioned and you don't get sore.

"It's like if you don't run for two years and try to pick up where you left off, you'll be in the hurt bag," Brad said. "I always felt good and didn't work out. I was active all the time."

The competition is never far from his mind, however. He keeps up with the professional rodeo standings almost on a daily basis.

"He's still very competitive and it's hard just to quit," Jackie said. "If you've ever heard that it's in your blood, that's a true statement. Some cowboys quit and they have nothing to do with rodeo anymore but that's not the way it is for Brad."

Jackie (Brown) Gjermundson grew up on a farm in Keene, N.D., located in the shadows of the Missouri River in the northwestern corner of the state. Her family always had horses and didn't miss many rodeos. Her dad worked in construction while the family tended to a few head of cattle. Jackie went to Watford City High School and Dickinson State, where she met her cowboy.

It's been quite a ride living the life of a rodeo champ. Perhaps a song called "Ride for Eight Seconds" written by Connie Gjermundson, Brad's sister, put it best:

"I met a bronc rider at a big rodeo I fell in love I told him so
But this was his answer to me, To ride hard and travel far I've got to be free
He said I'll ride for eight seconds, Gonna spur with all I've got

I'm gonna ride for eight seconds, Wanna be the man on top
He said I'll ride for eight seconds, Gotta lift on that buckrein
I'm gonna ride for eight seconds, Everybody's gonna know my name

I've tried to move on but it is hard; I've loved this man right from the start
I watch him ride broncs at the rodeo, Oh and he's the man that wears the gold

He's gonna ride for eight seconds, Gonna spur with all he's got
He's gonna ride for eight seconds, Wants to be the man on top
He's gonna ride for eight seconds, Gotta lift on that buckrein
He's gonna ride for eight seconds, Everybody's gonna know his name

He's the saddle bronc champion of the world, Oh if I could only be his girl

He's gonna ride for eight seconds, Gonna spur with all he's got
He's gonna ride for eight seconds, Wants to be the man on top
He's gonna ride for eight seconds, Gotta lift on that buckrein
He's gonna ride for eight seconds, Everybody's gonna know his name
He rides for eight seconds, and everybody knows his name"

That's eight seconds. Over and over and over again. For many years.

VIII. JFK, Vietnam and Bison Football

North Dakota State offensive guard Austin Kuhnert was one of four players present for the annual Friday press conference at Toyota Stadium in Frisco, Texas, the day before the 2017 FCS national championship game. Until then, there hadn't been many opportunities to talk with Bison players since their semifinal victory over Sam Houston State three weeks earlier. In Kuhnert's case, it was the first time he was made available to the media. I had one burning question: Did you pop your own elbow into place during the Sam Houston game?

The short video made its rounds on social media, a 10-second clip that appeared to show Kuhnert playing doctor — to himself. The camera angle caught Kuhnert getting up from the turf at Gate City Bank Field at the Fargodome and walking back toward the huddle with his left arm draped in obvious pain. Kuhnert took his right arm, cupped his left elbow and gave it a couple tugs as to force his dislocated elbow back into place.

It answered my burning question.

"The third play of the game, red zone, I probably fell on it funny; and I got up and noticed I couldn't move it hardly," Kuhnert said. "Just rotated it in, it popped and it felt better after that."

The assembled reporters, about 30 of them, looked at Kuhnert in silent disbelief, and then let out a collective nervous chuckle. As somebody who covered Kuhnert for four years, I was not surprised. The amazing detail is Kuhnert did not miss a play. His self-diagnosis and reaction did not alarm any of his Bison teammates who caught a glimpse of it, either. It's part of the toughness that linebacker Nick DeLuca described as commonplace with the Bison players.

"Our rams (offensive linemen) definitely pride themselves in being tough," DeLuca said. "Austin is a great representation of that. I've personally never had to do that. Doc Piatt popped my shoulder back in for me. There's some tough dudes, no doubt."

DeLuca overcame shoulder surgery performed by NDSU team doctor Bruce Piatt in 2016 that ended his season after three games. Kuhnert's analysis of his elbow came during a press conference where the questions usually address basic football talk like who's favored or the feelings of being in a title game. A player never talks about fixing his own elbow between plays.

"I was good to go," Kuhnert said. "Gotta be a man."

Kuhnert would fit the mold of the 1960s Bison perfectly. The run of six FCS titles in seven years beginning in 2011 was the result of NDSU's physicality and playing the game of football at a tougher level than the rest of the competition. Nobody wanted to go toe-to-toe for four quarters against NDSU because it took a toll. Their forefathers, the players who started the run of excellence in 1963, had to be proud.

Those '60s players were hardcore football guys. They grew the program in an era when the country reeled from the JFK assassination and the rise of the Vietnam War. It was a different time.

The Bison football players took on a similar in-your-face attitude. This wasn't Woodstock and free love. These guys were kids in their teens and early 20s disguised as men. One of the Sciacca brothers had a pet snake in his dorm room at Churchill Hall. He made a den for the slithery critter above his dresser.

"I saw a light bulb, some grass or something and this big-ass snake with a white rat in its mouth," said Lew Boyko, a student at NDSU at the time. "It freaked me out. I found it hard to sleep in the dorm room down the hall wondering if that S.O.B. got out, what and where would I go?"

NDSU defeated James Madison University 17-13 in the 2017 FCS title game. The Bison players celebrated on the stage of Toyota Field in much the same way they did the prior five times they won a championship. Then it was off to Dallas/Fort Worth International Airport for the routine charter flight back to Fargo. The Bison took a different type of flight after their 20-7 win over Grambling in the 1965 Pecan Bowl. That game wrapped up an 11-0 season and the College Division national championship.

That flight home had a nickname: "The Champagne Flight."

The team physician brought some champagne on board and gave a bottle to each of the 13 seniors. He rewarded the dog days of practice when the Bison offensive linemen would work as hard as they could on the "champagne drill." At the end of practice, the players would sprint 10 yards, turn around and rattle off a series of 200-yard runs. Their motivation: champagne after an unbeaten season.

"It goes back to that mentality," said Ardell Wiegandt, an offensive and defensive lineman on the '65 team. "You drive and you drive and you drive and you have that never-give-up attitude. We came back on the champagne flight. That's why we named that drill."

***

Those dorms were one of the first things Darrell Mudra kept an eye on when he first got the Bison head coaching job in 1963. Mudra knew he had to change the way the players went about their business, both on and off the field. His office was in the southwest corner of the Physical Education Building, which is now Bentson Bunker Fieldhouse that the Bison volleyball team calls home. His windows had a direct view across the street to Churchill Hall, where several of his players lived. In the morning, if he didn't see a light on in one of the rooms, he had trainer Denis Isrow knocking on doors to get the players up. There would be no sleeping in and missing class.

If there was one constant to the growing years of Bison football, it would be Isrow. Everybody called him Izzy. Sadly, he died in 2012 but his legacy lives forever within the program. He didn't have nearly the staff of assistant trainers and student trainers that NDSU does today, so Isrow would teach the players how to tape themselves. Bob Hyland, a Bison Hall of Famer, offense guard and captain of the '69 team, was majoring in physical education and coaching when he took a taping class.

"We would tape each other on road trips," Hyland said. "To hurry things up, we had to tape each other. I had to tape my right arch, which I broke in high school. Simple. Izzy would know if we were doing it right or wrong. You talk about a mainstay of the program, he was it."

When he was a senior, Hyland hyperextended his knee in a game at Northern Michigan. Upon returning to Fargo later that night, Isrow told Hyland to be in the training room Sunday morning at 11 a.m. He got there at 11:15, and by that time the ice was thick. Hyland told Isrow he didn't want to put his foot in there.

"He comes in, shoves my leg in there and holds it," Hyland said. "He was a grumpy father figure to us all."

The injury saga wasn't done. On Monday, Hyland got taped up and headed to the practice field in his practice jersey and shorts. Before he got very far, head coach Ron Erhardt spotted Hyland.

"You're a damn captain, what are you doing?" Erhardt told him.

Hyland, getting the message, went back into the locker room and got his full pads on.

"It hurt like hell but I limped around out there," Hyland said. "Erhardt then took me off the kickoff squad, so I went out there and threw the kid (who took his spot) out. If I'm good enough to play on the line, I'm good enough to come down on a kickoff. That was the end of it. I hadn't missed a kickoff in three years, and I'm not going to do it now."

Hyland figures most of his teammates played through injuries of some sort, most likely the result of practicing hard and playing hard. Hyland wasn't that big for an offensive guard but not many were in the '60s. He was fast and the Bison coaches wanted fast, athletic offensive linemen. He was a fullback at Wisconsin Rapids Assumption High School and reported to his first NDSU fall camp at 215 pounds. He was told to lose some weight, which kind of struck him as odd since he took fourth in the low hurdles at the Wisconsin state track meet and his brother was close to being a world class sprinter.

"They said we don't have 200-pound guards, you don't run fast enough right now," Hyland said. "I said wait until you see me run."

That competitiveness is still evident today – on a mantel in his home in Fond du Lac, Wis. Hyland became one of the most successful high school football coaches in the country, leading St. Mary's Springs Academy to 15 state titles heading into the 2018 season. He didn't start out that way. He was 1-15-2 in his first two seasons, but he also had the advantage of following the blueprint of his Bison coaches. Over the years, he accumulated game balls from those 15 championships, but ended up giving most of them away.

One ball remained.

The only touchdown of his NDSU career. It came on a special teams play because he had that combination of being a lineman who could get downfield faster than some running backs and receivers. Erhardt, in fact, made Hyland run sprints with running backs Tim Mjos and Paul Hatchett in practice.

The Bison were on punt coverage in his senior year at Northern Iowa. The punt returner, standing near his 5-yard line, attempted a fair catch when Hyland blasted into a blocker in front of him. They hit forehead to forehead, so hard the blocker ended up stumbling back and causing his punt returner to muff the punt, the ball bouncing in the end zone. For an offensive lineman, this was the stuff dreams are made of. There were two Bison players heavy on the prowl – Hyland and Jim Ferge. Hyland won that fight, got the touchdown, and has the ball to prove it.

Thanks to Izzy.

Isrow, sensing the rarity of a lineman getting a touchdown, asked the Northern Iowa sideline crew for the ball. They initially refused.

"Izzy said bullshit, I'll send you a check, I'll pay for it myself," Hyland said. "Nobody was going to get that ball."

The way they practiced ... would not fly today. It was a knock-out, drag-'em-out fight at times; starting positions won by the players who handled practice the best. The NCAA in the last few years has taken steps to avoid the all-day practice sessions and for the most part has eliminated two-a-day practices. The Bison of the '60s? They had three-a-days.

And they took pride in it. These days, it's called the "scout team," the group of mostly freshmen whose job is to simulate an opponent. In 1965, it was called the "Hamburger Squad." Cornerback George Kallenbach called it a physical experience.

"It was live for one bunch of people," he said, referring to the freshmen, "but you were not to damage the other side of the line. The Hamburger Squad ... we took pride in being on that team. Hey, you're winning, and winning becomes contagious."

Terry Hanson, the quarterback on the '67 team, once told my father about his knee problems throughout his career. He hurt his left knee during his sophomore season, got through his junior year unscathed but tore up his other knee before the season opener at Montana State as a senior. Izzy came to the rescue.

"Isrow would ice my knee before every practice and a half hour to 45 minutes before every game," Hanson said. "Then they would tape it from the waist down to the ankle. After practice or the game, they would ice it again. That went on all year. It held up OK and started getting better. Then, in practice for the Pecan Bowl, I hurt it again and had surgery after the Pecan Bowl."

There was no sitting out that game because of some lame knee injury. For the record, Hanson didn't play the entire game; so whatever presumed ligament was damaged probably finally gave out.

Hyland, after sitting out his freshman year like all freshmen did before the NCAA changed the rule in 1972, was second string behind John Heller when fall camp opened in his sophomore season. He knew the way to the starting lineup -- go after Heller.

"I had to physically beat him in practice whenever I could," Hyland said.

Hyland was the starter by the time conference play started. Heller also found his place on the team and was a standout at another position on the offensive line. The '60s Bison were not for everybody. When Heller and Kallenbach were new to campus in 1964, there were 85 freshmen who tried out. Only 10 remained when they were seniors. All 10 started; five on offense and five on defense.

***

Before there was-Joe Chapman, there was Herb Albrecht. Chapman was the NDSU president who ushered in Division I athletics when the school started the transition out of Division II in 2003. At least Chapman had some semblance of tradition and success to work with.

Albrecht had nothing.

He was hired in 1962, and he soon figured out people in Fargo didn't care about Bison football. The program was a disaster, hardly winning any games. Before all of 200 fans in attendance, he watched NDSU lose its final home game of the '62 season to Drake University (Iowa). It was a 40-6 thumping.

"I didn't appreciate losing that much," Albrecht said in a 1990 Forum story. "I always felt we could be good academically and athletically at the same time. We should be doing better."

The general consensus says the rise of the NDSU football tradition began when Albrecht hired Mudra as the head football coach on June 13, 1963. I would argue it happened before then. Not so much on the field, but the recognition of some students that the improvised dormitory for the football team resembled homelessness. I would argue the beginning came in 1956, when a kid had the guts to write about the living conditions of the players.

The rundown facility was home for several football players at the school known then as the North Dakota Agricultural College. The basement of what is now Bentson Bunker Fieldhouse resembled a jail cell at Alcatraz.

Picture an old black and white movie. The dressers, beds, and lockers were metal. The walls were concrete, except for a wood partition that separated roommates. The players called it "The Pit" and they made the best of it, enduring the constant thumps from physical education classes in the gym floor above. At night, dance class or school dances made sleeping an unenviable option. They were the kids of parents who grew up in The Depression and probably made the best with what they had.

It's hard for Wayne "Dempsey" Worner to remember how many roommates he had in "The Pit," but there were more than football players. Mice made it their home, also.

"It wasn't like they were waiting for us when we got home," Worner said. "But it wasn't unusual. We would see them running around."

The situation was addressed after Worner wrote a 1956 article in The Spectrum, the school's newspaper. Of all the investigative pieces written in this town over the last 100 years, the one written by a 17-year-old should have a place in history.

Half of the headline said it all: "Reporter Cites Athlete Degradation." Dempsey lived in the southeast corner of the building; the communal bathroom was in the northeast corner. The steam from the radiator left the air as Dempsey wrote "sticky and stale." The windows, the ones that weren't painted black, were nailed down.

It's no wonder the NDAC struggled in football until the 1960s.

The change from living in the basement of Bentson Bunker to the modern amenities of today has been gradual over the years. The old football locker room at Dacotah Field was no great shakes, either. The change had to start somewhere. It's probably a little presumptuous to say Dempsey Worner's Spectrum article on that spring day in 1956 was the start. But nobody can say it wasn't, either.

"I would love to think that it did," he said.

The Spectrum's editor was convinced. In an editor's note following Dempsey's story, he or she wrote the following:

"Are football players 'animals' to be put in what a dairy man would call a 'loose housing unit,' except when they are called upon to go out and play ball? Certainly no one can point to one thing and say, 'This is what is wrong with our football team.' However, one of the things that is wrong is the high mortality rate between the freshman and sophomore year. I attribute that high rate to a large extent to 'The Pit.'"

Dempsey left the NDAC after his freshman year and returned two years later. He figures that of the 36 freshmen football players that he came to college with, maybe six were still there. The living conditions were better when he returned, he said, and part of that may have been the result of a change in head coaches. Around that time Team Makers booster club started to get some legs and that may have helped.

These days, Dempsey is living in Blacksburg, Va., retired from Virginia Tech where he was a professor and Dean of the School of Education for many years. He works on occasion with the educational system in the state.

He comes back to the Minnesota lakes country in the summer. He's a proud Bison football alum, annually paying his $100 dues to the Bison

Football Players Association that former player Sean Fredricks started in 2016. He was a player who made a difference with his pen and The Spectrum article.

"I don't know that I was a social activist or anything but I liked to write and I wrote it like I saw it," he said.

Wayne Worner got his nickname Dempsey from his grandfather, who thought his grandchild was so active as a baby that he was more like boxer Jack Dempsey. As a college kid, Dempsey may have been the one to deliver the first punch to get NDSU out of the facility dungeon. It was quite the journey living with mice in the basement of Bentson Bunker to the Fargodome and Sanford Health Athletic Complex, the newly-renovated basketball arena.

Hundreds of players in the 1960s started the journey. These guys were farm tough, city tough, college tough – guys that never took no for an answer. As former player, coach, and current Team Makers executive director Pat Simmers always says, "before you become good, you have to become tough." Perhaps that's one reason Bob Hyland's St. Mary's Springs Academy has been so good over the years. Simmers was an assistant under Hyland for one season in the early '70s.

"He was very, very good and we got some things going," Hyland said. "It still goes back to your coaches. When they can work together and all be on the same page, then you can have some success."

Mudra started the work-together theme when he was hired during the summer of 1963, and there wasn't much time to get organized for the season. In the 34-year-old Mudra, Albrecht found a winner – he was 32-4-1 in four seasons at Adams State College (Col.).

Before Mudra was hired, Albrecht called in co-captains Joe Henderson and Jim Driscoll in the spring of 1963 to a meeting to gauge the players' feelings about the program.

"We're college students, as if we knew what was needed," Driscoll said.

The school needed a place to practice, a better game facility, more players and a good coaching staff. Driscoll, a Fargo Shanley graduate, figured the school was trying to hire legendary Shanley head coach Sid Cichy; but for whatever reason that fell through. Disappointed Cichy didn't get the job, Driscoll discovered immediately that Mudra was different. It was Driscoll's last season of eligibility and the thoughts of the 0-10 season of 1962 quickly disappeared. Players remember Mudra always saying "we haven't scratched the surface" constantly during practice, as if it were a visionary slogan.

"He was a doctor of psychology," Driscoll said. "The key to the whole change is he sold us on the idea that we weren't losers and that we could win."

The assistant coaches, a significant upgrade from the previous staff, preached as much. Mudra was quoted several times over the years he felt lucky to get the staff that he did. Buck Nystrom ran the offense and Ron Erhardt ran the defense. Erhardt went on to be a national champion head coach at NDSU and later to a career in the NFL, most notably as the head coach of the New England Patriots. Nystrom was a walk-on at Michigan State who became so worthy as a player that he was inducted into the Michigan State Hall of Fame in 2014. He played on two winning Rose Bowl teams in the 1950s.

He was not a coddled type. Nystrom was a two-way player as an offensive lineman and middle guard who once played all 60 minutes in a victory over fourth-ranked Notre Dame.

He was 5-foot-10 and 194 pounds.

"Buck Nystrom did not like big guards," Hyland said. "We played three guards on the '65 team, John Heller and the two Sciaccas; and not one of them weighed over 190 pounds."

Nystrom shunned a chance at the NFL because he figured he was too small, instead starting a career in coaching as the freshman coach at Michigan State in 1958.

"He only knows one speed and one way," said Driscoll, a long-time college coach himself. "He was very tough-minded but very fair-minded. He's a great teacher of technique, better than anybody I've ever watched. I've been to a lot of pro camps and different colleges and he's the best. So that's a major part of what happened at NDSU. From my point, Buck had so much to do with it."

It wasn't unheard of for one of the coaches to walk into practice and physically handle a player. You can't do it in 2018, but you could do it in the '60s. Erhardt was not only a gifted coach with knowledge, but he was strong enough to engage an offensive lineman.

Early in the '63 season, Nystrom wanted to make a point with his players with a "bull in the ring" drill. He would call a player's number and that player would have to go after another player in the center. Buck got in the ring.

"And Gene Gebhards hit him so hard that he flew out of the box," Wiegandt said. "He was black and blue."

When poor weather during spring football practice forced the team inside in the '60s, that meant Bentson Bunker Fieldhouse. Nystrom had his linemen go live on the stage of the gymnasium, meaning drills and hitting each other on the hardwood floor. The players that weren't linemen looked over at the stage and thanked the lord they played another position.

"The toughness I think," George Kallenbach said, "came from Buck Nystrom. Erhardt was very knowledgeable about the game. Mudra was the leader. He could take the money out of your wallet and that's what got Team Makers going. But Buck permeated the system."

Take the midway point of the 1965 season. The Bison started 5-0 and were an offensive machine scoring 59 and 55 in the first two games over subpar opponents Wisconsin-Milwaukee and Minnesota Duluth. They beat South Dakota State 41-13 and Augustana 47-7. All was good. That was followed by a 6-3 win over North Dakota, a victory that ended 12 straight losses to the Sioux. All was still good. NDSU flew to Montana State the following week and beat the Bobcats 14-7. The game in Bozeman was a war, Heller remembers, and the king warrior was running back Ken Rota. In the huddle late in the game, he had blood running out of his nose and his eyes were bloodshot.

"I'll never forget this: he comes out of the game in the fourth quarter and the Montana State crowd stood as one and gave him a standing ovation," Heller said. "Not because he had a lot of yards but because that game was so physical."

All was still good? Not in Nystrom's piercing eyes. The two straight low-scoring offensive outputs against UND and MSU didn't sit well with him. The following Monday practice was memorable for the wrong reason. Buck didn't like the way his offensive line was playing.

The team lined up for pre-practice calisthenics when Nystrom walked onto the practice field, red in the face.

"I want all the offensive linemen over here!" he shouted.

Mudra replied that the players hadn't warmed up yet.

"I want all the offensive linemen over here!" Nystrom shouted again.

The line went live for two straight hours of practice without a break.

The Bison defeated South Dakota 66-8 the ensuing Saturday. Message delivered.

When it came to messages from the players, nobody was better at it than Wiegandt. In 1958, he walked on to the Bison football team; but seeing he wasn't going to get a scholarship, he dropped out of school and joined the

Marine Corps. He came back to NDSU in 1963 when Mudra began the great turnaround. Nothing like a former Marine to instill some discipline in his fellow troops.

"When we got there, nobody dreamed we would be No. 1 in the country," said Wiegandt. "Nobody dreamed we would go to a bowl game. Mudra instilled into us that we can be one of the best there is. He provided that psychological advantage. He put that philosophy out there."

If Mudra was the coach who turned the program, Billy Sturdevant was the player. You can't win with one guy but the uptick in talent had to start somewhere. Sturdevant, a standout at the North Dakota State College of Science in 1961 and 1962, was recruited by the University of Minnesota. It was during the heyday of Gopher football, with the U not far removed from a Rose Bowl title and national championship in 1960.

Sturdevant was hanging around Minneapolis for two and a half weeks in advance of the start of fall practice, but never felt like he fit in. He felt lonely and called his parents asking to come back home to Wahpeton, N.D. Not officially enrolled at Minnesota, that's precisely what he did.

His brother, Terry Sturdevant and friend and former Science player Ed Pflipsen were playing at NDSU. They were on the field for the 1963 season opener when the Bison played Moorhead State. Hard to believe in the present-day Division I FCS, but the Dragons were a better program in the early 1960s.

They beat NDSU in 1962. The same thing happened in the '63 opener, and it wasn't even close. The Dragons won 31-14.

"We got beat by Moorhead State and that was a sad day," Driscoll said. "I'll never forget how tough that fall camp was and we needed to go through that. But then we got beat by Moorhead State."

The game may have ended, but NDSU's day on the field did not. Nystrom was furious and he took the linemen out of the locker room and back on the field for drill work. The stands had cleared, and Nystrom was putting his guys through a stance-and-start drill.

"We practiced until it was dark," Wiegandt said. "Mudra had to come out and get us off the field. That's a true story. That was our introduction to Buck Nystrom."

If the Moorhead State game was the downer, the game vs. the State College of Iowa (now Northern Iowa, a name that was changed in 1967) was the turning point. Erhardt's defense got its act together after the opening game debacle against Moorhead and shut out the Panthers 21-0.

"We were still low in numbers, still going both ways and Ron and Buck were really working us hard on base fundamentals and drilled us hard," Driscoll said. "The two of them were the hardest working coaches I've ever been around. That hard work was fine, but what we truly needed was that victory against the State College of Iowa. That win, I think, set the program from that point on. It was a different attitude."

The coaches demanded a different attitude. When Erhardt was the head coach, Hyland remembers fall camp being emotionally and physically draining. Those first two weeks were all football from dawn to well past dusk.

"You wanted to feel sorry for yourself," Hyland said. "Some people handled it better than others. Your body was just so tired. We had two-a-days and sometimes three practices a day. You were dead tired and it went on for two weeks. You just looked forward to it being over with."

It brought the players closer together. They're still close. Of the 13 seniors that took the Champagne Flight back in '65, four have passed away; but the other nine never waste a moment in talking Bison football with each other. You could say the same thing for the other successful teams of the '60s.

One player, however, was a strange case.

***

Paul Hatchett was the star running back from 1967-69 who left the school as the greatest running back to ever play at NDSU. He's still on the list as one of the greatest, and probably always will be. It was a haphazard career at NDSU, with some great performances overshadowed by some off-the-field troubles. My father in his book, "Bison Football: Three Decades of Excellence" tried to document it in one chapter. Dad passed away in 1993, but while going through some old family files I came across word-for-word transcribed interviews of several former teammates. When it came to Hatchett, each question from my father was worded the same: "Was Paul Hatchett used?"

Bruce Grasamke, the quarterback, said no. College football was a business, even back then. If a player accepted a scholarship, then everybody was being used. Marv Mortenson, an offensive guard, had virtually the opposite viewpoint saying "To me, looking back on it, it was using the kid. I don't know what they would have gained by getting rid of him, either, other than they would have gained the respect of some of the athletes and maybe some of the people in the community. That's what I meant when I said I had a lot of respect for Ron (Erhardt) and he was a fantastic coach; but I think he was at times willing to use people to better himself or the program."

Erhardt denied most of Hatchett's wrongdoings in an interview with my father, saying the players would know more about "that stuff" than he would.

In the summer of 2006, I took up the search to find Paul and with the modern-day Internet search engines, the process revealed a variety of websites, law enforcement phone numbers, and good ol' fashion reporting. Hatchett disappeared from any NDSU football allegiance immediately following his final game in 1969.

Somewhere, things went wrong for the record-setting running back, a man who in college was the director of a teen center in south Minneapolis. No one had seen him in years. Many stopped looking. Hatchett wandered the streets searching for cocaine in Georgia and Florida for years and was arrested for 10 various drug offenses between 1992 and 2000. He eventually served two years in a Georgia state prison.

"It's a mystery," said Karl Mabone, a former high school teammate at Minneapolis Central. "I don't know if he's dead or what."

Hatchett was gifted with a combination of speed and power; characteristics that helped raise the profile of a Bison football team that won seven NCAA Division II championships. Hatchett was now 57 years old. A Forum investigation into his whereabouts turned up a long rap sheet that began in 1971 when he pleaded guilty to using forged and stolen checks in Minneapolis. I contacted his sister and lone sibling, Laura Hatchett, who said at the time the last she had heard from him was 10 years earlier somewhere in Florida. She did not know where he was.

Roy Ann Combs, his cousin, said the last she heard was that he was living in Florida in the 1990s. "And all the older people who would know about him are deceased," Combs said.

Mabone, a friend of Hatchett's since grade school, said a lot of people just wanted an answer. "All of us guys at Central have been looking for Paul Hatchett for 10 years or more now," he said.

The last known identification of Hatchett was in October 2004 when he was charged with driving under the influence in Savannah, Ga. He pleaded guilty in Chatham County Court and was ordered to pay a $100 fine. A year earlier, he pleaded guilty to failure to report an accident. But charges of driving under the influence, failure to obey traffic devices, and leaving the scene of an accident were dismissed. Hatchett's attorney, Susan Fitzgerald of nearby Bluffton, S.C., in a phone interview could not recall Hatchett or the case.

He was living at 253 Brittany Street in Savannah. A neighbor said the place is a rooming house and that she had never heard of Hatchett. The last known sighting of Hatchett was four years earlier at Union Mission Inc., a homeless shelter in Savannah that specializes in support programs that help people get off the street. A receptionist at Union Mission said she hadn't seen Hatchett in a couple of years. She then put down the phone, mumbled something in the background and a man, presumably an employee, got on the phone.

"We have strict confidentiality here," he said. "We don't tell anything."

Bulldog Detective Agency, a private investigating firm in Savannah that was hired by The Forum, found no trace of Hatchett. I also questioned how hard the firm tried, if at all.

Paul grew up on the north side of Minneapolis. According to Mabone, Paul's mother, Margaret Hatchett, was never around. His father Fred was an alcoholic according to friends, and Mabone said Paul grew up with no firm parental guidance. That, Mabone said, probably led to Hatchett's problems with the law.

"I think he let out a lot of his troubles on the football field, the basketball court, and the baseball field," Mabone said. "When he wasn't in sports, that's when his mind took him to the native side of life."

Fred Hatchett died in 1977 at the age of 57. No records of Margaret Hatchett were found, though Laura Hatchett said she died several years earlier. Mabone said he never saw any sign of Hatchett's mother, not even a picture.

"And I was over there a lot," he said. "We hung out. I never did see any relatives at all."

Fred Hatchett was a janitor and Margaret worked as a maid, according to a player questionnaire Paul filled out when he arrived at NDSU. The Hatchetts lived at 3637 Clinton Ave., an address that remained in their name until the 1990s. A check of the house in 2004 found a gentleman who knew nothing of Hatchett or the family. Gregg Wong, a former St. Paul Pioneer Press sports writer and a teammate of Hatchett's at Central, said he used to see Hatchett at Vikings games up until the early 1990s. Wong said Hatchett had a seat below the Vikings press box.

From 1967-69, Hatchett amassed 2,309 yards – a career record that stood until running back Chad Stark and quarterback Jeff Bentrim led NDSU to three national titles from 1983-86. Talk to any veteran Bison football fan and they will say Hatchett was a force with the football.

"Another O.J. Simpson, they said," Laura Hatchett recalled, comparing her brother to the 1968 Heisman Trophy winner from USC.

Hatchett held 15 school rushing and scoring records. They included a season-record 1,213 rushing yards and 17 touchdowns in 1968. His 41 touchdowns was a Bison career record. The Bison went 29-1 with national championships in 1968 and 1969. NDSU finished second in the national wire service poll in 1967.

The Bison finished the '68 season with a 23-14 win over Arkansas State in the Pecan Bowl in Arlington, Texas. Hatchett rushed for 106 yards and was named the game's outstanding offensive player. His 18-yard touchdown run in the first quarter gave the Bison a 14-0 lead. NDSU capped a 10-0 season in 1969 with a 30-3 win over the University of Montana in the Camellia Bowl in Sacramento, Ca. Hatchett caught a touchdown pass in the game.

Hatchett tried to finish school at Augsburg College in Minneapolis. He was enrolled from September 1975 until May 1978, but did not obtain a degree, records show. His contact with former NDSU teammates all but ended the day he left Fargo. Erhardt said he hasn't seen Hatchett in many years.

Hatchett told a Forum reporter in 1969 that he wanted to go into social work, which would have been ironic since he ended up being on the other end of that equation most of his life. If Hatchett was homeless, he wasn't a problem for Savannah police. An officer who acts as a liaison between the police and the homeless said he had never heard of him.

He was working for Labor Finders in Garden City, Ga., when he was involved in a minor automobile accident in April 2002. Garden City is a few miles from Savannah. Labor Finders no longer exists; the company used a post office box in a Garden City police report. Hatchett's address was listed as 1106 East Duffy St. in Savannah. A neighbor across the street, Lorraine Coyle, didn't know Hatchett.

At the time, with his enrollment in the program at Union Mission, it appeared Hatchett was trying to rehabilitate from a series of charges – mostly in Florida, although the most serious was in Georgia. He was released in January 2001 after serving two years at Wilcox State Prison in

Abbeville, Ga., for possession of cocaine. An open records request of his prison records was denied by prison personnel. His prison status was inactive.

The number of arrests between 1989 and 1997 was astounding, numbering 41; almost all were misdemeanor homeless-type violations. After moving to Georgia, Hatchett was arrested by the Garden City Police Department for possession, manufacture, and purchase of cocaine in January 2000. Three months later, he was sentenced to one year in jail with all of it being suspended. It wasn't long before he was sent to Wilcox State Prison – his college career a distant memory. It paints a sad picture to those who knew him best. "My best memory of Paul is just playing ball with him," Mabone said. "It was all good. He wasn't in trouble. It was just all good."

The end of the sad saga came Monday, May 13, 2013.

That's when the book closed on Paul, but many of its pages were still blank. He died in relative obscurity in Savannah, leaving behind a life of homelessness and numerous problems with the law.

He was 64.

Hatchett died of natural causes, according to Julian Miller, the public affairs administrator for the Savannah-Chatham Metro Police Department, and there were no further public records. No funeral homes in the Savannah area had a listing for him. He disappeared. But in a way, he'd been gone for a long time.

We never got to speak to Hatchett about his All-American NDSU football career. Those who want NDSU's two national titles in 1968 and 1969 to remain untainted are probably OK with that. We'll never get to ask whether, or how, he was helped in any way, shape, or form to remain eligible. Records obtained by The Forum indicate Hatchett was a suspect his senior year at NDSU in two burglaries: a television theft from a local hotel and a stolen 1964 Chevrolet automobile from the parking lot of a local bakery. A series of police reports ensued with the intent of having the suspect come down to the Fargo police station and have his fingerprints taken to see if they matched a print obtained from inside the stolen vehicle. The last report, dated Oct 30, 1969, said the dean of NDSU called the station and said Hatchett is willing to have his prints taken and "will possibly be down in the a.m. if it does not interfere with his football practice."

Well, now, we wouldn't want to interfere with football practice.

There are those who believe Hatchett's nice side was close to steering him down a lawful path in the late '60s and early '70s. Margaret, his mother, wrote in a questionnaire on file at NDSU, the reason Paul picked NDSU was because "it is a great little school and he loves it." He was president of a Red Cross club in high school at Minneapolis Central. He worked with underprivileged kids at a community center in Minneapolis, according to a document from the NDSU sports information office.

With his teammates, however, Hatchett was one of the guys. What if he would have remained in Fargo after the Camellia Bowl? Would he have taken a different path in life? What if he didn't cut ties with mentors like Izzy? George Kallenbach was a sophomore when Hatchett was a senior and he recalls Hatchett being just fine around his teammates. Where he got into trouble in Fargo, people say, is hanging around a few guys from Moorhead State.

"He was the type of guy who shouldn't have gotten into trouble," Kallenbach said. "How did you get in trouble? Maybe because he wasn't surrounded by the right crowd, which he had here at NDSU. He needed the guidance from people like Denny (Isrow). He was always happy, a normal person with us."

Izzy. If people look for one definitive factor in the Bison of the '60s, look to Denis Isrow. That logo on the helmets of today? That was Izzy and former player Pete Lana. They designed the original version. Players, coaches, trainers, boosters and administrators have come and gone at the university since the '60s.

"The one attitude," Kallenbach said, "and I've thought about this, still permeates the halls of the athletic complex and that is Denis Isrow. The coaches up there today still feel the effect of Denis Isrow. If you're looking for toughness, his toughness is still displayed on these teams. When I look for reasons why the Bison keep winning, something that other schools didn't or don't have, it's because of a guy named Denis Isrow. There are bigger teams and a lot of coaches can X and O, but not many teams in this country had Denis Isrow."

IX. Gil

Mike and Chery DeLuca got the phone call they had been waiting for years. It was Friday night in Omaha, Neb., and they were told their child was born. Not wanting to jinx anything, they didn't buy many baby amenities, only a couple of outfits, a bottle, a blanket, and a car seat still in its box sitting in the basement. Sleep wasn't going to happen on Saturday night, because on Sunday morning – on Super Bowl Sunday of 1995 – they were set to go to Methodist Hospital in Omaha. Chery remembers being awake at 2 a.m. Then it was 3 a.m. A few hours later, there was still no phone call telling them the adoption was off, so that meant it was on.

They were waiting in a front entry area of the hospital when a nurse walked by with what Chery called the cutest baby.

"We were like, 'Oh, I hope our baby is going to be cute like that,'" she said.

Later, they were called to another room to meet their new son. They walked through a set of double doors and there he was.

"That was him," Chery said. "The cute baby."

That baby they've been wanting for years.

Mike called it becoming a parent overnight, "so I wasn't sure what to expect."

The name was another matter. Above his crib was written "Gil," which Mike said was disappointing because he thought the baby already had been named Gil. Gil? Having a baby boy is great, but it was their hope they could choose their own first name, something that has a nice ring with DeLuca. Gil DeLuca wasn't doing it for them. A little later, they breathed a sigh of relief.

Gil wasn't his name after all. It was an acronym for Given In Love, a term for adoption. Gil's new parents got to decide on another name.

They decided on Nick.

I got to know Mike and Chery in the years of covering Bison football while Nick was in the process of becoming one of the all-time greatest linebackers in school history. Dom Izzo and I had a Bison Media Blog pregame video web show that usually aired three hours before game time, and was usually live. The DeLucas were gracious guests on occasion. Mike was a guest on our Saturday morning radio show. And one question that none of us really wanted to ask but were wondering: how can the parents be the size of me (around 5-foot-5) and their son be a 6-foot-3, 245-pound NFL-type linebacker?

The answer was adoption.

It's been a beautiful thing over the years for a few standout athletes from North Dakota. It can make one play the what-if game. What if a loving family did not take in a baby who was in need of a home? What if Nick DeLuca went to a home where nobody really cared for him? Would he be the same great athlete on the field and the same gentleman off it?

What about Tony Satter, one of the all-time great running backs in NDSU football history. What if his adoption didn't go like it did, and he ended up somewhere that didn't nurture and develop him as a player and student?

Conceiving a child was hard for the DeLucas. As the years went by, each one seemingly more painful than the previous, Chery and family medicine weren't working. Every month when the time came to see if anything worked, hope turned to grief.

"Just grief for this child you didn't have," she said. "Why? Why? Why?" Chery would look at friends, neighbors or anybody out and about with a family, and wonder: Why me?

Why couldn't she have a little boy or a little girl? She wanted to be a mom; and even with all the fertility advances, with her mid-30s within sight, she felt like her clock was ticking, if not expired. She and Mike explored adoption, but it fell through. Then came that phone call on a Friday night, right after work, asking if they were interested in another try at adoption. Knowing a previous attempt failed, they didn't tell anybody.

They gave it another shot.

"When you look back on it, you realize it wasn't your plan," Chery said. "God had a plan for us and we didn't realize it at the time."

That plan was for Nick to play football at NDSU, and be a four-year starter, a force in the Bison's title years. He was always one of the biggest boys for his age growing up – he was more than 30 pounds as a 1-year-old – and that didn't stop when childhood turned to adulthood. Nick had the size with speed, an uncommon combination for a player by the time he was a senior at NDSU. He talked to only a few of his teammates about his adoption and didn't have any friends who went through the same situation. Like his two parents, he said, "I'm a firm believer in everything has a plan."

"I think I was placed in the best situation possible as far as my upbringing," Nick said. "Obviously being adopted is a different upbringing. It's not usual, but I couldn't picture my life in any other way."

Mike and Chery were always open with Nick about his birthing situation, telling him over the years it was going to be up to him as to what he wanted to do with it. Chery said she's seen other people keep the adoption a secret and that never turned out well for anybody.

When the topic came up, for instance, Chery was always referred to as the real mom and Mike as the real dad.

"We refer to her as the birth mom," Chery said. "Through the years, I've wondered if they tried to find him or not."

Moreover, the lawyer the DeLucas hired to represent the birth mother passed away. The situation took another tough turn early in 2017 when Nick found out his birth mom died of cancer.

"I was very upset when I found out, I was absolutely in tears," Chery said. "It was always the plan that when Nick was 21, it would be his information to decide."

Chery said Nick was unsettled but took the news better than she did. She said he also wondered if he had any siblings.

"It was a shocker, it's so hard," Nick said. "You have all kinds of emotions when you hear stuff like that. It's different because you don't know anything on that side of your family. You don't know what she was like or any of that stuff. It was obviously very sad."

The news, he said, threw a wrench in thoughts of tracking down his birth mom's family.

"I haven't found the right time and haven't found the right way to approach it," he said. "Maybe down the road, it's hard to say."

One thing that's easy to say: Both mom and dad didn't waste many minutes being with Nick over the years. When Chery used to throw the football to Nick when he was little, he always told her to "make him dive" for the ball. In the 2015 FCS title game in Frisco, Texas, Nick made a diving interception against Jacksonville State (Ala.) that the Bison turned into a 17-0 lead, an advantage that was never threatened on their way to a fifth straight national championship.

"After the game, he and I both looked at each other and started laughing," Chery said. "I said, 'Mom, make me dive.' And he said that's exactly what I thought of when it happened."

They became parents at 34 years old, so they were probably more appreciative than most of that diving play.

"Over time and throughout his life, he's constantly teaching me more than I'll ever teach him," Mike said. "He's an old soul that is very giving and very selfless. He doesn't have a braggadocios bone in his body. That's just the way he is."

The way he is, whether his name could have been Gil or is Nick.

"I've joked about that, there are a few guys on the team I've told," Nick said with a laugh. "That would have been different."

What isn't a joking matter is the benefit Mike and Chery got from adoption. When both were asked the question about what it meant, words were hard to come by. Putting so many years' worth of words into a few sentences is impossible.

"Through the years and to this day we have always talked about how much they must have loved him to have made the most difficult and most loving choice to place him for adoption," Chery said. "That couldn't have been easy. He was an absolute beautiful baby. One glance at him and you were in love. My heart has hurt for them through the years that they didn't get to watch him become the wonderful, kind, and talented young man that he is today; but they have always remained in my daily prayers of thanks for giving me the best gift of my life. The gift of my son and the chance to be his momma."

The momma of a player with NFL aspirations.

DeLuca was thought to be draft-pick material until a shoulder injury forced him to redshirt as a junior in 2016 after three games. At least he went out with a bang in that season, helping the Bison to a 23-21 upset win at the University of Iowa. DeLuca played that game with one arm, having surgery afterwards to repair a torn labrum – an injury that required a four- to six-month healing period. His injury was so pronounced that even a brace couldn't stabilize it. Nobody outside of the team could tell he was hurt. In the game before Iowa, against nationally ranked Eastern Washington, he had 15 tackles and returned an interception for a touchdown.

His 2017 season was injury-riddled when he was hit in the knee by a teammate's helmet during practice the week of the season opener at Eastern Washington. The team reported it was a "non-ACL" injury, meaning he wouldn't be out for the season. The following Monday, he underwent a procedure to address the problem, whatever it was, and returned to the playing field by the end of September. Still, how healthy was he? The answer: he gutted it out.

That's what came to be expected from Bison football players. In the championship years, after they were done with their careers, stories of guys playing with excruciating pain were common. Some were so mentally tough it's doubtful they felt any pain. In DeLuca's case, he finished the season, was selected to a college post-season all-star game, and was invited to the NFL Combine at the beginning of March. He appeared on pace to be drafted by somebody. It didn't happen, instead he was signed by the Tennessee Titans as a free agent.

***

Bricker Satter was a month old when he started to struggle. The first child of Jim and Paulette Satter, nothing could be more crushing to two parents looking to start a family. Jim said his baby was dusky-colored, and he knew something wasn't right. Jim was teaching and coaching high school football at Frazee, Minn., when the local doctor came into the room at the clinic and said the child needs medical care that he couldn't provide.

The Satters took their baby to the University of Minnesota medical care facility. The diagnosis: Bricker Satter's heart "was completely transversed," Jim said. Doctors performed a procedure to open one of the ventricles to get better blood flow. Still, Bricker's blood pressure went down and at that point, the doctor approached the Satters with some tough news.

"I can still see the surgeon's hands," Jim said. "He walked in and said, 'I don't know what to do?' Our son passed on."

Bricker Satter, the first child of Jim and Paulette, died. It wasn't an easy time on anybody.

They went back to their home to see a bassinette sitting in an empty room. After time passed, the question they asked each other was simple: What's next?

Looking for another option, Jim and Paulette started looking at the adoption route. They contacted Lutheran Social Services, and were told that to adopt a white, healthy baby would probably take years. Jim said he was told bi-racial babies were available; and if time was of the essence, that would probably be the best way to go.

"At the time, bi-racial children were kind of stuck," Jim said. "They weren't white, and they weren't black. Kind of a lost group."

The Satters were not deterred. They forged forward and adopted their first child, Brock, who was born in the Twin Cities. They drove to a Minneapolis hospital and took him in immediately after he was born. Brock is the son of a mother, who to this day lives in Belfield, N.D., and a father from Nigeria who died from a blood disorder on a flight back to his native Nigeria.

The Satter parents were not done with adoption.

"With the loss of Bricker, we sat there and said, gee, there are all kinds of children that need homes," Jim said. "Why in the world would anything hold us back? You get the question, yes, they're not yours. That couldn't be further from the truth. Children need homes and we were in the position to give them a home so let's do it."

Little Tyrone lived in a foster home in Louisville, Ky., for two years before Jim and Paulette Satter saw a picture of him with a ball in one hand and a big smile on his face. They were smitten.

"Does Brock need a brother?" Jim asked. "Let's do it."

There's still videotape that has 2-year-old Tyrone getting off a plane in the Minneapolis-St. Paul International Airport with a social worker from Lutheran Social Services. The boy has a ball and truck in one hand, and is introduced to his new parents.

"Here's your new mom and dad," the social worker says.

"Hey mom and dad," the boy replied.

"He was just right at home now," Jim recalled.

Like Gil DeLuca wasn't a fit for his parents, the Satters contemplated a name change of their own. They chose Anthony. Sports fans in the Upper Midwest know him today as Tony Satter. All Tony knows about his past is he was born in Louisville, Ky., in 1969 to a couple of mixed race, and that's all he wants to know. His parents bought him an ancestry kit in Christmas of 2017, and DNA results suggested he's 48 percent British.

"King of England," Tony jokes.

There's no knowing what life would have been like back in Kentucky, or wherever he could have ended up, but there is no denying he found a loving home at first in Morris, Minn., and later in Fargo.

"You could argue I'm one of the luckiest people around," he said.

That is true, but the luck goes both ways. Adoption often times is a win-win for all involved. The Satter clan consists of Jim and Paulette and their three children: Tony, Brock and Bridgette, who is the biological child. But magically take away the skin color and nobody would know it. Tony is a chip off the old block of Jim, and it's almost scary.

In his college days, Jim Satter was a first-line sophomore running back for Concordia College on the Cobbers' 1964 national championship team. Jim was initially recruited by the Bison; but it was a period in which NDSU was not a winning program and he wanted nothing to do with that. He figured he was better off being a bigger cog in a smaller wheel.

Jim had good feet, a player who would see an opportunity to make a cut and make something of it. If the defensive end was slow, that player was no match for Jim in getting around the end into some space. He averaged 6.1 yards per carry. He broke a bone in his foot during that national title year, but returned to make the travel squad to the title game.

He may not be the biological father of Tony, but both played the same way. Both had the same style of running. The similarities were haunting.

"I would watch him and say, cut, cut, cut and he would make the cut," Jim said. "He was a lot better than I was ... but Tony was really a chip off the old block. There was always the question how heredity is involved and what they're exposed to. It's amazing how he thinks like me and responds to me."

Tony developed his love for football in Morris. Jim left Frazee to become the head football coach and teacher at Morris High School. From there he developed a friendship with University of Minnesota-Morris head coach Al Molde. Wanting to get in the private sector, Jim left the public-school system for a job with an agricultural chemical company, a position that had flexibility in terms of work hours. Molde approached Jim about becoming the offensive backfield coach.

In a small town with not much else to do, the coach's kids were constantly at practice. It was common for Tony to play catch on the sideline with the backup quarterback.

"He caught the ball, and he was just a natural athlete," Jim said. "We knew we had to work with him and get him to understand this God-given ability."

The Morris years ended when Tony was in the middle of fourth grade. The family packed up and moved to Fargo. In those days, Fargo was less diverse; and Tony felt the pain as a sixth grader at Agassiz Junior High. He was the victim of bullying, before anybody really talked about the term.

"Every day," he said.

Every day.

One kid threw a padlock at him, barely missing his head, the force so hard it probably would have knocked him out. The worst hour, however, was when school was let out for the day.

"That's when you run," Tony said. "School is out, and they started picking on me, and I'm like, OK, what am I going to do? Sports was always a great escape for that. I always tell people that you know why I run the way I run? It was running home from school, running through the neighborhood because the older kids were bullies. They don't understand it."

He was bullied because he was a rare kid of color at Agassiz.

"Some of it was bigotry or whatever you want to call it," Tony said. "You just fight through it."

He did. It was around then that Tony started to get his football legs under him. He had an ex-college coach in Jim, after all, coaching his youth football team. Jim still knows his record as an F-M Athletics football coach: 54-2-1. Other parents accused him of cheating the system, although that was puzzling considering the coaches didn't pick the kids on a team. No, Jim Satter coached youth football like a college team.

"We didn't fumble the football," he said. "They were sixth-graders who could do anything a college kid could do; the only difference was their attention span was so short. It was amazing what little guys could do if you gave them the opportunity."

At South High, the bullying went away for Tony and athletic excellence started to escalate. It reached a point where he had to figure out what sport he wanted to play in college: football or baseball. Football won out, and NDSU and head coach Rocky Hager had a Division I recruit playing Division II football. Molde, at the time, was at FBS Western Michigan and wanted Tony. Wyoming, Iowa, and Minnesota all sent the recruiting pressure his way. He considered Western Michigan because it had a good baseball program and, initially, Molde said he could play both sports. That thought faded after his campus visit, Tony said.

"Minnesota had Daryl Thompson as their running back and I thought, why would I go to Minnesota and be behind Daryl Thompson and lose every other game?" he said. "We won more in one year at NDSU than the four years I would have been there."

That is true. At NDSU, Satter was a big wheel in two Division II national championship teams. The only downside was his lack of carries, the result of a talent-laden veer offense backfield. Even Jim Satter was confused, at one point talking to Hager about the lack of carries by his son. Tony was averaging nine attempts per game. Rocky told him that 20 to 25 a game would wear Tony out.

"Rocky, you're missing the point, 15 carries, get him 15 carries and he'll score a touchdown," Jim said. "We need a little happy medium here."

Tony was dynamic. When he got the ball, things happened. He finished his career as the second-leading rusher in school history with 3,212 yards in the regular season. He went over 100 yards 21 times, which was a school record in a program that prides itself on running the ball. In 1989, he had 1,907 all-purpose yards in just 175 attempts that averaged 10.9 yards every time he touched the ball. As a running back, he averaged 7.5 yards per carry. He was named by Sports Illustrated as one the state's 50 all-time sports figures.

He was one of the final cuts with the New York Giants in their training camp; and perhaps if he was with another team, he might have had an NFL career. The Giants had Otis Anderson and David Meggett in their backfield so cracking that lineup was an uphill battle.

"It wasn't the luck of the draw," Jim said. "He called me one day and said Otis Anderson and Lawrence Taylor were at camp at this little college, and there was only one phone. Tony was with Otis and Taylor, and they asked him to take their stuff to the bus because they were staying in town. Otis says to Tony to take his keys to his car, it has a phone in it, and said go head and use it as you need. So, he called me and said, I'm in Otis Anderson's car."

That was life before cell phones.

That was the life Jim and Paulette Satter gave Tony because they had it in their heart to adopt a boy who was living in foster care.

He is their Gil.

Bricker Satter is buried in Fargo and seeing the moist eyes in Jim when talking about it, I'm certain the pain never goes away. How can it? But when Tony showed up in the Minneapolis-St. Paul airport, it was a win-win for all involved. One of the greatest players in NDSU football history is the result of a married couple who wanted to start a family. They didn't care about the color of the skin. Nor should anybody.

X. One Night in Madison

The University of North Dakota won the NCAA national hockey championship in 1982, a season memorable for many reasons. It was the year of the Sioux vs. the Badgers. They played seven times with UND winning three of four in the regular season. They played twice in the Western Collegiate Hockey Association playoffs, back-to-back games the Sioux wanted to forget. The first was a 9-0 loss; the second a 3-1 defeat.

Both reached the NCAA tournament and the championship game at the Providence Civic Center in Providence, R.I. Predictably, the score was tied 2-2 heading into the third period. But UND's Phil Sykes scored his second and third goals of the game, which sandwiched a goal by Cary Eades, and the Sioux won 5-2.

The second title in three years re-established the program's presence as a national power that was missing for most of the 1970s. How did UND do it? The Sioux went back to the basics. They recruited players with a different work ethic and developed that mindset over the course of their careers. They found players in smaller communities that other coaches probably didn't know existed. While the University of Minnesota was sticking to its flashy players from in-state, the UND coaches were driving the small two-lane roads in the United States and Canada.

"Guys who were big, strong, and played very aggressive," said head coach Gino Gasparini. "The game was called different in those days. If you watch the game today there is more of an emphasis on skating and tempo. Back in those days, there were some tough guys in our league. It was very aggressive. Michigan had a big, tough team. The league was pretty good-sized in terms of players. We always had a philosophy that sometimes you were able to beat teams that maybe you weren't as skilled as they were, but you would play harder and be as tough or tougher. You were committed. Those were the attributes you had to play with. Winning was as much attitude as it was skill. You have to have the right attitude to be successful. And so you were always looking for those players. You can be the best coach in the world but you can't invent skill. When you're standing on the bench and you're down one goal; if you don't have skill, chances are you won't be able to score. You have to have skill, and in addition you have to have the right attitude."

And there's no backing down. That's what happened in that One Night in Madison. Before winning in Providence happened, Jan. 30, 1982 had to happen. It's referred as the "Water Bottle Game," a Sioux vs. Badgers collision at Wisconsin's Dane County Coliseum that lived through generations with such popularity the phrase is now capitalized.

It was the defining moment in a decade of prominence for Sioux hockey.

"It was one of those things," said UND's Jim Archibald. "As a team, I think it kind of made us realize and figure out that everybody had everybody's back. It brought us closer together. We really gelled after that."

The fight ignited when Wisconsin's John Newberry squirted UND's Cary Eades with a water bottle as Eades skated by the Wisconsin bench. The two were rivals from the British Columbia Junior League in Canada. Eades saw the door to the Wisconsin bench was open, so he figured it was time for a neighborly visit to his old friend Newberry.

"I stuck my stick to his throat and said don't mess with me," Eades said. "It happened. It happened for a reason. We felt their team was disrespecting us and it was the heat of the moment."

The fight is legendary for hockey fans on YouTube.com. There are no secrets on social media websites, a reality Eades acknowledged while sitting behind his desk at Scheels Arena in south Fargo. He's the head coach of the Fargo Force of the United States Hockey League. The video is grainy, mostly black and white with a hue of color like those classic, old NFL films that illuminates a further sense of nostalgia.

With legendary sportscaster Ed Schultz at the play-by-play, the video begins with Archibald going into the Wisconsin crowd after a fan.

"Archibald is getting after some guy up in the stands there. Archibald's hurt!" Schultz shouts into the microphone. "I think Archibald's hurt!"

Moments later, Archibald threw a punch at a Wisconsin player near the crowd. That was followed by quick police presence, which was noted by Schultz and his color analyst, Tim O'Keefe. Archibald said after the brawl briefly settled down, he was near the beer gardens back underneath the stands.

"Then he got away from the police, came back across and cold-cocked the first guy he saw," said Virg Foss, who covered the Sioux for many years for the Grand Forks Herald newspaper.

Meanwhile, it got heated in the area where Schultz and O'Keefe were broadcasting. It was the first two games as a color analyst for O'Keefe, a former Sioux player. The Dane County pressbox was too small to accommodate the broadcasting duo, so they were seated at a table in talking distance of Wisconsin fans. During the fight, it turned into shouting distance.

"Ed was calling it like a prized fight," O'Keefe said. "A left. And a right. A left."

Badgers fans began throwing crumpled paper cups at Schultz and O'Keefe. Schultz tapped O'Keefe on the shoulder, which was the signal for O'Keefe to start talking. Schultz took his head set off, stood up and yelled at the fans.

"Who threw that! You want go? Come up here!"

The network took a commercial break.

"Ed," O'Keefe said, "have you ever been hit before? I have, it hurts and I don't like our odds here. It's 2,500 to 2."

Moments later, Schultz was hit between the eyes with a rolled-up paper cup. More heckling led Schultz to not care about being on the air.

"I'd like to bop that bozo," he said.

The skirmish lasted about a half hour. O'Keefe said it felt like it would never end.

"To me, the 1982 team was clearly the best team North Dakota has ever had," O'Keefe said. "The '82 team was so deep, both up front and defensively. We were so gritty and an extremely tough team to play against. No question what happened in Madison was something that was binding for the players."

The fight was the same night a Wisconsin player scored from 185 feet away on UND goalie Jon Casey, who saw the puck take a strange bounce in front of him and hop over his shoulder.

"There were a lot of moving parts in that game," Foss said.

In 2012 Grand Forks Herald sportswriter Brad Schlossman wrote a 30-year anniversary story of the "Water Bottle" incident. Brad Berry, UND's head coach and former player from the '80s, said Eades was a player who "lived and died with the program, and still does." Former player Doug Smail called Eades and Dean Dachyshyn "the greatest Fighting Sioux warriors to ever wear a Sioux jersey." Schlossman's 2012 description of the 1982 incident, in part, read like this:

The teams have played for MacNaughton Cups, Broadmoor Trophies, and even a national title, but one incident that occurred at the Dane County Coliseum has, over the years, defined the North Dakota-Wisconsin hockey rivalry more than anything else. Cary

Eades rarely goes a week without someone asking about the Water Bottle Game, which will turn 30 years old on Monday.

"Unfortunately, it's almost daily sometimes," said Eades (then an assistant coach with UND). "It's got a lot to do with YouTube."

While preparing his team for this weekend's renewal of the rivalry between UND and Wisconsin, Eades recalled the famous brawl that has been viewed more than 100,000 times on YouTube. (It was 129,000 as of the spring of 2018). The Badgers led the series finale 3-0 as Eades skated past the Wisconsin bench on his way to make a line change. Wisconsin's John Newberry squirted Eades in the face with a water bottle — for the second time during the game.

"Their door was open, so I went in to have a talk with him," Eades said.

Wisconsin defenseman Pat Ethier saw this exchange, ran down the bench and landed a punch on Eades that set everything off. UND emptied its bench and a massive brawl ensued in Wisconsin's bench. It spilled out down the hall into the beer garden area, where UND's all-time penalty leader, Jim Archibald, got into it with fans.

"They're fighting out in the aisles and everyplace else," the Badger announcer exclaimed. "They're fighting with the police! They're fighting with the fans! North Dakota has done it again."

Eades, Archibald and Dan Brennan received game disqualifications for UND. Newberry, Ethier and Steve McKenzie of Wisconsin also were given DQs. Later, the Western Collegiate Hockey Association added two-game suspensions for Newberry and Eades and a five-game suspension for Archibald.

While everyone remembers the brawl, Eades prefers to think about and talk about the other aspects of the rivalry that season.

"From my personal standpoint, (the brawl) kind of overshadows a lot of good things I accomplished in my college career," Eades said. "I was very fortunate to have a lot of good teammates and good seasons, but that's the only thing anyone wants to talk about. I'd rather talk about the four goals in one period, but there's no video of that. The fights and controversy and uproar are what people talk about at the hockey games and the beverage places afterward. Hopefully, with the 30 years, we can put it in a casket and bury it."

Eades was the wrong guy to pick on. Gasparini called him a hard-nosed player who was not afraid to stick his nose anywhere. He said he wasn't the best skater but his instincts made up for any deficiencies.

It was one squirt of a bottle. UND went on a winning streak after the fight. The Sioux were eight points behind the Badgers with eight games to play. They won the next seven.

"We came together," Eades said. "We had a lot of team unity throughout the year but I think (the fight) cemented it. Actually, I think that inspired our team. We had a little mental edge after that for whatever reason. In the end, it's about winning hockey games."

The decade of the physical Sioux that began in '78-'79 was in cruise control in the 1980s. Video killed the radio star with MTV, and college hockey was a man's game.

"It was real," said Smail, from Moose Jaw, Saskatchewan. "Everybody thought college hockey was for pussies. I didn't realize how tough it was until my rookie year. I got into a scrap during training camp and got eight punches to the head. It made me realize quickly that college hockey wasn't what everybody said it was. It was a lot different than junior hockey."

Add the intensity of rivalries with Wisconsin and Minnesota and lightning struck at any moment. It was more than players, too. The head coaches were three intense and legendary leaders. Gasparini won three national titles with the Sioux. Herb Brooks was the head coach at Minnesota. Bob Johnson had the same job with the Badgers. The battles with Wisconsin took on a life of their own.

The Water Bottle Incident changed the way college games were officiated. In Madison, the setup was one linesman and two officials with the linesman having the job to break up scuffles.

"The officials sat back and pulled out notepads rather than get in the middle of things," O'Keefe said. "In college hockey, that fight or series of fights that evening was a black eye on college hockey in the view of a lot of people. It spurred a discussion on how to prevent that from happening again."

In 1989, a few years after his UND career ended, former player Frank Burggraf was kicked out of a bar and grill in Madison after the owner said he recognized him.

"No, you don't," Burggraf said.

"Yes, I do," he replied. "You and your brother. I remember you."

A bouncer escorted Burggraf out saying the Sioux weren't welcomed in his place. The Burggrafs have a notable history with UND. Frank's brother Charlie Burggraf was a two-year captain from 1977-79.

Brooks had a celebrated history with hockey, having led Team USA to the "Miracle on Ice" gold medal in the 1980 Winter Olympics. He had that pedigree in addition to the Gophers' philosophy of solely recruiting in-state Minnesota players. UND had the stereotype, in most cases true, of having older Canadian players and overlooked recruits from anywhere in the country. It was a clash of styles.

Gasparini built a recruiting network across Canada and the United States from his time as a Sioux assistant. He made connections with lower-level hockey coaches. He took a different path than most of the major coaches with his recruiting philosophy.

"The reality of our program is players came from different walks of life," Berry said. "Just having an affiliation with the program was for the greater good of the team. That was a big deal. It was a situation where everybody had to accept a role as far as trying to win games. Big-time egos never got in the way. The players knew right away. The big thing was entitlement not being a big thing here. Those were hard teams. 'Hard skill.' We called it 'hard skill.'"

Hard skill was defined with players like Smail, Archibald, Eaves, Troy Murray, Mark Taylor, Dan Brennan, and Bob Joyce. There are many more. Twelve players from the '82 title team had an NHL look, if not a long career.

"They were skilled and they played hard," Berry said.

Hard skill.

Hard skill with a UND team that had a hard edge; especially being the smaller school from the rural state against the mighty Big Ten Conference duo of Minnesota and Wisconsin. Those two had the big budgets. UND had what it had. Minnesota was from the big city of Minneapolis. Wisconsin was from the trendy city of Madison. UND was from Grand Forks, where the main attractions were Whitey's Bar across the river in East Grand Forks, Minn., and the local college hockey team.

"We're North Dakota, you talk about North Dakota tough, we were not the Big Ten," Berry said. "We're a team that has to earn everything we get, even respect. When I think of those special rivalries, you have to earn respect."

Bob Johnson would play any situation up. He insisted on a police escort when the Badgers traveled to Grand Forks. A college hockey team in Grand Forks needed law enforcement assistance about as much as Eades needs it at Scheels Arena. But that was Bob.

"Bob Johnson was an intense guy," Gasparini said. "Herb Brooks was an intense guy. Gino Gasparini was a very intense guy. I tried not to cross the edge but sometimes I crossed the line. It was a pretty intense time. The rivalries were really, really heavy. It was the old WCHA. I remember the commissioner of the league came and talked to Wisconsin and North Dakota and said if it doesn't settle down, they'll have to cancel the series for a year. That's the way it went. But eventually it settled down and got to be a good series. When you look back through the '80s, you have Minnesota, Wisconsin, and North Dakota who were always going to the NCAA at that time. Those three schools. It was a battle."

It was a different time in America. The rebirth of UND hockey came as the Carter administration and its failed policies came to a close. The country was in a major recession in 1981 and 1982 with some of the worst economic times since the stock market disaster in 1929. Interest rates were high, making buying a house hard on the budget. The Iran hostage crisis of 1979 and the Soviet intervention of Afghanistan further heightened global fears. The uncertainty of the Vietnam War and the Watergate scandal were in the rearview mirror for that generation of college kids, but they still didn't grow up with affluent tastes. It made tough-guy hockey all the more vogue and all the more accepting.

Ronald Reagan was elected president in 1980 and promised to restore the country's military power, which was in a major decline since the end of Vietnam. Reagan crushed Jimmy Carter in a landslide, and the brute presence of America was said to be restored. It's part of the theme of the Olympic movie "Miracle on Ice."

UND didn't need a miracle; it needed the right recruits.

"We were a group of guys who had a lot of trust and a lot of respect for each other," Archibald said. "That's why I think we did so well."

Gasparini didn't do it alone. Rick Wilson, a former Sioux player, was an assistant. He coached 19 years in the NHL. Dean Blais got his first assistant college coaching job at UND in 1980. He led the Sioux to two national championships as the head coach in 1997 and 2000.

"He was the common denominator to our success," Archibald said. "He knew the certain type of players that he liked. You talked to those guys and you got the feeling they were genuine. They were going to take you under their wing and get to where you wanted to go. We were student-athletes and with Gino there, he stressed student first and athlete second. I think that was a big deal."

College hockey in the '70s and '80s was different. Players could get into a fight and receive only a double-minor or a triple-minor penalty. Drop the gloves, start landing upper cuts and the penalty was consecutive two-minute minor penalties. It wasn't much of a deterrent.

Every team had its bouncers. UND had Dachyshyn (pronounced like Decision), who Foss said was notorious for getting into brawls in the penalty box.

"He wouldn't let it go," Foss said.

After the 1982 season, the WCHA made it mandatory for all teams to install a glass partition between each team's penalty boxes, affectionately known as the "Dachyshyn Partition." It later became an NCAA rule. The next time one goes to a college hockey game, take a gander at the penalty box area and think Dean Dachyshyn.

The penalty minutes added up, but not to historic proportions. Don't forget about the "hard skill" factor. Archibald is far and away the school's all-time leader with 540 penalty minutes in four years; but of the top 10 in UND history, only two were from the late '70s and early '80s. Dachyshyn is 10th. Howard Walker was a menacing figure with his frame and facial Fu Manchu. He's not in the top 10 in penalty minutes. Walker was 20 years old when he enrolled at UND as a freshman. Brooks called him "a 35-year-old" when the Gophers played the Sioux.

"UND is playing at Minnesota for the WCHA title in 1979," Foss said. "It's late in the game and the Gophers' Neil Broten is taking the faceoff. It was an important one. Walker skates into the circle and tells Broten, if you go into the corner for the puck, it will be the last thing you do in your life. He was a scary guy."

That move backfired. Two weeks later, in the NCAA title game in Detroit, Broten scored the winning goal for the Gophers in the 4-3 victory over the Sioux. That goal hurt in another way. Broten, from Roseau, Minn., was on his way to signing with UND along with his high school teammate Frank Burggraf until the last minute. Burggraf was downstairs at his home when the phone rang at 11:35 p.m. It was Broten, who told him he was switching his commitment to the Gophers.

"That's the way it goes," Burggraf said.

Burggraf signed his scholarship with Gasparini the next day.

"There were a lot of tough customers recruited to play college hockey," Foss said. "It was just a far different time in hockey than it is now. Even the NHL now is trying to enforce fighting. In college hockey there is not much of it at all."

Archibald came to UND from Craik, Saskatchewan, population in 2011 of 453 people. His penalty minutes are well documented, but the guy could score. In 154 games, he had 75 goals and 69 assists in a career that included

12 game-winning goals. Gasparini knew he had a winner. He played the game at a peak level of intensity and if that included penalties, so be it.
If it included defending his team One Night in Madison, so be it.

***

Walk into the new Ralph Engelstad Arena in Grand Forks and first-class amenities are visible with every step. The marble floors. The leather stadium seats, each adorned with a Sioux logo. The lighting. The state-of-the-art scoreboards. The sound system that delivers a perfect pitch. The suites, each with elegant décor on the inside. Nobody really knows the final cost of construction, which was completed in 2001, but estimates put it higher than the official Ralph Engelstad Arena website figure of $104 million. Officially, there are 1.1 million bricks, 3.2 miles of brass accents on the floor, 2,200 logos (and shrinking after the NCAA forced the UND to give up its Sioux nickname), 50 suites, and 300 televisions. I know a guy who helped with the mechanical engineering of the building and he put seven air exchangers in the UND locker room, which he said would make it the best-smelling locker room in the history of hockey.
It was considered the grandest hockey arena in the United States.
The upgrade from the old Ralph Engelstad Arena, which was built for $2 million and opened in 1972, was significant. Funding for that project consisted of $800,000 in student bonds, $500,000 from the Edmond A. Hughes Estate, $460,000 from a local fund drive and $240,000 from UND alumni. There was no piecing together funds for the new arena with Ralph writing the checks.
The old Ralph could get rockin'. Berry said it was "incredibly loud" with a tinny-like atmosphere because of the reverberation of the sound.
"I'll tell you this," Gasparini said. "The incline of the seating at the old Ralph was pretty steep. The slope was steep. When that place was full and the students were standing on the far side, they looked like they were right on top of you. The visiting teams used to complain it was quite intimidating."
Gasparini was hired as the head coach in 1978. He was a UND guy having played for the Sioux from 1965-68 and returned to the university as an assistant after a brief career with the Toledo Blades of the International Hockey League. Ironically, he was not a popular choice, and of the three finalists was the clear No. 3 of the group.

The other two were Union (N.Y.) head coach Ned Harkness and Denver head coach Marshall Johnston. O'Keefe wrote a letter to UND President Tom Clifford promoting Gasparini as the best choice. O'Keefe noted Gasparini's background as a Sioux player and assistant coach.

The favorite in Foss's opinion was Johnston, a former NHL player and a former captain for Team Canada in the 1968 Olympic Games. He had an 89-63-7 record in four years as the Pioneers' head coach. He had a lake home near Bemidji, Minn., and many Grand Forks hockey people knew him.

"But his wife said no way in hell we're moving to North Dakota," Foss said.

Johnston withdrew. That moved the attention to Harkness, a former head coach with the Detroit Red Wings who was tasked with building Union hockey in its first year as a varsity sport. He was the preferred choice with the UND students despite quitting as the Union head coach halfway through the 1977-78 season. Nobody gave an official reason. Rumors circulated about a tussle with the Union administration, perhaps over recruiting violations. Still, he had resume of two national championships with Cornell in 1967 and 1970 and one runner-up finish in 1969.

Clifford offered the job to Harkness. Foss said Harkness countered with a demand of free tuition at the university for his kids. UND athletic director Carl Miller refuted those demands. The job was offered to Gasparini.

"He was the unpopular choice to be the head coach," Foss said. "The guy nobody wanted. Nobody could believe it that they ended up with the assistant coach."

Local sportscaster Robb Leer, a UND graduate, voiced his displeasure on the air, reportedly tearing up a season ticket package and saying "If UND doesn't care about the program then I don't either." The station disciplined Leer.

The student body wasn't impressed. A sign in front of the Alpha Tau Omega fraternity house said, "We Would Rather have Rube." It didn't sit well with the players like Smail, who lobbied for Gasparini. It's debatable what the sign actually said; a couple former fraternity members believe it said "Why Carl Why," in reference to Miller hiring Gasparini.

"We were getting together, we were going to leave Walsh Hall, rip the sign out and beat the hell out of anybody who tried to stop us," Smail said. "We wanted Gino. We felt he supported us and we were ready to give him our heart and soul. We believed in ourselves. We believed that what was being built was the right team. We were sour."

The players' demands came on the heels of the program going through a long dry spell. Since defeating Denver 6-5 in the 1963 NCAA title game, and later losing to Denver in the 1968 championship game, the program went silent under head coach Rube Bjorkman. He was a legendary name in Grand Forks yet had seasons of 6-28 in 1974-75, 15-21 in '75-'76 and 15-22-1 in '77-'78, his last year.

A few players didn't think Bjorkman was engaged with them. The fans were still showing up but wins were not coming at an expected clip

"The program had been down so far, limping along and not getting any place," Foss said.

Todd Anderson was a Grand Forks Central High School graduate who played one year at Cornell in 1975. He transferred to UND, tried out for the team in 1978 and '79 but didn't make it. An avid Sioux hockey fan, he wasn't impressed with Bjorkman either.

"It was almost a joke," Anderson said. "It really was. I went to practices when I was in high school, watched them, and it was just kind of like a joke. He had some decent players, but not compared to the rest of the league. Gino used to run things as the assistant. Gino saw what was happening, and he could tell that more than likely a change was going to be made."

Hiring Gasparini was a stroke of luck for Miller. An intense coach who favored the more physical style of play, he put together some teams in the 1980s that nobody expected. After getting the promotion, his first order of business on the recruiting trail was a player's mental makeup.

"Attitude became part of their growth and maturity," Gasparini said. "Freshmen are freshmen but when they get to be a sophomore or junior, then you see the growth of the individual. That attitude evolves, becomes a product of the environment that they're involved in. You're always looking for skill, but that giddy-up in the game – the worker guy who is committed. Some players evolve and develop and some never develop. It's like the old saying, if you can't get one contract, you won't get the second, third, or fourth."

The table was set in Bjorkman's last year with Gasparini at the recruiting controls. The Sioux signed freshmen Smail, Dave Christian from Warroad, Minn., Marc Chorney from Thunder Bay, Ontario, and Paul Chadwick from Merritt, British Columbia. The following year, Eades, Walker, and scoring ace Kevin Maxwell came from a junior team in Penticton, British

Columbia, population of about 30,000. The first speech Eades heard from Gasparini after he arrived on the UND campus went something like "I'm tired of losing, I'm tired of being stomped on, and it's going to be us that will be doing the stomping."

"There was a fierce culture of brotherhood that came quickly," Smail said.

Smail was sold right away. Gasparini, Smail, and Erwin Martens from Cartwright, Manitoba, met at Level 7 restaurant and bar in East Grand Forks with both players receiving a clear message. They were here to win a national championship.

"Erwin Martens was one of the most passionate players I ever played with," said Smail, who had a 13-year professional career, 11 with the Winnipeg Jets. "The whole team was like that. It was infectious. We weren't all the same personality, but when it came to playing and supporting each other and the Fighting Sioux logo, it was incredible."

Goalie Bob Iwabuchi came from Edmonton and Sykes from Dawson Creek, British Columbia.

"The chances to score short-handed were excellent," Anderson said. "Maxwell, Taylor, Smail, and Christian on the penalty kill and then you add in Sykes. It was a this-is-our-house thing now."

Eades' first preseason training camp in 1978 lasted six weeks, an abnormally long time before a first game. It wasn't easy. There were consistent battles between teammates on the ice. The first exhibition game was against Minnesota and Herb Brooks in Minot, N.D., a game the Gophers won 6-5 but a game marred by a handful of fights. It may never be known if Gasparini approved of the scuffles, but it's generally believed he wanted to send a message. The University of North Dakota was going to be the aggressor under his watch.

"It changed just like that," Anderson said, snapping his fingers. "These guys came in, and they came in with an attitude, and Gino let them go with that attitude. It was borderline 'Broad Street Bullies.' Change was coming. Tough hockey."

Eades said Gasparini quickly became "the Little General."

"As tough as he was and as demanding as he was, he was a real father figure to many of us guys," Eades said. "He had that rare combination. Back in those days you could inflict a lot of fear in players, which doesn't work as well with today's athletes. But he also had a softer side. Guys feared him but they also loved to play for him. He liked a variety of players on his team; it wasn't all skill. He knew it took many different instruments, and he likened it to an orchestra. You have your lead singers, your bass guitar, and drummers as well. His big thing was recruiting character, and some of the guys were indeed characters."

Frank Burggraf called the 1978-79 season the spark. The 1980 team was the explosion that ended with an NCAA championship. After the '79 season ended with the 4-3 loss to the Gophers, the players walking out of the locker room made a commitment to the following season.

"Everybody was responsible," Burggraf said.

The students attending games took note. Smail will never forget students from western North Dakota or rural Canada wearing cowboy hats to games. Berry came from Bashaw, Alberta, population about 800 in the central part of the province. Like a lot of Canadians, he dreamed of playing professional hockey at a young age but had to hit the road to do it. Bashaw had a team until he was about 14 years old, then it took mom or dad to drive him 30 miles one way to play at the next level. He was 16 when he moved away, destined for junior hockey and eventually UND.

Canadian players were already at UND spreading the word in their provinces that Grand Forks was a destination. Berry heard from the likes of Troy Murray and Dave Donnelly, James Patrick and Gord Sherven. Patrick, Donnelly, Sherven, and Dave Tippett left UND to play on the Canadian Olympic team, which had a program that took players a year in advance of Olympics.

"I said to myself, if they're getting the opportunity through the University of North Dakota to go to the Canadian Olympic team, there must be something pretty good down there," Berry said.

In preparation for college, Berry visited Wisconsin, Northern Michigan, and Boston University, among others. UND was his last scheduled recruiting stop.

"Something internally triggered for myself where I thought I would fit in here," he said. "The people were down to earth, and that's how I grew up. I remember thinking about the word 'care.' They cared about you. When you walked into a room, you would get the handshake, and they would look you in the eye. There's a sense of care within that. Not that I didn't feel it in other places, but I had a strong feeling when I came here."

Virg Foss knows. He was sent to Dallas in 1999 to cover the Stanley Cup between the Dallas Stars and the Buffalo Sabres. There were seven UND alums in the game on both teams; and when Foss got there, he went to the Dallas practice rink to talk to Ed Balfour, Craig Ludwig, Tony Hrkac, and

Rick Wilson. Foss was stonewalled at the facility, told it was the Stanley Cup and the only interviews being granted were for the three or so players who were to appear at a press conference. Great, Foss thought to himself. The Herald sent him to Dallas to write several stories on the Sioux alums, and he wasn't able to talk to them. This reminded me of the time The Forum sent me to Phoenix for a spring training story on No. 1 overall Major League Baseball draft choice Darin Erstad from Jamestown, N.D. It was to be a three-day major enterprise project. But Erstad had some sort of medical rehab on Day 1 and wasn't around. Day 2 was his day off. Great, I thought to myself. The Forum wanted this big project and I hadn't seen Erstad. It worked out on Day 3.

As for Virg, he asked one favor of a Dallas Stars employee.

"Mind calling down to Wilson's office and tell him I'm here?" he asked.

Wilson answered the phone.

"Virg is here?" he said. "Send him right down."

Foss was given as much time as he wanted with the UND alums.

"That's the loyalty and rapport you had with them," he said.

XI. 'When Cinderella Wore Spikes'

The baseball team from Drayton, N.D., boarded a Northwest Orient jet at Minneapolis-St. Paul International, and for many of them it was their first time on a plane. For some, their first trip outside of North Dakota or Minnesota. The destination was Oklahoma City, where the team would land on a trip that would take them to Hobart, Okla., the site of the American Legion sectional championship. Drayton was one of 12 teams in the country still alive for a Legion baseball World Series title.

The year was 1958.

The first impression in getting off the plane in Oklahoma City was the heat. Searing hot, unlike anything the players felt all summer in the Red River Valley of North Dakota. The second impression was the dirt. Red dirt. Back home in the agricultural rich lake bottom of old Lake Agassiz, the dirt was black.

"We thought, what the hell is this all about?" said center fielder Dick Johnson.

The temperature continued rising during their first day, and the players were getting edgy. A very old hotel in Oklahoma City was another kick in the face -- the rundown nature of the structure. At least one good fortune hit the team. Johnson was walking around outside the hotel when he stepped on a roll of money. It amounted to $50; and in 1958, fifty bucks was a jackpot. After going through the steps of telling the coach and the hotel office, where nobody claimed it, Johnson treated his teammates to a Coke and bought himself a nice pair of cowboy boots.

The next morning, the team boarded a bus for the 120-mile trip to Hobart, but before reaching the highway the bus picked up the team from Cincinnati. There were three teams in the tournament: Drayton, Cincinnati, and Maplewood, Missouri. I'm not sure what the difference was in population in 1958 between Drayton and Cincinnati, but the oddity of those two in one of the final four Legion baseball tournaments in the country must have been striking. There was one other difference. The Drayton boys were well-mannered; the Cincinnati boys not so much.

"They turned out to be a bunch of jerks," Johnson said. "They get on the bus, they open the windows in an air-conditioned bus and start singing. Here we are quiet North Dakota kids putting up with all of this, which we did all the way to Hobart."

Drayton reached its motel in Hobart to find another inconvenience. Only two or three rooms had air conditioning, with one of them being assigned to the team coaches. The first team meal didn't make the day any better. Grits, a main course kids from Drayton were not accustomed to. The team batboy, Pete Halcrow, was in a line with his metal tray when he approached a lady serving grits. When little Pete pulled his tray back at the last second, the grits fell to the floor; and that was OK with the kid. The Drayton kids later in the day went to a local hamburger joint where once again they ran into the jerks from Cincinnati. Nothing changed from the bus ride; they were obnoxious and loud repeatedly singing "Rock 'Em Robin."

"We hated them," Johnson said.

Back at the hotel, it was time for rest before the next day's opening round game. Nobody could sleep, it was so hot. Some of the players went into the coach's air-conditioned room and slept on the floor. It was not what anybody had in mind to properly prepare for a game of such importance.

Maplewood dealt Drayton a 12-5 opening-round loss. Then came an elimination game against the hated Cincinnati team, and Drayton started like it had enough of the big-city smack talk. The kids from North Dakota led 5-2 after seven innings in the nine-inning game, but misfortune struck when starting pitcher Doug Halcrow developed a blister on the index finger of his throwing hand. It was the break the Cincy boys were looking for, and they rallied late to take a 9-7 victory.

Cincinnati, the defending national champs, went on to win the Legion World Series for a second straight year.

It was over for Drayton.

What a run. A season unlike any other in the history of North Dakota school-aged baseball. A run that will probably never be seen again.

Drayton, North Dakota.

Most people recognize the name because it's on an exit sign on Interstate 29 between Grand Forks and the Canadian border. Drayton just sits there, a mostly north-south layout with a population of 824 in the 2010 census. The Red River borders it on the east and the highway acts as a fence to the west.

The Methodist, Catholic, Lutheran, and Assembly of God churches are prominent in stature. Main Street has the drug and grocery stores, Kodak Bank, insurance agency, post office, resort and bait shop, and, of course, a couple of bars. Most of the buildings lie across the street from the Red River. Finding evidence that recognizes one of the most amazing small-town stories in the history of North Dakota athletics is tough, but a small monument that looks new rests in the ball field at Schumacher Park. The field was once home to the greatest assembly of small-town baseball players in state history. It says:

Baseball Capital of North Dakota
Region 9 American Legion Champion
1958
Class A State American Legion Champions
1958 and 1962
State High School Champions
1958 1959 1960
1961 1962 1963

"This was where a small slice of baseball history was made," said former player Ray Long.

Well, a big slice of history. In the magical summer of 1958, the Drayton American Legion baseball team, after petitioning to move up a class to play the state's large cities, won the North Dakota Class A state title and the Region 9 tourney. The team advanced to that national sectional game in Oklahoma, which is the equivalent of today's American Legion World Series.

Sixty years later, the team's second baseman can be found ushering at Fargo-Moorhead RedHawks games. Adored by fans, Ray Long has enjoyed the job since he retired from teaching junior high in Detroit Lakes, Minn., in 1998. He's stationed near the RedHawks dugout, and fans know when he's not around. In the fall, Ray can be found working North Dakota State football games near the NDSU student section, a spot in the Fargodome he loves because the former teacher likes being near the students. He's had a front row seat to some of the greatest Bison football games in the history of the program. As of 2017 they were on a run of six FCS national titles in seven years.

I knew Ray from those two venues, but I had no idea he was a member of that Drayton team. A couple of friends from my church in Fargo, Bob Rohla and Bob Lamp, brought it up while I was talking about this book project. Bob Lamp remembers listening to one of the playoff games on radio while he was riding a tractor on his farm near Edgeley, N.D. I was still in disbelief -- American Legion national tournament? Yeah, they claimed. I was flabbergasted at the accomplishment and embarrassed this sportswriter didn't have a clue. Drayton, that little town we drive by on the way to Winnipeg?

Guys like Ray Long are like that, though. They don't advertise their past greatness because, well, how do you do that? It's not the nature of North Dakotans to talk about their successes.

"You just don't keep bringing it up, life goes on," Ray said. "You don't keep reliving it. Maybe we just didn't realize at the time how much fun we were having."

If this chapter can do anything for Drayton, please, somebody erect a sign somewhere at the entrance of town honoring the amazing feat of the 1958 baseball team. Who cares if it was so long ago? It will never be done again. I really believe that. A town that small reaching that level of tournament baseball will never be done again as long as the current population of the state remains relatively the same. The big cities are bigger and the small towns are smaller; there is too much of a gap. Smaller schools will be able to come up with a great player or two, but to find a roster full of great players to compete at a state level like Fargo, Bismarck, Minot, Dickinson, West Fargo, and Grand Forks and a regional level of Omaha, Des Moines (Iowa), Twin Cities suburban teams, Sioux Falls, or Rapid City is just not possible.

Two programs in North Dakota have reached the American Legion World Series: Grand Forks in 1967 and Fargo in 1969, 1989, and 1992. Drayton's run was so forgotten that a 2017 story in the Grand Forks Herald, the biggest newspaper closest to Drayton, listed the Grand Forks '67 team as the first from North Dakota to qualify for the World Series since it started in 1928. Technically, that would be correct. After winning the regional, the next step for Drayton was the sectional. In today's eight-region format, the regional winner heads to the World Series.

How did Drayton do it? They were a group of kids who grew up together playing the game at an early age. Nobody moved to another town, so the core group never wavered. Shortstop Myron Albrecht's family moved into Drayton in 1953, but other than that, the team was constant.

As young kids, a couple of families built mini-baseball fields in their yards where sandlot games were played as long as there wasn't too much snow on the ground. These boys had talent, many moving on to baseball after high school. It was the perfect storm.

Head coach Dick Davison brought a high-level of teaching to the Legion team. Long, Johnson, Albrecht and Bill Brosseau played at UND. Albrecht and Brosseau were captains of the 1964 Sioux team. Doug Halcrow went to Mayville State to play baseball and basketball. Pitcher-first baseman Tom Knoff was signed by the New York Yankees after high school and spent two years in the minor leagues.

Left fielder Frank Brosseau and catcher Mike Halcrow played at the University of Minnesota. Frank, who was a 6-foot, 13-year-old in the 1958 season, played on the Gophers' 1964 College World Series championship team. He was an all-Big Ten Conference outfielder in 1966 and was signed by the Pittsburgh Pirates. Frank had the strongest arm of any of the Drayton kids.

"If he wasn't throwing a baseball, he was throwing rocks as high as he could against the elevator or rocks at birds, he was always throwing," older brother Bill Brosseau said. "He was throwing tennis balls against the side of the school house pretending he was the shortstop. He would throw, throw, throw."

Frank was about to attend UND when Minnesota head coach Dick Siebert heard about him through the Gophers' student manager, who managed the Drayton Legion team when Frank was a senior.

"Frank comes to UND to play ball with me, and then he finds out he can go to the University of Minnesota; and so he goes down there and gets the first full ride I understand for baseball at Minnesota," Bill said.

Frank was one of three starting pitchers for the Gophers. He was the winning pitcher in the second game of the '64 College World Series, a 12-0 win over Maine. He went five innings and allowed one hit, making him the only North Dakotan to win a game in the CWS. He signed a minor league contract with the Raleigh (North Carolina) Pirates of the Class A Carolina League as an outfielder, not a pitcher. Bill traveled to Raleigh to watch his younger brother play. Other Raleigh players told Bill stories of Frank throwing runners out from the center field wall. That arm was developed throwing everything he could in Drayton.

"He said Joe Brown is flying in to talk to me," Bill said.

Joe L. Brown was the general manager of the Pittsburgh Pirates who built two World Series champions and five divisional winners in the '60s and '70s.

"Brown says, 'Frank has the only arm equivalent to Roberto Clemente,'" Bill said. "'If you keep your batting average up, you're going to come up and be his backup.'"

It didn't happen. Frank hit .176 in 61 games in 1966 for Raleigh. He hit .211 and .232 the following two seasons for Class A Gastonia of the Western Carolina League. At Gastonia in 1968 a strange twist in Frank's career took place. Gastonia was in need of batting practice pitchers so the manager asked the players if anybody was capable of throwing. Frank volunteered. After about 10 minutes, the manager asked him why he wasn't a pitcher out of college instead of an outfielder.

"Because I signed as an outfielder," Frank said.

The manager replied, "You're a pitcher now, go sit down."

Frank Brosseau morphed into a pitcher who in 1969 got on the mound for two games for the Pirates. He threw 1 2/3 innings giving up two hits and two runs. He was sent down to Class AA York, spent 1970 with Class AAA Columbus and 1971 with Class AAA Charleston (Ill.). His career ended in 1971, but not without getting into one more game with the Pirates. He pitched two innings, giving up one hit and no runs. His major league baseball statistical line reads three games, 3 2/3 innings pitched, two earned runs, two strikeouts, two walks and an ERA of 4.91.

After Minnesota, Mike Halcrow played for the minor league Grand Forks Chiefs and another team in the Cleveland Indians organization.

The top two pitchers were Doug Halcrow and Knoff. There wasn't a radar gun in those days, but estimates in later years by teammates put their fastballs in the high 80s mph. The 6-foot-4 Doug Halcrow was a thinking-man's pitcher who would study opponents, uncommon for kids that age. He could hit his spots with the fastball and had great control with his off-speed pitches.

Knoff was the ace. The players were friends all those years, perhaps not inseparable, but friends nonetheless. Knoff had his moments of being aloof, however, and not everybody was on board with his attitude. His childhood goal was to pitch for the New York Yankees.

"In those days for Tom, it was all about Tom," Johnson said. "If he didn't have a couple of good tournaments on the hill and he didn't hit squat, I think the pressure got to him. It showed when he got to the minor leagues."

Knoff signed with the Yankees in 1959 and was assigned to Class D Kearney of the Nebraska State League. He appeared in nine games throwing 25 innings giving up 19 hits, 15 earned runs, walking 40, and striking out 12. He went 1-0 and had a 5.40 ERA. The poor strikeout-to-walk ratio must have been a red flag to the organization.

He began the 1960 season at Auburn of the Class D New York-Pennsylvania League where he was 1-2 with a 5.66 ERA. He threw 35 innings walking 24 and striking out 18, a better ratio than the prior season. He finished that summer at St. Petersburg of the Florida State League going 0-1. That is where his pro career ended.

"He came back to Drayton and played town ball with us," Johnson said. "The funny thing, he had this great curve but that fastball was gone, that thing I could hear whiz from center field. Just gone and I don't know why. But for some reason he could throw this huge Bert Blyleven curve."

Knoff started to distance himself from other people. Some called him a recluse. To the townspeople, he turned into a mysterious figure who lived alone in the country for the ensuing decades. One theory is he never coped with the sudden death of his father, Raymond Knoff, from a heart attack. Raymond was involved in his son's baseball career at every step. When Tom was on the mound, Raymond nervously paced with every pitch, smoking a cigarette. He guarded against Tom throwing too much so he wouldn't have arm trouble. That was unheard of in those days.

"His dad was very protective of how much he was throwing," Bill Brosseau said. "His dad had those kinds of insights. I mean, my younger brother would throw until his arm fell off. I don't think kinesiology and all of that didn't come out until the '70s."

Tom Knoff wouldn't answer the door if people made unannounced visits to his house. He would consider opening the door if somebody called in advance. One time at a yard party in Drayton that Johnson was hosting, a couple people asked about going to see Tom at his farm to see if they could bring him back to town.

"Sure enough he came to the door and it was hi, goodbye, nice to see you," Johnson said.

Raymond Knoff died when Tom was trying to make his way through the minor leagues. Bill Brosseau believes Tom was one of a few pitchers destined to make the next level of minor league ball when the sudden slide hit him. He got this information from Jim Knoff, Tom's younger brother, who Bill coached a couple of years after high school. They were playing a game at Wahpeton when Bill removed Jim Knoff from the game.

"He was crying in the dugout," Bill Brosseau said. "I walked up to him and said, 'What's the matter Jim?' He says he was thinking about Tom and he says, 'You know, Tom was one of three pitchers destined to be brought up and then his dad suddenly died. Just collapsed.' Jim said Tom just lost it and the next spring, those other two pitchers broke spring with the big club and Tom came home to the farm. Supposedly, Tom was ranked higher before his dad's death."

In 2010 when the 1958 Drayton team was inducted into the North Dakota Sports Hall of Fame in Jamestown, Johnson called Knoff to gauge his interest in attending the event. It was a short conversation that ended with Knoff saying, "I'll think about it, goodbye."

He did not attend. The Knoff family has a legacy of athletic ability. Tom's cousin, Kurt Knoff, was a standout athlete at East Grand Forks, Minn., as well as an All-American football player in 1975 at the University of Kansas. He had an NFL career with the Minnesota Vikings, Denver Broncos, and Houston Oilers. Curious about his distant attitude with the great '58 Drayton team, I tried contacting Tom at his house in the country. Our phone conversation was brief.

Doug Halcrow died in 2014 after living his adult life in northern California. Before he passed away, he penned a short story on what it was like growing up in Drayton.

"Drayton, back then, there was nothing to do but play ball in the summer. We were always playing, morning till night. We might have short summers up there, but we crammed a lot of baseball into them. Baseball was popular everywhere, but I can't imagine the game's collective enthusiasm as focused in other towns.

"All of us wanted to be something special, something above the rest, and we seized the opportunity. I was a skinny, sickly child who went into the hospital almost every summer with a bout of asthma. The 'me against the world' attitude I developed as a result wasn't a monopoly, however. The kids I grew up with, I think they tired of Drayton being beaten up in sports and decided to do something about it."

Doug grew up as a neighbor to Dick Johnson and they both talked before the 2010 induction into the Hall of Fame honor that assured the legacy of Drayton baseball.

"Otherwise we would be gone with the wind," said Johnson, now living in the Denver area. "Doug said he realized then what an impact we had. Fifty-two years later, it was nice that it sunk in with Doug. I never realized the impact the story had outside of Drayton. I know we were an exceptional team. I've come back to North Dakota over the years and the people from distant towns, if they heard of Drayton, they knew about the baseball team. We were a modest group. I was probably the least restrained of them all and even I didn't tout it."

***

Drayton fans hopped on the bandwagon starting with the 1958 high school season. With pitchers Doug Halcrow and Tom Knoff, Drayton dominated the state tournament winning the first of six straight state prep championships. That stands as an unbreakable record in North Dakota high school baseball. There were teams that won three straight (Hatton 1969-71), Cavalier (2002-04) and Minot Ryan (2007-09). Since North Dakota instituted Class A baseball in 2000, no team won even two straight titles in the next 18 years.

Drayton won the '58 prep title at Jamestown McElroy Park, a field that was a home away from home for the players because of all the tournament games it hosted. The four-hour trip home was taken on a Lake of the Woods Busline. It was dark and the players were settling in after the post-game celebration. Toward the front of the bus, head coach Davison was having a conversation with a few of the players. He posed the question, "What would you think of challenging Class A in Legion ball?"

Johnson believes that question was already answered between Davison and the guys at the Drayton Legion club. Davison was probably looking for his final answer with the players.

"I think we all bought into it right away," Johnson said. "Nobody said, oh geez, we might lose. We were all enthusiastic about it."

Maybe not all. Ray Long figures a few of the players were "a little hesitant about it" but they eventually came around. To move up a class, the Legion post had to petition the state Legion board. Nobody knows the tone of those conversations, but it was approved.

Davison, in a letter describing his experiences, wrote "I didn't see much competition in Class B ball, and thus there would be no motivation for me to push the athletes to the max. I wasn't interested in returning to coach players who would be satisfied with the minimal effort it would take to win a Class B title. But the players on that bus wanted to be the best. That trip was like a time warp. We left Jamestown as a Class B lineup and sometime, as our bus was knifing through the darkness, those youngsters became North Dakota's Class A team of destiny. My assessment of the team at that point was that we had two, and possibly three front-line pitchers; a big, young catcher savvy beyond his years; a lineup of fearsome hitters top to bottom; a solid defense that was getting better, and a hole in left field that I'd try to fill with a couple of 'rookies.' But Heaven spare us any injuries. Our bench was shallow, filled with junior-high kids whose future as Curt Gowdy might say 'is ahead of them.' Nevertheless, Drayton's starting lineup was as good as any that I could imagine in Class A."

Davison said he spoke with Doug Swenson of the Drayton Legion post to talk about moving up. The next day, Davison went on vacation for a week driving to his hometown of Lawton, N.D., near Devils Lake, and later to Washburn, where his brother lived.

"During the drive, the team never left my mind," Davison wrote. "We would have to have time to develop the catcher, morph a seldom-used reliever into the number three starter and figure what to do in the corners of the outfield. "

Swenson called Davison at his brother's house in Washburn and told him all systems were go on moving to Class A. Two days later, he drove back to Drayton to get the season in the higher class started.

"I was as excited as the kids," he wrote. "It was the role that I had dreamed of."

Scheduling Class A competition didn't go as anticipated, however. Drayton got some games with Grand Forks and what Davison called first-rate teams from Thief River Falls, Minn., and the Warsaw independent team near Grafton. Grand Forks was coached by Marv Skaar, who made a name for himself as the head coach of the North Dakota State men's basketball team in the 1970s.

"Marv Skaar used to send his 'B' team to Drayton and we would flatten them," Johnson said. "Finally, he was the only guy who would schedule us."

That summer, the Drayton players got into the comparable score game because that was about the only way they could gauge themselves against the Class A teams. Davison and a couple of players including Long made one scouting trip, traveling to Fargo to watch the Post 2 club. When they got back, Johnson asked Long what he thought of Fargo.

"And Ray started giving me this long explanation that their pitching is really good, their hitting is not so hot and then I said, 'Damn it Ray, can we beat them?'" Johnson said. "'That's all I want to know.'"

"Oh yeah," Long said, "we can beat them.'"

It was a hectic summer for Davison, who was in charge of the Midget and Pee Wee levels of baseball in Drayton in addition to coaching the Legion team. That meant he was accountable to the practice times of every team. It took a toll on his health; and by tournament time, he was enduring stomach issues that caused him to throw up before most games.

"Funny but the players didn't feel good unless I upchucked," he wrote. "They said that if I didn't spew, they wouldn't win. A strange good luck charm, but real ballplayers are superstitious. It was true. During the tournaments, the only time I didn't lose lunch was before the Sioux Falls game and we lost."

Drayton went 13-2 in the regular season losing 2-0 to Pembina and 7-2 to Warsaw. They beat Grand Forks twice in a doubleheader 7-2 and 12-8. The baseball field in town was the place to be; one of the Legion commanders before every game would put a speaker on top of his car and drive around town promoting the upcoming game. Fans routinely packed the bleachers behind home plate, down each foul line and sat in their cars in the outfield. There was no home run fence, which made for some interesting plays when Drayton batters crushed a ball a country mile into the vehicles. Johnson once hit a ball that ended near an exhaust pipe, a play that turned into an argument between Johnson and the umpire, Don Halcrow. He was Doug Halcrow's dad.

"He made up some rule that the hit was illegal and I wasn't going to get into an argument with my next-door neighbor," Johnson said. "He probably knew I had enough hits by then anyway."

Schumacher Park, located on the west edge of town, had a dirt infield on land that was donated by a farmer. Drayton finished the regular season with a 10-3, 15-0 doubleheader sweep of Warroad. It was on to the playoffs, time to see if moving up a class was the right move. Drayton hosted Wahpeton in the Class A Challenge Round, a best 2-of-3 series to get into the Eastern Division tournament. A wooden snow fence was installed to make Schumacher Park in compliance with tourney regulations.

The team had no trouble with Wahpeton, winning 14-1 and 17-1. Drayton opened the Eastern Division tourney with a 4-2 win over Jamestown, which set up the big matchup with Fargo at the old minor league ballpark home of the Grand Forks Chiefs. Before the game, Davison got in front of the team and gave it one of those "win one for the Gipper" speeches.

"Play your game," he told the players. "We pull our pants on just like they do. We're a solid team and we've seen better pitching than this. If you're feeling unsure of yourselves, don't be. Go out there and win."

"It was the turning point if there was ever any doubt you could beat Fargo," Johnson said. "They only had one pitcher in Ed Kelly and I would always like to argue that Ed Kelly couldn't make our team."

A popular Drayton joke for years was Bob Kostka could have made the team -- on the Drayton bench. Kostka was inducted into the Fargo Post 2 Hall of Fame in 2015.

The Fargo vs. Drayton matchup got nasty; the teams smacked-talking each other. Fargo started a "Where's Drayton?" theme. On the flipside, Drayton fans filled the Grand Forks stadium giving it the home-crowd advantage.

Drayton won 5-3.

"Of course, after the game, we were yelling 'where's Fargo!'" Johnson said. "Fargo had some wide-eyed looks on their faces."

Jamestown came back to end Fargo's season, a game the Drayton kids listened to on radio. The small-town kids won the Eastern Division title taking down Jamestown again 11-2. It wouldn't be the last time Drayton faced Jamestown, either. Both teams advanced to the state tournament at McElroy Park in Jamestown. The last time Drayton left McElroy it did so as high school champs and the talk of moving up.

Now the team got a chance to be crowned the king of state baseball.

Drayton fans came to Main Street to see the Lake of the Woods Busline off to Jamestown, taking pictures and wishing their boys good luck. Drayton knew nothing about Williston, the opening-round opponent. Williston was good in football and fielded a baseball team with big players.

Williston led after seven innings. Drayton rallied. Johnson's triple was the go-ahead RBI, and he scored an insurance run in a 5-3 Drayton win. Drayton sent Jamestown to the losers bracket with a 9-6 win with Jamestown coming back to knock Williston and Bismarck out of the tournament.

The state title game was no contest.

Drayton 14, Jamestown 2.

"We were elated to win but it wasn't unexpected," Johnson said. "Here we were, we knew we were a Class B town but people said we were a Class A team from a Class B town. We knew how to put a baseball uniform on. We didn't look like some of these farm kids who would dress like they were changing a tire or something. We got that from watching the Grand Forks Chiefs."

The Region 9 tournament was in Bismarck, so Drayton didn't face a long road trip to a tournament that hosted the state champs from North Dakota, South Dakota (Sioux Falls), Minnesota (Minneapolis Grain Exchange) and Wisconsin (Green Bay). The fans in Bismarck were on board with the small fish in the big pond story. The Drayton games drew crowds of 3,000, with kids hanging from fences to get a view.

Drayton beat Sioux Falls 6-3 in the opener. Sioux Falls had ace pitcher Jerry Crider, who went on to a career in minor league baseball and a couple years with the Chicago White Sox and Minnesota Twins. Probably not taking Drayton seriously, Sioux Falls opted to start another pitcher and paid for it with a loss. That brought a matchup between Minneapolis and Drayton, which would be the first classic David vs. Goliath matchup of the postseason.

"But I don't think anybody said, boy, we're in trouble, we're playing the Yankees," Johnson said.

Drayton handled the Grain Exchange with ease winning 7-1. Green Bay was the first to get eliminated, giving Sioux Falls another crack at unbeaten Drayton. Crider was on the mound this time, and Sioux Falls took a 5-1 victory setting up the Region 9 title game between the same two teams. In a close game, Drayton won 4-3 and became the darlings of Legion postseason baseball. It was the first time since 1940 a team from North Dakota advanced beyond the regionals.

"We were getting lots of press," Johnson remembers.

Baseball fans across the state knew what happened. Word was out.

"On the bus back to Drayton, they were just building the interstates so we would go through all these towns," Johnson said. "People would come out and honk their horns. Heading into Drayton, people started following us about the last 10 miles outside of town."

The next day, Drayton left for the section tournament.

As Dick Johnson wrote, "When Cinderella wore spikes."

***

In the summer of 2018 the Grafton Legion baseball team is playing the Fargo Jets Class A Legion team in a regular season doubleheader, but excuse the Jets if they were confused as to who they were playing. Grafton was wearing Drayton jerseys.

The "throwback" uniforms were a tribute to the Drayton run of excellence. Drayton and Grafton are separated by 21 miles with Drayton contributing two players to that Grafton team.

The subject got legs thanks to Grafton head coach Chad Kliniske and Drayton resident Andy Duncklee, a 71-year-old retired doctor who played on the last two Drayton high school title teams in the early 1960s. Drayton dropped its Legion program after the 1963 season. It resurrected the team in 1994, but that lasted 10 years.

"An old-timer in Drayton in the last year we had a program said before I die, I want to buy new uniforms for the kids," Duncklee said. "He died before he got to see the uniforms. They wore them one year and were sitting in boxes ever since."

The uniforms resurfaced in 2018. Grafton wore them later in the year in a Class A state tournament game against Park River.

"It honored the memories of the Drayton players over the years," Duncklee said.

He was 11 years old in the summer of '58 and has some recollection of that team. One wonders how many people in Drayton still have any remembrance the '58 team, or even think about it. Many folks have died. There will forever be items in the North Dakota Sports Hall of Fame in Jamestown. There will always be Dick Johnson's writings.

Andy Duncklee's greatest contribution to the legacy is in the form of cassette tapes. His mother recorded Drayton's tournament games on radio including the regional title victory and the Cincinnati game. Andy still has them.

That was some year. That was some team.

XII. The Skipper

Rectangular city streets are rare in Charleston, W.Va. That's probably fine with Doug Simunic, whose 42 years in minor league baseball was full of twists and turns in every corner of the United States. Home is a modest house with a driveway a kid could use for a sledding hill. If it were Fargo in the winter, bags of salt and sand would be required to get a car into the garage.

Simunic's bi-level house formerly served as an offseason office in his 22-year job as the manager of the Fargo-Moorhead RedHawks, the city's first minor league team since the Fargo-Moorhead Twins folded in 1960. The desk is gone, but the room is stocked with RedHawks gear and memorabilia. His old RedHawks No. 33 jerseys hangs on a clothes rack. On the wall is a framed No. 35 USA jersey from his stint in 2002 in Monterrey, Mexico, with the United States minor league players. The U.S. entry in the "Series of the Americas" played countries like Cuba. Team photos and framed newspaper articles of selected moments in his RedHawks tenure are everywhere. There's a cherished photo of his late father and his older brother at a RedHawks game.

Simunic is 62 years old and hanging out in Charleston, a city that has lost population over the years but still maintains a sense of West Virginia history. The Appalachian Mountains are visible anywhere in the city, a surrounding landscape that is opposite of Fargo. It's a strange feeling for Simunic. He's never lived in his hometown in the summer months, spending most of the time since the mid-1990s at a rented apartment the team paid and furnished in south Fargo. His golf game has never been better. He's hitting the ball longer off the tee with his driver than he has in years and his approach game to the green is sharper. The putter could be better, but that may be a matter of time before he figures it out.

His Type 2 diabetes is under control, with visits to his endocrinologist once every four months instead of once every three. He asked a local hotel bartender for the best place to get a beer at 10 at night. The kid told him a street where the trendy college kids hang out. That wasn't the answer Simunic wanted. He's not a trendy guy. He's old school.

Charleston is an old and historic town situated along the Kanawha River. Simunic married into it; it's the hometown of his wife, Stefanie. They raised their only daughter, Allasyn, in Charleston, and the trio made the best of Doug's job over 1,100 miles away at Newman Outdoor Field in Fargo.

The team's manager since its inception in 1996 until 2017 seemed happy, despite moments in the last year when the relationship with the club turned for the worse. Baseball is an addiction, he said, and withdrawals from the game don't come overnight, if ever. He constantly looked at his phone, a habit he's trying to kick. Minor league managers are on their phones day and night because the job requires daily maintenance of player evaluation. If the team is struggling, there is little time for patience and managers need to have a pulse on what players are available.

"Forty-two straight years in it, so for me not to be in it is a little weird," he said. "It is what it is. You have to know that at the end it won't be pleasant for you. I'm not bitter about it. I'm OK with it."

After his run with the RedHawks, he figured he would land another job in baseball. The New Jersey Jackals of the Can-Am League made a pitch for him, but he didn't like that he never got a chance to talk to the team's owner. He wasn't comfortable with the front office staff running the team that was young and most likely inexperienced. He didn't want to train twentysomethings on the ins and outs of minor league ball. He had already done that in his career and didn't want to do it again at 62 years old.

The job he wanted was managing the fledgling Chicago Dogs of the American Association, the same league as the RedHawks. Simunic had extensive conversations with Dogs team owner Shawn Hunter, and he figured he was on track to get the job. The contact with the Dogs started in June of 2017 when it was apparent the RedHawks were not offering Simunic another three-year contract, which was to expire after the '17 season. Both parties appeared fine with that, too. Simunic said a meeting with RedHawks team owner Bruce Thom in August of 2016 ended with an agreement 2017 would be his last as manager.

"I went into his office, and he said, 'What do you see moving forward for Doug Simunic?'" Simunic said. "I said building a few more championship teams because I still have a desire to do it. And I want to try and get the best personnel I can. Thom's words were, 'It's not going to happen here, we're not offering you a contract after the 2017 season.' So, I said, 'All right, OK.' I wasn't totally shocked. I said, 'We're going through the 2017 season?' He said, yeah, '2017 will be your last season.' OK. I said, I understand we're parting ways; but if something new comes along that I know about or a team is vacating a manager, I have to be able to negotiate or talk to them during the 2017 season."

Thom's response, according to Simunic?

"Not a problem," Thom said. "Not an issue."

Simunic said there were indications a role with the team in some capacity could be on the table after he was done managing.

"I said, 'If I don't land another job, let's talk about that,'" Simunic said. "And that was the end of it. I walked out, didn't say much about it and moved on."

He moved on to building his 2017 team, a process that is mainly done in the winter months. In June, with the season in the early stages, Simunic said he and Hunter started talking about the new Dogs franchise. They spoke once a week, sometimes twice. They e-mailed each other. Hunter asked questions on how to build a franchise. That's what Simunic did with the RedHawks. He took the team from scratch and built it into a Northern League championship franchise.

"I knew Bruce knew because I told him," Simunic said. "I needed another job for 2018. And he said, 'No problem.'"

That job wouldn't be with the Dogs. The communication with Hunter came to a halt after the American Association vs. Can-Am League All-Star Game on July 25 in Ottawa, Canada. The team owners held their mid-summer meeting in conjunction with the game; and it was there, Simunic said, RedHawks president and chief executive officer Brad Thom told Hunter to stay away from Simunic.

"'You're tampering with our manager, and it's against the rules,'" said Simunic, quoting Brad Thom. "'We don't want you talking with our manager because we're not sure what we're doing with him.' I think there was some collusion in my inability to get that job, but there's nothing I can do about it. I didn't get why I didn't get that job. Evidently, they didn't want anybody who knew the league, knew the players."

The end of his RedHawks reign came two months later, 22 years after the Fargo-Moorhead franchise was awarded without a finished stadium. Newman Outdoor Field was not completed, so opening day was played at Fargo American Legion Post 2's Jack Williams Stadium. At least the on-field leadership was finalized with the team's pursuit of Simunic.

He had finished his second year as the manager of the Winnipeg Goldeyes, his team having lost the Northern League championship to the St. Paul Saints. Afterward, Simunic and assistant coach Jeff Bittiger went to the house of Goldeyes owner, Sam Katz, to discuss a new contract. Katz laid it on the line. If the team doesn't win the Northern League title next year, forget about any two-year deal.

"Right there I said I'm leaving," Simunic said.

Bittiger had a contact in Fargo, and that's how the Simunic tenure with the RedHawks began. Bittiger and Simunic met with Bruce Thom and RedHawks announcer, Jack Michaels, at the old Grainery restaurant in West Acres Mall in Fargo. Why Jack Michaels? Simunic says Michaels was the only person Thom trusted with baseball knowledge. Ever heard the cliché of deals being written on bar napkins? That's how this one was done. Simunic was all in with the Hawks not only because Katz soured him on the title demand, but also he wanted to get back to managing in the United States.

So, it began.

A memory was born every day, like the time former RedHawks player, Ricky Freeman, visited the team when Fargo-Moorhead was playing at Kansas City. Freeman greeted Simunic in the visitor's clubhouse. After talking about old times, he asked Simunic if he and his son, Zach, could sit in the dugout with the team during the game.

"Sure, not a problem," Simunic said.

The manager asked Freeman an odd question.

"Do you want to put the uniform on?" Simunic said. "I have one veteran spot open right now and am in the midst of trying to fill it."

"Absolutely," was Freeman's response.

Freeman borrowed a pair of baseball cleats from another player. To make it official, Simunic had Freeman sign a one-day contract. F-M had the game in hand in the later innings when Simunic made that one-day contract real. He told Freeman to grab a bat and pinch hit.

"I haven't played in eons," Freeman said.

His last season was 2003, where he played just one game. His seasons of note were 2001 and 2002 when he hit .303 (23 home runs, 83 RBIs) and .301 respectively. Freeman quickly searched for a pair of batting gloves and headed to the on-deck circle.

"He had a marvelous power swing," Simunic said. "He fouled the first two straight back. I mean, he was right on them, and he didn't miss by much. He ended up striking out, but he was so grateful in giving him a mid-life opportunity. We released him after the game, he and his son thanked me ... I'll never forget it. Great story."

Not many in the stands the day the St. Paul Saints played the RedHawks in St. Paul will forget Simunic vs. Marty Scott, the Saints manager. Both were ejected in the early innings and ran into each other in a hallway underneath the stadium. They were talking about the game, mostly about the umpires, when they saw a pair of inflatable Sumo wrestling suits used for a between-innings promotion.

"Can we get into those?" Simunic asked.

Saints owner Mike Veeck started the franchise with actor/comedian, Bill Murray; the duo open to any promotion or gimmick in their ownership years. A phone call was made to the press box to alert team management and the public-address announcer that Simunic and Scott were up to something. Between innings, with Sumo suits on, Simunic and Scott went onto the field to duke it out. They hit each other three times, both falling backward, when umpire Don Grimalski, who had ejected both of them, walked over.

"You're in trouble." Grimalski told both of them.

"He didn't find it too funny," Simunic said.

Funny was common with Simunic and the Hawks. Like the time pitching coach Jeff Bittiger was using binoculars at an opposing stadium. With Bittiger not knowing, Simunic took eye black and rubbed it around the outside of the scope. Bittiger grabbed the binoculars, looked at something in the stadium, before walking to the mound to visit his pitcher. He had black circles around his eyes.

"The players were roaring," Simunic said.

Everybody was roaring, except relief pitcher Barry Nelson, on the night in St. Paul when Nelson thought he won the Powerball. The jackpot reached $100 million in 1998 for the first time in lottery history, so several of the players banded together to buy tickets. Somebody from the RedHawks wrote the winning numbers on a piece of stationary that had Twin Cities television station WCCO at the top to make it look more official. An intern took that paper and delivered it to the RedHawks' bullpen at Midway Stadium to show the pitchers who bought tickets. Nelson matched the numbers with his ticket – and imagine the immediate pulse that penetrated his mind. It was a tight game and Nelson was warming up thinking he won the $100 million Powerball. He wanted to call his mother to tell her not to close on a house she was about to buy. After the game, Nelson brought his luggage to the locker room, at which time bus driver Cordell Sinding asked him why he needed it. Nelson told him he won the Powerball and was staying overnight in St. Paul, instead of traveling with the team. Nelson made reference to buying the bus and buying the team. To add to the prank, a radio announcer from the Saints, who was in on the joke, did a "fake" interview with Nelson talking about the Powerball ticket.

The episode ended when Nelson went to his locker. On the door was a pink slip that read: "Got you."

"Listen here motherfuckers," Nelson said, "at least I know what it's like to win the Powerball."

The team on one trip learned what it was like not to have air conditioning. In the heat of summer, the team was driving south when pitcher Gene Caruso took off his clothes in the back of the bus, walked unannounced to the front behind Sinding, and asked while standing naked: "Anyway we can get some air back there?"

The bus rides got tougher on Doug with each year. He was diagnosed with diabetes eight years into his job with the RedHawks, a condition that made it hard to sit still for long periods of time. In minor league baseball, road trips can take many hours.

Simunic powered through them. It wasn't his nature to be coddled. He grew up modestly in the small development of Washington, Mich., located north of Detroit. His father, Joe, was a carpenter. His mother, Edith, drove a school bus. The couple bought a small piece of land and built a house, a dwelling that was nice, but small for the three Simunic boys. Doug and one of his brothers slept in a den. His parents made a good enough living, however, for Doug to play hockey and baseball at Romeo High School, located six miles away.

Doug's two older brothers followed their father's blue-collar footsteps. Keith, the oldest, was a carpenter. Mike was a painter. Doug had other thoughts when it was time to decide on a career.

"I'm not doing any of that shit," he told his dad.

"I'll make you a deal," his father replied. "I'll subsidize you as long as you want to play."

Joe Simunic knew the importance of baseball to his son. Doug attended St. Clair County Community College in Port Huron, Mich., instead of a four-year college because he "screwed off too much" in high school and his grades suffered. He redeemed himself, later, getting his education degree from West Virginia State. He was drafted in 1975, starting a 10-year minor league career that reached the Class AAA level. A catcher with an average bat, he was valuable to the minor league teams because of his ability to handle pitchers. One of his highlights came off the field when he met Stefanie Masinter at a downtown Charleston bar. They've been together since.

He was an organizational guy, not a major league prospect, playing in 813 career minor league games with 550 hits in 2,231 at bats; a .247 average. His best year at the plate was his last in 1984 with Class AA Chattanooga, where he hit .281 in 44 games. The minor league career fizzling out, he went to Canada with pitcher, Bill "Spaceman" Lee, to play in a senior baseball league. From there it was over to Italy to manage a team for a couple of years. He returned to the U.S. catching on with the Houston Astros organization for one year and the Los Angeles Dodgers for two years.

Independent baseball was gaining momentum around then. In 1993, Simunic got the job managing the Rochester Aces in the new Northern League. A year later Winnipeg called. Then it was Fargo, where he brought his gritty, determined style of play to fans who got to experience pro ball for the first time.

Oh, the times and the players.

The RedHawks won Northern League titles in 1998, 2003, 2006, 2009, and 2010. Those teams were the result of Simunic knowing the Major League Baseball player release market better than anybody else in the league. It was a year-around challenge. He called it "the chase." He could recruit. When players got released from a Major League club, independent managers like Simunic would sell them on their franchise and city much like a college football team wooing a five-star high school prospect.

"When baseball season rolled around, I knew it was 137 days you had to be on the job site, including training camp," Simunic said. "I'd get in at 8:30 every morning and start working on it."

Assistant coaches, for many years Bucky Burgau and Kole Zimmerman, arrived later in the morning. "We would end up cooking out a lot, but also working on the team," Simunic said. "After the game, we would have a couple beers in the clubhouse and talk about the game: how we can improve, who's underachieving, who needs to go. Sometimes the game would end at 10 a night, and we wouldn't leave until after midnight. Then you go home to bed and do it all over again the next day."

There was no shortage of personalities in the clubhouse. Names rattled off like a who's who of RedHawks baseball: Daryl Motley. Chris Coste.

Joe Mathis. Brian Traxler. Rich Becker. Motley, Traxler, and Becker were players with Major League experience. Traxler was on the ground floor with the RedHawks in 1996 and 1997. He passed away in 2004 at the age of 37 from liver problems, a probable result of alcoholism. He was a cult hero in the minor league system with his rotund look and powerful left-handed bat. His cause of death was reported by the Japan Times newspaper, which followed his journey because Traxler was a popular player in Japan in the mid-1990s. Simunic sensed issues with Traxler's drinking, but said it never affected him on the field.

"But he always had some troubles and I think it kept him from a career in the big leagues," Simunic said. "He was a winner. A fun guy and he came to play."

Fun guy, fun times. Traxler, Coste, and Simunic were part of a public relations RedHawks caravan that spent a night at the Shooting Star Casino in Mahnomen, Minn. The three were in one room when Traxler laid down a ground rule: "If you don't get some sleep for me," he said, joking that he was planning on gambling late into the night while the other two weren't, "then you're in trouble."

Coste was the hometown poster child, getting his start in pro ball with the RedHawks and parlaying that into 13 years in the minor leagues. He was rewarded for his persistence making the Philadelphia Phillies roster and winning a World Series ring. The start came with Simunic and the Hawks on the first day of practice.

"You want to see me hit?" Coste asked Simunic.

"No," the manager responded.

Then Simunic asked a question.

"Have you ever caught?" he said.

"No," Coste replied.

They were working out at a batting cage at Concordia College in Moorhead. It was in need of repair, so Simunic was about to get in his car to drive to a hardware store when Coste spoke up.

"I'll ride with you," Coste said.

Coste hopped in the passenger seat, and the baseball conversation continued. How does a guy spend 13 years in the minors and make a Major League Baseball roster? He didn't know the meaning of the word "no." Simunic said Coste kept asking questions, like what position would suite the kid best.

"Wait your turn and see what happens," Simunic said.

After the hardware store stop, they headed back to Concordia.

"What role do you see me playing?" Coste asked him.

"Wait your turn; there are a lot of pro guys here," Simunic said.

The RedHawks went through training camp with Coste as the bullpen catcher. They played one regular season game when F-M's starting catcher, Mike Crosby, was picked up by another ball club.

"I took Coste around the corner and said, 'Are you ready to step on 'em?'" Simunic said. "He says, 'Put me in coach.' It was on-the-job training. He was raw but he was OK."

In Coste, Simunic saw a lot of himself. Coste was a good handball player at the downtown YMCA in Fargo because of his quick hands. Behind the plate, he caught every ball. That may sound elementary, but good catchers don't let pitches get by them. None. Simunic loved that in Coste. As a coach, he liked that Coste was clutch with the bat.

"I mean, real clutch, man," Simunic said. "He never complained. And then he started to become a pretty good catcher by his second year. He started to throw guys out."

Coste was from Concordia College. So was pitcher Greg Salvevold, another Simunic favorite. He was 54-32 in eight career minor league seasons, going 10-1 with a 3.06 ERA with the RedHawks in 1999.

"One of the top winners in RedHawks history," Simunic said. "He learned on the fly."

Simunic got a kick out of shortstop Jeremiah Piepkorn, who played at North Dakota State. The RedHawks clinched a league title in Winnipeg, with the celebration ending at a bar in the city called Earl's. The drinks were flowing. The team ordered food. Before the party ended, Piepkorn ordered an expensive shot of alcohol for everybody – on the team's tab. The bill came to $2,400, to the dismay of team ownership.

"That was Pep, he knew how to run up somebody's tab," Simunic said.

Pitcher Justin Fletschock was from Munich, N.D, and NDSU. He played six years with F-M and was 53-23. Mike Peschel, a lefty from NDSU, was 36-17 from 2003-08. He wasn't overpowering, but crafty. Jake Laber, from Fargo North and NDSU, was more about power. He was the anchor of the staff, and led the team in superstitions.

"He'd bring his own water, his own everything," Simunic said.

Laber was 59-43 from 2008-14 and left as the franchise's career leader in wins, games started, innings pitched, and strikeouts. The day he unexpectedly passed away in August of 2016 from natural causes was a night when Simunic went back to his empty hotel room, sat at the edge of the bed and cried. Zimmerman, a close friend of Laber's, took it the hardest.

"I lost Zimmerman the rest of the time that year," Simunic said.

We all were at a loss. I knew Jake. I get it. The kid was a gem and left us way too early.

***

The end of the 2008 season was a case of foreshadowing. Simunic was suspended for the first six games of 2009, the result of "inappropriate behavior" during the RedHawks' 2008 playoff series against the Kansas City T-Bones. Pitching coach Steve Montgomery was interim manager during the suspension.

"I've known Doug for 17 years," Northern League Director of Baseball Operations Harry Stavrenos told The Forum. "I respect him and what he's done with that ball club. But, just like any manager, he's got to adhere to the rules."

Stavrenos said Simunic was tossed for complaining to umpires his team did not receive properly rubbed-up baseballs. Typically, new baseballs are rubbed with mud before a game to dull the shine. Simunic left the clubhouse more than once after being ejected, Stavrenos said. Players and managers are required by the league to remain in the clubhouse after being ejected. The Forum reported Stavrenos said Simunic got into an argument with the Kansas City left fielder after leaving the clubhouse in street clothes.

It was the second lengthy suspension resulting from a tormented end to 2008. He was suspended for four games in August for repeated criticism of the league in the media. "I have put it behind me," Bruce Thom said. "The suspension is being served. This is last year's business, and I'm much more concerned with this year's business."

That year's business became monkey business later in the season. Simunic never had much love for the Goldeyes, but matters got out of control on the night of Aug. 19, 2009. Goldeyes coach, Tom Vaeth, and Simunic got into a fight.

About a decade earlier, I covered a boxing match between Virgil Hill and Donny Lalonde at Winnipeg's old baseball stadium, and that victory went to the North Dakota boxer in a unanimous decision. Call Simunic vs. Vaeth a draw.

Simunic came face-to-face with a charging Vaeth after Goldeyes pitcher Ace Walker threw behind RedHawks hitter Nic Jackson in the fourth inning. After exchanging words, Simunic slapped Vaeth with an open left hand and attempted to hit him three times with a closed right fist.

The altercation was the culmination of a contentious first three innings. RedHawks starter Garry Bakker threw a pitch over Winnipeg batter Kevin West's head in the second inning, then hit West in the helmet in the third inning.

"(Vaeth) got a little too close. You're not going to go with your hat in my face," Simunic told the Winnipeg Sun newspaper. "That's all I've got to say. Take it for what it's worth. The rest is history. There was no need. I was going out there to ask the umpire what the warning was all about."

"Who expects that? What manager acts like that," Vaeth told the Sun. "Simunic felt he needed to voice his displeasure at one of our guys, and I didn't want him talking to our players like that. The next thing you know we were standing face-to-face, and he hit me with an open-hand slap."

Neither Simunic nor Vaeth were suspended by the league. Stavrenos regretted not taking action.

"The bottom line is this: I blew the call," said Stavrenos, who was in charge of fines and suspensions for the Northern League. "I don't know what I was thinking. Both of those guys should have been suspended. Days ago, I told them nothing would happen, so I can't go back now."

Said Simunic, "If someone's going to threaten me and push and shove me, I'm going to deck you. Sorry. I'm not proud of it. I'm defending my team, defending my people, and defending myself. He put his hands on me first."

Vaeth was tossed again the following game for arguing with umpires. It was the first time in league history a coach had been ejected on consecutive nights.

Vaeth was suspended by the Northern League years earlier for a physical altercation with an umpire. Meanwhile, Simunic's run-in with Vaeth was caught on camera and immediately made the rounds on the Internet. The video was viewed more than 4,000 times on YouTube.com in a span of one week.

While sitting at a restaurant overlooking a hilly Charleston golf course in June of 2018, Simunic chuckled at the Vaeth fight.

"We had a little altercation back in the day, over silliness," he said.

The problem started when Goldeyes manager Rick Forney disappeared from the dugout, with Simunic believing he was in his office trying to make player transactions. That's minor league ball. If a team needs a player, there is no waiting, even for the end of the game. Vaeth took over for the Goldeyes, and the fireworks started. Simunic said that his pitcher was not throwing at the Goldeyes' batter, but the insinuation by the Goldeyes turned into a lot of mouthing off.

"I tried to calm it down, and the next thing you know he and I are swinging it out," Simunic said. "It was not a proud moment."

Simunic and Winnipeg had a contentious relationship. Hardcore Goldeyes fans saw a manager who deserted them for a better job in the States. It was common for fans to harass Simunic in most games played in Winnipeg. At one point, he received hate mail that was serious enough for the RedHawks to put Simunic up in a hotel that was different from the team.

"I mean, we didn't think anybody would kill him," said Brent Tehven, who worked the clubhouse for the team in those years. "But would somebody get in his face and cause something? Yes, absolutely. Or would they try to say something to his family? It was a bitter rivalry."

Tehven got an early education in minor league baseball. He was the team's bat boy in 1996 and 1997, and also having the title of assistant clubhouse manager in '97. He became the clubhouse manager as a 17-year-old in 1998.

"Doug just had that grit, his mental toughness and just grinding it out every day," Tehven said. "He's a guy who would be in the hotel lobby at 8 in the morning going through stats."

Tehven once got a stint as first base coach, which started as a joke. Burgau, the first base coach, couldn't make a three-game trip to Gary, Ind., leaving the RedHawks to fill that position. The first game was on Tehven's birthday; and before the nine-hour bus ride to Gary, Simunic asked Tehven what he wanted for his birthday.

"I want to coach first base," Tehven said.

After batting practice and 20 minutes before the first pitch of the opening game of the series, Simunic asked Tehven why he didn't have his uniform on. Clubhouse guys don't wear uniforms.

"You're coaching first base," Simunic told him.

Tehven didn't believe him. Before long he was coaching first base. The RedHawks won the game, so Simunic handed Tehven the same job in Game 2. The clubhouse guy was on a roll. The Hawks swept the series with Tehven at first base; and it was on to Edmonton, Alberta, for another three-game series. The good vibe of the first base coach ended in Canada. F-M hitter Brant Krause crushed a pitch to the outfield gap that scored a runner from first. The throw to home plate wasn't close, with the ball sailing well over the catcher's head. At the same time, Tehven told Krause to go to second base. Tehven didn't see the pitcher backing up home plate, but his throw to nab Krause at second was wild. Krause made it to third base. Simunic, however, wasn't happy Tehven sent Krause to second in the first place. It was raining, which was part of Tehven's defense.

"The turf was wet, I knew he wouldn't be able to grip the ball and get him," Tehven said, with a laugh.

The RedHawks lost. Tehven never coached first base again.

***

It was a serene Sunday morning in Fargo-Moorhead, with temperatures in the 60s and light winds. Friends gathered in a private room at Herd & Horns Sports Bar and Grill by the NDSU campus to say goodbye to Simunic. The former manager was in good spirits, telling everybody he'd be fine, and it was time for him to do something else. For a goodbye party to do justice to a manager who made Fargo his home for 22 years, people would have had to fly in from all over the country.

Upon returning to his Charleston home, with Fargo permanently in the rearview mirror, Simunic penned a letter to the editor to The Forum newspaper thanking the fans. It wasn't the way he wanted to say goodbye, but at least it was a way.

To the fans,

Thank you Fargo for the twenty-two years that you allowed me to call your community home every summer. Starting in 1996 at Jack Williams Field to finally making our opening at the Nest, thank you for those great memories and support.

Thank you for being there for five championships and supporting all the great players and coaches that came to your great area all these years. Thank you to all the great people I got to know and spend summer nights with at Newman Outdoor Field. The people and those nights will be lasting memories that I never will forget.

Finally I wish I could have said good-bye to every fan that supported what I was doing all these years. A tip of the cap or meeting everyone at the front gate on fan appreciation night will only be a memory. Though I had been dreading saying good-bye to all the fans on the final night knowing that my contract wasn't going to be renewed, now my biggest regret is that I was not able say good-bye.

Thank you Fargo. You will always have a place in heart.

Doug Simunic

The letter ran on the front page of The Forum's sports section, which was a rarity. Letters normally run in the opinion page in the A1 section, but the unique circumstances of the week led sports editor Kevin Schnepf to keep it for himself.

Simunic had support in the media. Nobody came out in favor of the firing. Even Simunic's fiercest rival, the Winnipeg Goldeyes, were perplexed. The Winnipeg Free Press newspaper ran a headline "Say it ain't so, Simmy..." Sportswriter Mike McIntyre called it a stunning move by the RedHawks and wrote the timing of removing Simunic as manager was bizarre.

Even Forney, the Goldeyes manager who had his share of run-ins with Simunic, was puzzled.

"It's definitely a surprise, knowing you're this late in the season," Forney told the Free Press. "I'm not sure what the benefit of doing that at this point is. The man has had a helluva run down there in Fargo and in independent baseball. Nobody's won more games or championships."

McIntyre's article ended with a reference to Simunic's last appearance in Winnipeg. The RedHawks manager was tossed after arguing two straight balk calls against his pitcher. To say Simunic expected to get ejected was probably an understatement. Simunic mocked the umpire's "you're out of here" sign doing the same thing with his own arm at the same time.

Winnipeg fans sang "Na na na na, hey hey hey, goodbye" as Simunic exited the field.

The letters and emails from fans came pouring in. Doug Tehven, whose two sons including Brent, worked the clubhouse in the early years of the franchise, wasn't happy. He wrote a letter to The Forum after the Herd & Horns farewell.

There was a small, almost intimate gathering Monday evening at Herds and Horns (managed and co-owned by my oldest son) to get together with our friend Doug Simunic on the eve of his flight out of town as he was recently relieved of his duties as the manager of the FM RedHawks.

I felt compelled to share my respect and admiration for the guy who many of us only knew as Simmy. This man came into our community 22 years ago and gave everything he had to win baseball games, five league championships, and entertain us each summer in a way that will never be matched. His passion for the game, his team and the entire Fargo-Moorhead community was evident—just ask any umpire who he went nose-to-nose with. He was a fighter and a believer in what was right.

I fully understand baseball at this level is not just a game. It is a business and no one knows this better than Simunic. Throughout his years here, he has called dozens, if not hundreds, of young men into his office and told them they were being released or traded. Sorry to say, this is just part of the game. What makes this so different is the timing. With three weeks to go in the season and still a chance at making the playoffs, I fail to see how you can fire the "face of the franchise." Win or not, the stands were still full.

As a result of the ownership's decision, there are devoted fans who have said they will never attend another RedHawks baseball game again. This is the ultimate lose-lose deal. Nobody wins. In the end, the community loses and Simmy ends up saying his farewells to some friends at an almost secret party behind closed doors. The fans at Newman should have had the divine right to stand on their feet and offer their sincere thanks and appreciation for everything he has done for this community. And how do you not allow Simmy to tip his hat one last time at Newman to the fans and friends where he has spent and devoted his past 22 summers?

As I left Monday's gathering, I thanked him for helping raise our two sons who both had the privilege and opportunity of working for him. Our oldest son was 14 when he became Simmy's first batboy and continued to work for him for several years as the club house manager. Next May I'm going to miss asking my son: "Is Simmy back in town yet?"

Doug Tehven

The contentious relationship between Simunic and the RedHawks wasn't done with his leaving Fargo. A few months later, in Charleston, he revealed his side of the story. I've known Simunic as a straight shooter. So did Mike McFeely, Eric Peterson, Dom Izzo, or anybody in the media who covered him on a regular basis. The guy spoke his mind. When it came to McFeely, the columnist who at times was tough on the RedHawks manager, Simunic said, "He was hard, man, he was a columnist. He was hard. He would turn it inside out, make a story out of something that wasn't there. I like him, he was alright. Controversial."

Simunic admits to the RedHawks playoff drought that reached four seasons by the time he was fired. Back-to-back records of 65-35 and 62-48 in 2012 and 2013 were followed by 43-56 and 44-56 records. The Hawks went 52-48 in 2016. The North Division of the American Association was highly competitive with veteran managers like Simunic, Forney in Winnipeg, Montgomery in Sioux City, and George Tsamis in St. Paul. The Saints had the best stadium in the league. The competition for players was intense with new facilities making for a nice recruiting tool.

Simunic said the controversial scenario of his dismissal began the day after the team was swept by the Kansas City T-Bones. Simunic told his staff that he sensed something was "eerie" around the clubhouse.

"I knew something was up," he said.

On Sunday, Aug. 12, Simunic was having breakfast at Kroll's Diner on 45th Street South in Fargo when he got a text message from Bruce Thom. He was told to go to Brad Thom's office when he got to Newman Outdoor Field. He finished his food, walked to his car and called his wife Stefanie.

"This is the last ride to the stadium," he told her.

"What are you talking about?" Stefanie replied.

"Something is going to happen," Doug said.

She told Doug that she hoped it would be another contract, since the RedHawks had won 11 of their last 14 games.

"Not a chance," Doug told her.

He drove to the stadium and went into Brad Thom's office, as instructed. Simunic said Brad was in a corner of the room, Bruce Thom was straight ahead and general manager Josh Buchholz was sitting on a couch wearing a baseball cap, so low that it almost covered his eyes.

"He had tears in his eyes," Simunic said. "I knew what was going on. Bruce had his RedHawks white shirt with the logo, he looked bad, he looked like he really didn't want to do it but he said to me 'As of today, we're going to relieve you of your duties.'"

"That's like I'm being fired, right?" Simunic said.

"Yeah," Bruce Thom replied.

According to Simunic, what happened after that was blunt and disrespectful.

"They said we want you to leave town by 3 in the afternoon," he said. "That's what Bruce said to me. That day. We'll pack all of your stuff and send it to you. We want you out of town by 3 o'clock. And I think that's all he said."

That's not the way Brad Thom remembered it.

"We just told him we wanted him out of the stadium before the game began, and we wanted to know when he wanted to get home," he said.

Simunic looked at Buchholz, extending his hand to him.

"It was a hellavu run, wasn't it?" Simunic said.

"Yeah it was," Buchholz said.

He shook Bruce Thom's hand.

"Who are you going to get to manage?" Simunic asked him.

The answer was assistant coach Michael Schlact.

"You're kidding," Simunic said.

Simunic had his loyal assistants like Burgau and Kole Zimmerman. He didn't regard Schlact as one of them.

"I walked down to my office and Schlact was sitting on the couch, staring at the floor with his baseball hat on," Simunic said. "I looked at him and he wouldn't look up. So, I bent down, so he could see me, and said, 'Are you fuckin' happy you got what you want?' He never said thank you or nothing. I said 'You're gutless.' I grabbed my shit and left, went to my house and got things in order."

The RedHawks played Gary that night. Simunic returned to Newman Outdoor after the game, figuring it was late enough that everybody was gone. He was driving south on Albrecht Boulevard on the North Dakota State campus when the Gary bus was going north. Simunic flashed his lights in an attempt to stop the bus. It worked. Gary manager Greg Tagert, seeing it was Simunic's car, walked off the bus. Simunic got out of his car and the two hugged.

By now, the relationship between Bittiger and Simunic had deteriorated. The two, who were so critical in getting the franchise on its feet in the late 1990s, no longer spoke to each other. Simunic said Bittiger wasn't a big fan of Brad Thom early in their partnership "but he buttered up to Brad at the right time. I never buttered up, never knew Brad that well. I had to thank through (an advertisement) the newspaper all the people of Fargo, who are great people."

"I used to be his boss," Simunic said of Bittiger. "Then all of a sudden Brad comes on, and he became my boss. I was leaving anyway."

Simunic said he knew the end was imminent in spring training when he wasn't part of a meeting with the Thoms and Bittiger. The three parties always talked, but not this time.

"(Bittiger) wouldn't tell me anything before he left, he flew all the way back to Philly," Simunic said. "And I got him on the phone and asked, 'What happened?' He said, 'They're going to keep the cheaper of the two.' And I said, 'OK, you're the cheaper of the two, right?' And he didn't say anything so I figured it out. That was in spring training, and I knew I was doomed; but I knew I was doomed anyway because my contract wasn't being renewed. So when I got fired that night, (Bittiger) called me; and I said, 'Really, they had to do it with 24 games left in the season?' He kept saying, 'Owner's decision. It was an owner decision.' And I said, 'You want me to be honest with you? The owner's not competent enough to make that decision at his age. He would have seen it through, I know he would have. And he said, 'It was an owner's decision.' So I said, 'All right, whatever.' And he said, 'By the way, you've made enough money here,' as to say it's time for you to get lost. And then we got into who stuck up for who when it came time for jobs."

Simunic's biggest regret was not having the rest of the 24 games of the season to say goodbye. He was preparing for that moment for a year anyway, dating back to the contract non-renewal meeting at the end of the 2016 season. Plus, with the team winning, he wanted to lead it into the playoffs in the last 24 games.

Brad Thom said Simunic "not necessarily" was told 2017 would be his last.

"We told him we had to see vast improvements, have a winning record and get into the playoffs again," he said. "And if that wasn't going to happen, we were probably going to make a change. Mainly it was him and Bruce that would talk."

I scratch my head at ownership demanding a winner every season. Attendance at RedHawks games over the years was stable. This isn't Bison football, where winning is demanded. The RedHawks are a nightly vacation in the summer with affordable tickets and concessions. Football is intense. Baseball is relaxing.

Yet, Simunic said the directive from Bruce Thom in the last several years of his tenure was to win at home.

"I was threatened the last five years, 'Buddy, I don't care what you do on the road, you better win at home,'" Simunic said, in mimicking Thom's voice. "Baseball doesn't turn on and off that way. That was my pet peeve – you have to win at home. The fans in Fargo are cooped up all winter. They want to get out on a Friday night, have a beer and catch some baseball on some green grass. He was a little disconnected."

There were issues with Simunic's cell phone and unemployment compensation from the state of North Dakota after his firing. The RedHawks cut off his team-issued phone around Labor Day. The team had no interest in accommodating its ex-manager despite the two-plus decades Simunic put into the club.

"They didn't like me talking to certain people," Simunic said. "I said, can I ask you one favor? Could I keep the number on my new phone? They said absolutely not. You know what that did to me? That set me back with all my contacts. All the people in baseball. I had to re-establish myself. It took me a few months. Just weird stuff."

Eighteen years of accumulating phone contacts were erased.

Brad Thom said the phone contract was closed because Simunic continued to call RedHawks staff members.

"It was a RedHawks cell phone; it wasn't Doug's cell phone," he said. "We paid for the communications, and we paid him though the end of his contract which was September. And we asked him not to contact our staff which he continued to do so we shut down the cell phone. It was as simple as that; it was our cell phone."

Brad Thom was asked why Simunic wasn't allowed to keep his number.

"It was our number," he said. "I don't even remember if he requested to keep it, but we discontinued it."

The unemployment episode surprised Simunic. He was fired on a Sunday but did not want to leave Fargo until the Herd and Horns sendoff on a Tuesday. On Monday, he drove to Job Services of North Dakota and talked to two people working behind a counter.

"We know who you are," one of them said.

"Oh yeah, you've been to Newman Outdoor a time or two?" Simunic replied.

"Yeah," one of them said, "and we're sorry to hear about your misfortune."

Simunic asked one of the employees, Jerome Billups, about drawing unemployment.

"How long did you work there?" Billups said.

"Twenty-one and three-quarters years," Simunic said.

Simunic was asked about his contract and if he was terminated immediately. The RedHawks agreed to pay him until Oct. 1. Job Services told Simunic to go online on Oct. 2 to sign up for unemployment, which he did with the help of Stefanie.

"We had to call them once a week," Simunic said. "So the third week in, like the end of October, I get a letter that says Fargo-Moorhead RedHawks baseball club and Bruce Thom are going to challenge your request to receive unemployment from the state of North Dakota."

Simunic sought the advice of an unemployment lawyer. The lawyer's advice to Simunic was to stick to his guns.

At the hearing, which was done via phone, Bruce Thom was on one line and Simunic on another.

"He starts saying the players didn't like me, nobody in town liked me anymore, I was bad in the clubhouse," Simunic said. "I wanted to interrupt a couple of times, is this really being said?"

The lawyer asked Thom if he was changing his testimony that was previously written. Simunic gave his closing statement, saying he was blindsided on the 13th after 22 years of loyal service. He was told a verdict would take five to seven days.

"I went online the next day and they ruled for me," he said.

He received 26 weeks of unemployment compensation.

"The thing Thom didn't like was that his premium goes up," Simunic said. "That's why he did it."

Brad Thom denied it was over a premium. He said that the club wanted to get verification from the state because it wasn't sure of state labor laws.

"When you pay him through the end of his contract, does that constitute unemployment as well or is it just done with the contract," he said.

***

The hope is the mess from 2017 will disappear and time will heal. And "The Skipper," a nickname given to Simunic by several people in Fargo, can be recognized as of one of the greatest and toughest sports figures in the city's history. That's a lot of years every summer at Newman Outdoor Field. In an instant, 22 years vanished.

"I tried to do my best on a nightly basis," Simunic said. "My goal was to get my team to as close to a Major League baseball team as I could so people didn't have to get in their car and drive almost four hours (to see the Twins). Like I said, I'm not bitter about it. I'm OK. I'm happy in the next phase of my life."

Everybody involved knew it was time to move on. The Skipper knew it. He was fine with it. Twenty-two years is a great run for any coach or manager, especially in professional baseball where managers often live a revolving-door existence. There is no finer way to spend an evening in the summer in the Red River Valley than to catch a RedHawks game. The grass is so green fans can smell it. The stadium is functional, nice, and efficient. The beer is cheap compared to Major League Baseball. The tickets are affordable.

For 22 years, it was the home of The Skipper.

s

XIII. State of N.D. vs. Don King

The temperature was 102 degrees in early August and Medora, N.D., was cooking. In the Old West, when it's hot, it feels like history. Shelter is an air-conditioned building away; something cowboys didn't have when traveling by horse. Perhaps they hung out by the Little Missouri River, cooling themselves with water from the quiet stream that winds through Theodore Roosevelt National Park.

Try taking a photo of the majestic bluffs with a cell phone. Digitally capturing the perspective of the historic western buildings against the red, sandy horizon is nearly impossible.

It's a unique area of the country. Golfers know that. Bully Pulpit Golf Course is a scenic gem that carves its way through the heights of the Badlands on the back nine holes. The difference in elevation on a couple of holes makes a player wonder if knowledge in rock climbing is required. My son and I, on a father-son trip to the Badlands, played with a married couple from Alberta, who said they ran into golfers from Scotland. How a developer hiking through the property could configure a setting for 18 holes of golf is beyond me. The first nine holes is a nice experience. The experience of all 18 with the picturesque back nine are nature-painting-meets-sports moments.

Teddy Roosevelt and Harold Schafer had it right. Roosevelt was the 26th president of the United States who hunted and ranched the Badlands. Schafer was the North Dakota entrepreneur and founder of Medora. It's a perfect place to shut out the world for a few days. For the last 42 years, one man got away every summer. Bill Sorensen says the worst part of a summer in Medora is a lack of national and world news. Visible TVs in town are rare. It's also the best thing. Happiness for Sorensen is not having to worry about the anxiety of the nightly newscasts.

The nightly Medora Musical in the Burning Hills Amphitheatre is Sorensen's yearly oasis, a show that starts with laid-back preparations in mornings and afternoons and gradually builds in hype the closer to showtime. The cast call was around 6 p.m., when singers began their warmup routine.

Sorensen was the co-host, the narrator who orchestrates transitions from one song number to the next. He was the father figure, conveying the same stately presence of Teddy Roosevelt. There was raw emotion in his delivery when paired with Chet Wollan, the star of the show and host. A touching moment came when both paid tribute to Cowboy Lyle Glass, a long-time musical cast member who died earlier that summer at the age of 67.

Billed as the "best show in the West," the backdrop of the Badlands in the distance is unparalleled for live theatre. The show uses horses trekking up steep bluffs tracked by spotlights at night. Medora is in the midst of an economic revival and primed to get bigger as more attractions become part of the town scene.

Sorensen, 67, is best known in the western part of the state as the mayor of Bismarck from 1990-2002. He was a stickler for well-run meetings that created avenues of growth in the capitol city. His true calling is show business; those 42 years of summers in Medora comprising over 3,000 shows. He's been a part of over 5,000 shows in 39 states; the next event being the biggest. There are no days off nor does Sorensen want one. Of 100 days in Medora, he was scheduled to perform in 97 of them, the other three filled with other commitments. There's no shortage of enjoying life. He's a survivor. Sorensen beat stage 4 throat cancer and kidney cancer, and overcame seven heart bypass surgeries, the last in 2008. Doctors told him with his level of heart failure there was an 80 percent chance he would die within two years.

"I've been sailing past that," he said.

Walking around Medora, Sorensen paused at the sight of anybody he knew, or thought he knew, to give an awe-shucks greeting. He was a recognizable star in the musical.

It was a big production. Sorensen changed costumes frequently to depict the theme of the current act or song. There was a black suit with western-looking purple shoulder highlights in the opening scene. He wore a green-glittered suit coat during a game-show theme set. That turned to khaki pants and a light purple vest when the lights dimmed for another number. He portrayed a journalist wearing a fedora hat, tan vest, and white shirt. A black cowboy hat and light blue coat was the intro for another number. With the sunset and the natural beauty of the Badlands behind the theatre lit with spotlights, he wore a white overcoat facing the landscape while the Burning Hills singers sang "Ghost Riders in the Sky." He concluded the show with a bright red, knee-length coat and black pants.

It was G-rated, wholesome family entertainment.

Bill Sorensen is the same guy who went toe-to-toe and stared down the most imposing, R-rated and bullying figure in boxing history: Don King. The guy who greeted an 80-year-old with grace on a Medora street corner is the same guy who took the worst insults and threats from a boxing promoter whose slogan is "Only in America."

"Don King takes legitimacy away from the sport," Sorensen said.

Sorensen was the manager for North Dakota boxer Virgil Hill during Hill's assault on world light heavyweight and cruiserweight titles from 1987-2007. To earn title belts, to reach the top boxing pay scale, the Hill camp had to align with King. As much as the Hill team didn't want to do it, King had contracts with HBO and Showtime, the premier pay-per-view boxing networks.

Negotiations were tense, combative, dishonest, and unbelievable. Sorensen was never shy in letting people know how he felt about King, being quoted in Sports Illustrated "the only thing straight up about Don King is his hair."

"Don negotiates through intimidation," he said.

In Las Vegas, both parties were figuring a way to get Hill in the ring. They were seated at a dining room table when King crossed one leg over the other thigh exposing a gun in a leg holster just above his shoe.

"I just laughed," Sorensen said. "That would drive him crazy. Every time he went berserko, I would smile and that would make him even more mad."

A gun surfaced another time during a Hill fight weekend in Bismarck. King and his people and the Hill entourage were out to dinner at local restaurant East 40 Food & Drink.

"And Don had this guy Cecil with him," said Al Larsien, Hill's assistant trainer. "Cecil made it clear that he had a gun. I don't know if he thought we were going to bum-rush him or something or what. He was commenting on how white North Dakota was, and he was thinking something could happen to him out here. I'm like, you don't have to worry about anything out here."

One time, King called Sorensen wanting to make a deal. Itchy to sign papers, King said he was sending his private jet from Las Vegas to Bismarck to pick up Sorensen. He declined, saying he would travel on his own dime. Sorensen took a commercial flight with the stipulation only those two would talk about another fight, agree on the terms, and let the attorneys handle the legal language. Sorensen went to a suite in the MGM hotel in Las Vegas, where he sat at a dining table waiting, waiting, and waiting. King always made him wait. King finally walked in pacing back and forth talking on the phone. Sorensen waited some more.

Sorensen soon had company when four men sat next to him.

"Who are you?" Sorensen asked one man.

It was a man with the last name Abrahamson.

"What do you do?" Bill asked.

"I'm Don King's personal attorney," he said.

Sorensen asked the other man the same question.

"I'm the attorney for Don King Promotions," he said.

Sorensen asked the third man, who replied he was an attorney, too.

King got off the phone, and Sorensen took advantage of the brief silence.

"OK, we have a problem," Sorensen said.

"What's that?" King said.

"You said you and I would meet and do this discussion and not deal with the attorneys," Sorensen said.

"Yeah," King said, "but let them listen to us so they hear it first hand and get it right."

Sorensen and King started negotiating anyway, when the Abrahamson fellow chimed in.

Sorensen turned to Don and said, "Who's negotiating here? Why are these guys here?"

King goes berserko again. He says he has no time for deals.

"Don, we have to figure out the bedrock of the contract," Sorensen said. "Finally, he sat down and negotiated. (The other attorneys) didn't leave the room but they shut up."

King continually tried to take advantage of Sorensen's inexperience in boxing. Little did he know Sorensen studied the sport relentlessly, and that included details of the foreign television market. The two sides were $225,000 apart on a deal one time that tested Sorensen's boxing acumen.

"I can't give you that kind of money," King screamed at Sorensen. "You have to be reasonable. Work with me. We're a team here. You think I'm making all this money?"

King told Sorensen he would be lucky to get $100,000 from the foreign TV market. Sorensen made a proposition. The Hill camp would take $100,000 less than King was offering in exchange for sole rights to the foreign TV money.

"King goes berserko again," Sorensen said.

King gave in to the $225,000 difference.

"He's calling me an S.O.B. and all of that," Sorensen said. "But I knew there was at least $300,000 in the foreign TV market. We did enough research on that."

About then Hill was coming off two years of inactivity thanks to Don King.

"Two years of my life just gone," Virgil said.

The Hill camp went into training seven times, only for a fight to be postponed or canceled. It was frustrating to Larsien, who had to make sure his fighter was peaking for a fight. One time, everybody's bags were packed for Switzerland when a call came that morning. Unpack. For a boxer like Hill competing in a sport that doesn't appreciate age, that mental hopscotch was tough on his body.

"This individual had so much control over my life," Hill said of King. "The last six months of the contract, I just kind of lost it. For any athlete, that's a long time not to be doing anything."

When the two parties signed the $2 million, five-fight, 20-month contract in May, 1994, all was golden. But the honeymoon was short and the marriage, which publicly appeared blissful, immediately developed in-house problems.

The reasons for the demise with King were two-fold: One, Sorensen wasn't certain King had a sincere intention to live up to the contract. And two, the "Battle of the Badlands" between Hill and Frank Tate, among other bouts, wasn't as financially successful as past Hill fights. The biggest quandary was the minimum value of a fight. Sorensen said the contract for Tate called for $250,000.

"The first thing King did after we signed was offer $100,000 less than the minimum," Sorensen said. "Then I'm doing everything in the world and not hearing anything. Then he offers significantly less, and he said I was unreasonable."

In the end, the Hill camp went overseas for the last fight in the King contract, a matchup with Drake Thadzi in the fall of 1995 at Wembley Stadium in London. It didn't go off without controversy; the snag this time was over the difference between a boxing agreement and a promotional agreement. One of them said if Hill won, King got the rights to the next three fights.

"I said I can't sign this," Sorensen said. "This was not part of the discussions or the negotiations."

Sorensen believed King was hoping the Hill party would sign the documents without reading the fine print. There was still no resolution at the weigh-in the night before the fight. To find privacy, Sorensen and the Hill camp attorney, Joel Gilbertson of Bismarck, huddled in a broom closet in a hotel next to Wembley Stadium. They decided if the contract doesn't change, Hill wasn't going to fight Thadzi.

"I tell everybody we have a problem with the contract, and Virgil may not be part of the fight," Sorensen said. "All these media people that were there ... the rumors had gotten out about it."

At a reception following the weigh-in, Sorensen saw Hill talking to Carl King, Don King's son. Sorensen figured Don King sent his son to the reception to soften Hill hoping Hill could convince his management team to sign the contract. Hill gave Sorensen a "come over" motion while he was talking to Carl King.

"Bill, I want to introduce you to Carl King," Hill said. "Carl, this is Bill Sorensen, my manager."

"Of course, I know Bill," Carl King said. "I've known him for a while."

"If you know him, why are you talking to me?" Hill said to Carl.

"Bill is getting in the way of negotiating and not being reasonable," Carl King told Hill. "We want what is best for you."

That didn't sit well with Hill, who throughout his lengthy career let his management team do the managing. Sorensen won the contract battle that night. The language that gave Don King the rights to Hill's next three fights if he won was scratched out, with both parties penning their initials next to it.

"I've never seen a guy walk into a room and suck up all the oxygen and electricity," Hill said of Don King. "He's not a little guy; he's like 6-4, and that's not with the big hair. The weirdest thing was it was a love-hate deal. He just had that street-hustle thing, and you never knew who the real guy was."

Larsien called King "a guilty pleasure." He liked being around him, calling King funny and intelligent. King could rattle off the Nos. 1 through 10 contenders in any weight class without notes on a daily basis. That's over 100 boxers at his immediate recall.

"Just jaw-dropping intelligent," Larsien said. "His problem was he would rather steal a penny from you than make an honest dollar. He was that kind of a guy. He kind of got off on making people crawl."

Larsien was equal to King in the intelligence department. A well-read individual, he brought Shakespeare on the road and was the brains and consistency behind the training operation for all those years.

Don King, on the other hand, enjoyed the control of boxers he had under contract. Most of the big-dollar fights that King put on, like the Mike Tyson events, had a behind-the-scenes subplot of other King fighters showing up looking for a bout. One such case for Hill was in 1995 when Tyson had a fight at The Spectrum in Philadelphia. The fighters looking for work were literally waiting in a line to talk to "Mr. King," and that included Hill, Larsien, assistant trainer Ray McCline, and newly-crowned middleweight champ Bernard Hopkins.

In front of that group was middleweight Julian Jackson having a conversation with King that everybody overheard.

"Don is standing there in his underwear spouting blah, blah, blah," Larsien said. "And Julian Jackson is literally saying, Don, I have seven kids, I need a fight. He's begging. He was begging for anything, anywhere on any card. It was uncomfortable so Virg and I were like, we'll come back another time. We saw this over and over again in dealing with Don. This scene repeated itself all over the world."

So why did the Hill camp sign with King in the first place? Because King controlled many of the top contenders, and boxing rules call for the champion to have a mandatory defense against the top contender.

Besides, it wasn't the first time Hill was around a boxing circus. The Thomas Hearns fight in 1991 was Example A of the cruel business side and how resilient a fighter has to be to survive.

***

Hearns was Hill's first opponent with big-time credibility. The Bobby Czyz bout in 1989 in Bismarck ranked high on the popularity meter, but the Hearns matchup was high on the payday meter. It was a mess for Hill. He arrived in Las Vegas for the pay-per-event at Caesars Palace with a broken nose suffered on the last day of sparring in training camp. Sorensen, who wasn't his manager at the time, questioned manager Gary Martinson if Hill should even fight. Hill also had a hyperextended arm injury known only to the trainers. At the pre-fight press conference, Hill wore makeup to hide the bruise on his nose.

The nose was the biggest concern. Freddie Roach, Hill's trainer, was hopeful Hearns lost some power having moved down a weight class to light heavyweight.

"And as fate would have it, right away Hearns hits him square in the nose," Sorensen said. "Virgil ... his eyes were just watering."

The Hearns fight would be the last with Martinson, a North Dakota native. Hill made $1.3 million, his first seven-figure pay day. But that money vanished over the course of the next few months. It appears Martinson made at least one bad investment with the earnings.

"Virgil loses the fight to Hearns, it was his biggest pay day, and then he finds out he's broke afterwards," Sorensen said.

Those were tough times.

Hill loaned Martinson an undisclosed large sum of money before the fight that spawned frank discussions in the Hill camp. That included Scott Nelson, Hill's accountant. One question Hill's handlers debated: Does Hill pay Martinson his fee as manager up front or take it out from his loan to Martinson? Nelson advocated for the latter.

"He's in financial trouble, and you won't see it again," Larsien quoted a Hill team member saying.

Hill said Martinson gave him his word he would pay him back, a statement which ultimately caused Nelson to resign as his accountant. Hearns won the fight in a unanimous decision, able to endure Hill's patent jab with enough offensive force.

"He wasn't broke after that fight but it was almost like ... losing that fight was a real emotional thing and he went into a tailspin," Larsien said. "He was only 27, but it was his first loss as a professional, and it was a fight that knee-deep in the heart he knew he should have won."

There were several steps Larsien would have done differently. It's one reason the good trainers are generally older. The job can be so complex that the only teacher is experience.

Roach, a former boxer who had 53 professional fights, was new to the training gig. Experienced assistant trainer Thell Torrence was scheduled to come into training camp for the last three weeks, but Roach didn't call him. Larsien said Torrence would have stabilized the team.

At that point, Roach and Larsien were to be paid a percentage of the purse.

"Then Gary comes to training camp and tries to talk Virg into putting Freddie and I on salary," Larsien said. "It was open warfare at training camp. Wait a minute, we've gone through all this stuff in getting a big pay day, and you try to pull the rug out from under us? That created a rift big time between Freddie and Virg. Trust was kind of gone and it was sad."

Roach moved on to other fighters, most notably training world champion Manny Pacquiao. Hill and Larsien, meanwhile, disappeared to Australia; one of the best moves Hill made in his career.

The move resulted from a friendship between Hill and Australian lightweight Jeff Fenech, a three-time world champion. Five months after the Hearns fight, Fenech flew to Las Vegas with billionaire Australian media tycoon Kerry Packer for the Evander Holyfield-Mike Tyson fight. Tyson withdrew from the bout citing a thumb injury, but that didn't stop Hill and Larsien from hanging out with Fenech.

"Packer had this gigantic suite, his own private casino up there," Larsien said. "He was losing and winning millions every day, literally. Virg was still playing softball, and he had a tournament and left town. I was hanging with Fenech. I told him it seems like Virg has kind of scattered, is not very happy, and is lacking direction right now. We were struggling to get back on track."

Fenech made the offer to the Hill camp to train in Australia. He offered the services of his trainer, Johnny Lewis. Fenech talked to his promoter Bill Mordey, who arranged for a rented house for the Americans to live.

Hill needed to get away. Shortly before Christmas of 1991, he and Larsien flew from Los Angeles to Sydney.

"By that time, money was tight, we were training and not doing a lot other than that," Larsien said. "He got refocused. Rededicated. It was a wonderful time out there."

While getting refocused in the ring, Hill called Sorensen to get his out-of-ring matters refocused. He wanted Sorensen to be his manager.

"I know nothing about boxing," Sorensen said.

Hill didn't flinch, pointing out Sorensen helped him with former managers Martinson and Marc Ristman. Sorensen said no, again. Later, Hill made another call to Sorensen.

"I'm going to retire," he said.

"That's fine," Sorensen replied. "What are you going to do?"

"I don't know," Hill said. "But before I retire, I would like to have a shot at the title."

Sorensen explained to Hill he would fall out of the boxing rankings if he didn't fight soon. Hill fought once in Melbourne, Australia, against Aundrey Nelson, winning by unanimous decision. Once again, he turned to Sorensen to keep him in the boxing loop. Sorensen gave in.

"I'll put together an event to keep you in the rankings," Sorensen told Hill. "If you want, I'll help you find a manager because you need somebody who knows more about it."

That next event was against Lottie Mwale in 1992 at the Bismarck Civic Center, which resulted in a fourth-round Hill knockout. The referee was holding Hill's arm up as the decision was being announced when Hill turned to Sorensen, who was standing in the corner. Hill motioned for one more fight.

"The long and short of it, we did a one-fight deal for the next 12 years," Sorensen said.

The Hill train was back on the track after the Mwale TKO. He had the dependable engine in Larsien and the box cars led by Sorensen to carry the management freight. Hill defeated Frank Tate to regain the WBA light heavyweight belt. He won five straight fights in 1993 starting with a crushing of Adolpho Washington at the Fargodome, a mauling in which my white shirt at press row had faint dots of Washington's blood. That was followed by victories over Fabrice Tiozzo, Sergio Daniel Merani, Saul Montana, and Guy Waters – each time to retain the WBA belt. Hill was named the WBA's Fighter of the Year.

The Waters fight was in December. In January, Hill was scheduled to face No. 1 contender Drake Thadzi in Grand Forks for his mandatory defense. A win over Thadzi and the Hill camp had the upper hand in negotiating for a fight. But during training in Grand Forks, an earthquake struck the Northridge, Calif., area on Jan. 17. Hill's wife was living near the epicenter.

"There was no stopping him, Virg flew to L.A.," Larsien said. "As we're going to the airport, I'm still trying to talk him out of it. What can you do what emergency workers can't do? He said he needed to be there for his family, and I can respect that."

When Hill returned, Larsien could tell his fighter hadn't been training. Weight was an issue, and there wasn't much time before the fight. Running outside in the middle of winter wasn't optimal for shedding pounds, and the boxer struggled to reach the maximum 175 pounds. During the weigh-in, Sorensen told Larsien to stay on Hill's right side. He told trainer Mike Hall to stand on Hill's left side, and Sorensen said, "I'll stay behind him in case he falls over."

"We made weight for the fight, but he basically killed himself in making weight," Larsien said. "He got sick. All the fluids he took in after weigh-in, he threw up. We had to take him to the hospital and get him on IVs."

Promoter Cedric Kushner was at the hospital pushing for Hill to fight the next day. It didn't happen. He was too sick and the fight was canceled. So much for being in control of the next fight.

"And that's what made us sign with Don King," Larsien said.

Hill would fight only once in 1994, twice in 1995 until meeting Lou Delvalle in 1996 at old Engelstad Arena in Grand Forks.

***

I'll never forget traveling to Atlantic City, N.J., in 1996 to document Hill's training before the Delvalle fight. The champ gave me great access, letting me follow him around the "Las Vegas of the East Coast" for a couple of days.

We were in traffic in his white Suburban with North Dakota license plates, stopped on Illinois Avenue. Hill let another vehicle pull out of a parking lot in front of him. This was the East Coast. There is no driver etiquette on the East Coast. Locals do not stop a visitor on the sidewalk at Pacific Avenue and ask how's it going? They don't care. The only time they'll stop somebody is to ask for money. It's called getting mugged. Not once, but twice, the big Suburban with 75,000 miles let another car pull ahead.

The driver was not from the East Coast. Virgil Hill called North Dakota home. He was a boxing champion and movie critic. He scorned the film "Fargo."

"I hated it," he said. "It pictures us as all we ever do and say is, 'Yah, sure. Uh uh.'"

Yah sure, there was another WBA light heavyweight championship coming up. You betcha, for the 21st time in his record-setting professional career, Hill was ready to put the belt on the line, this time against Delvalle. Hill was 32 years old, and he wanted to unify the title in the division and retire financially secure.

"I think how they measure whether you're a success in my sport is how much you have in the bank," Virgil told me. "Not on what you have accomplished."

His accomplishments were not an accident. If there was a motto at 400 West Brighton in Pleasantville, N.J., the address of the Pleasantville Recreation Center where Hill trained, that would be it. There was no such thing as an accident.

"It never ceases to amaze us the lessons we count as accidents," trainer Mike Hall said. "I believe nothing is an accident."

Hall was a good ol' guy. He was genuine, the sweat master at gyms. It saddened me when he passed away in 2014 at the age of 69. Larsien was asked to say a few words at the funeral. He made it to the third word and broke down. The news devastated Hill, who shortly after his death said that he learned more about the sport of boxing from Hall than from former trainers Eddie Futch and Roach combined. Those were heady words. Futch and Roach are both in the Boxing Hall of Fame.

Hall, Larsien, and assistant trainer Ray McCline made sure Hill didn't cut corners at the Recreation Center. Situated amid an older section of homes in Pleasantville, eight miles west of Atlantic City, it was the training-camp base for the champ.

There were two moods in the gym: laughter and business. It was all fun when the workout began in Hall's office. As Hall meticulously taped the hands of Hill, the atmosphere was boxing's version of happy hour. Even if a joke or comment wasn't funny, it seemed funny. The office looked more like a basement boiler room. The ceiling was unfinished sheet rock. The floor was concrete, spattered with drops of dry paint. The desk was old. The refrigerator was ancient. But it was home.

The boxing room was so revered that there were not 10 commandments, but 12 posted on a wall. Break one rule and somebody may break you:

1. No hats.
2. No profanity.
3. Respect staff.
4. Treat others like you would want to be treated.
5. No food or drinks in gym.
6. No horseplay allowed.
7. No loitering.
8. No spitting.
9. Staff is not responsible for personal belongings.
10. No music during boxing hours.
11. Boxing hours are 5 p.m. to 8 p.m.
12. No littering.

Between mouthfuls of cheese balls, a 5-year-old boy named Richie asked Hill if he hit Richie's father in the face during a sparring match.

"Yeah, I did," Hill responded, in a pitying but sarcastic tone. "I'm sorry."

"Are you mad at Virgil for hitting your dad?" Larsien asked.

"No," said Richie.

Everybody laughed. Richie went to play with other kids. The big kids, Hill, Larsien and Hall, got ready for business. The Pleasantville boxing hall bristled with activity in the late afternoon and early evenings. The sound of punching bags, jump ropes, encouragement, and timing buzzers filled the room. Life came to a standstill when Hill and his sparring partner, heavyweight Maurice Marshall of Atlantic City, went a few rounds. Eight boxing protégés stopped their workouts and watched.

"One thing about Virgil," said Bob Wimberley, a 69-year-old volunteer, "he takes the time with the kids. Virgil works with a lot of them; it's a big thing for them."

"Anytime somebody gets in there with the champ, everybody's curious. Word gets around," Larsien said.

Hill had a good rapport with youngsters. One woman at the Recreation Center overheard his name and said, "Virgil Hill? He got our pompon team going." Several yards away in the basketball gymnasium, several teen-age girls practiced a pompon routine. Hill's donation was one reason the squad existed. Hill donated $10,000 to a Grand Forks track club. In 1995, the family of 12-year-old John Brewster of Bismarck credited a visit by Hill for the turnaround in their son's recovery. He was inadvertently shot in the chest.

Larsien brought two hand pads to finish the workout. Hill hit them until his arms ached. His face had a look of pain. After one final hit, the clinching blow, he collapsed to the floor. Working to exhaustion is how he got as far as he did starting with a silver medal in the 1984 Olympics. Many big bouts followed.

Hill worked over Delvalle for a unanimous decision. With King out of the picture, the camp headed to Germany to face German legend Henry Maske, a fight with the International Boxing Federation and World Boxing Association belts on the line. Maske was the Muhammed Ali of his country and the prospect of beating him on his own soil was not good.

The Hill camp began training camp in Medora in September, a decision they regretted. They trucked out a ring, heavy bags, and all the boxing training equipment. That included the training crew and sparring partners, who drove from New Jersey to Medora. Hill tore his calf muscle running on the third day, and the situation quickly became a mess. The camp was moved to downtown Bismarck at the old National Guard Armory.

The crew stayed at the nearby Sheraton Hotel, where Sorensen unwittingly played a key role in getting Hill ready for Maske. Larsien felt like Hill was missing a hard edge attitude and was looking for a spark.

"Bill said to Virg, we should have a talk," Larsien said. "Bill asked Virg if he was scared to fight Maske. It's a miracle Bill is still alive today. It's a miracle Bill got out of the hotel room without getting beat up. Virg was mad as hell and he didn't even want to talk to Bill."

Later, Hill told Larsien about the conversation.

"You know what Bill asked me?" Hill said. "He asked me if I was afraid to fight Maske. Can you believe that?"

Larsien couldn't have been happier.

"He just poked the bear," Larsien said. "It was perfect. It was like taking a bat and hitting a hornet's nest."

Larsien figured it was going to be his job to rid of the training camp of distractions like the switch in venues and the injury. Sorensen did it for him.

The crew flew to Germany in November. They were treated like kings staying at a five-star hotel in downtown Munich, with Hill's suite costing around $2,500 a night. The fight was at Olympic Stadium in front of a full house of 16,000 fans. Hill shocked them all winning by a split decision.

"That was just the most unlikely thing ever," Larsien said. "Virg goes in to fight an undefeated Olympic gold medalist in his backyard and we win."

***

Those were the greatest days in the many years of a friendship between Hill and Larsien. They grew up in Grand Forks. They went to the same Ben Franklin grade school.

Their locations were in different junior high school districts, but Hill was able to change that and attend South Junior High with Larsien. It required Hill to oftentimes walk or run the 2.5 miles from his trailer park to the school from 1977-79, and there were mornings it was a frigid commute. The average low temperature in January of 1977 was minus-12. In February it was minus-5.

Hill and Larsien were wrestlers, both doing drills together in the same weight class. Practice began at 7 a.m. and if Hill didn't have a ride, he ran the 2.5 miles at times in sub-zero temperatures. Part of the route was across a snow-filled Grand Forks Red River High School football practice field.

He took advantage of icy conditions on the streets or sidewalks to speed up the commute.

"It would be run, run, run, slide," Hill said.

The Hill-Larsien friendship spanned the globe. It got testy. Larsien figures he was "fired" at least once every training camp. On the flipside, Hill said that Larsien sacrificed his career, like following the boxer to Australia.

"We were attached to the hip," Hill said. "He was closer to me than my brother. He's very, very bright and extremely opinionated."

He was the trainer in the corner who helped get Hill into the International Boxing Hall of Fame.

"What Virg did and the way he promoted North Dakota," Larsien said, "there were a whole bunch of us who grew up out here and felt inferior. I think he lifted a lot of people's perception of North Dakota and boosted a lot of people's pride. He's a world champion and proud to be from North Dakota. I was always amazed by that."

It wasn't by accident. The Hill family made sacrifices when Virgil was a young kid; his father Robert Hill often driving him to amateur fights in North Dakota, South Dakota, Wyoming, and Montana. The family car was never new. Cash wasn't prevalent.

"My dad was a plumber, he worked from check to check," Virgil said. "He probably spent more money than he should have most of the time. I can remember my first trip, went to a restaurant and I ordered steak and eggs. I'm like around 15 or 16. The lady asked me how I want them? I said, steak and eggs. She said 'over easy' and I had no idea what that meant."

The routine was driving to a boxing card on Friday, fight on Saturday and trying to catch another bout on the way back to Grand Forks either Saturday or Sunday. Hill had almost 300 amateur fights. His final pro boxing record was 51-7-0.

"If it hadn't been for boxing, god knows what I would be doing," Hill said. "I was fortunate to come across it and fortunate to have the people that I had involved in it. I was lucky."

Virgil has remained in boxing, training fighters at his Quicksilver Hill Sports Academy in Simi Valley, Calif., about 30 minutes from his home in Santa Clarita.

He hasn't gone the way of Bobby Czyz. The fans were so loud the music was barely audible that 1989 day when Hill took the ring against Czyz at the Bismarck Civic Center. Czyz was a rock star, a good-looking dude who brought the aura of big New Jersey money to Bismarck. He was smooth.

So was his East Coast promotor Ernie Latisiano, who wore a long mink coat around Bismarck.

Years later, alcohol and other issues contributed to Czyz's downfall. He was reduced to bagging groceries in 2018 at a New Jersey grocery store. A story by NJ.com documented Czyz's medical bills totaling $1.6 million above what insurance would cover from an auto accident that left him in a 28-day medical-induced coma.

"I've got lots of regrets. I have more regrets than you have thoughts," Czyz told the reporter, before explaining why he was fired as a network boxing analyst. "They canned me because, they said, of my fourth DUI. The first three didn't bother them, I guess. Don King was a convicted two-time murderer. He was the promoter with an exclusive contract with Showtime. That didn't bother them."

Oh, Don King.

In 1954, a jury ruled it was justifiable homicide when King shot a man during a robbery. But in 1967, he served almost four years in prison for manslaughter before being pardoned.

Oh, Don King.

Those days are a distant memory. The only involvement Sorensen has with boxing is trying to get Hill as a recipient of the Theodore Roosevelt Rough Rider award. It goes to a notable North Dakotan, an honor that is not necessarily given every year. I agree he's worthy. Hill is in the International Boxing Hall of Fame, the highest honor in his sport. He labels that induction night his career highlight.

"I don't know anyone who has worked harder to promote North Dakota," Sorensen said.

Sorensen's best example happened the day before the second Maske fight in 2007 in Dresden, Germany. It took 11 years for the rematch with Maske. The pre-fight press conference was packed with at least 800 media and over 40 TV cameras. Mike Hall leaned over to Sorensen and said it was time to end the questions because he had to get his boxer to the gym for a final workout. Sorensen told the moderator to wrap it up. Hill had yet to promote his home state, something he customarily did in a press conference.

Hall knew it.

"Bill," Hall said in a whispering voice, "this is the first press conference ever where Virgil hasn't gotten a North Dakota plug in."

"You're right," Sorensen replied.

The last question, through a translator, addressed Hill's age.

"Mr. Hill, the average champion keeps the title for just over two fights. You've defended it 17 times, what do you attribute your longevity to?"

"That's easy," Hill told the crowd. "It's because of where I'm from. In North Dakota, people don't care what you did yesterday. They care what you do today. Every morning, I got up, put my boots on and went to work. It's the work ethic I grew up with, so I learned to work hard and not take things for granted. I was fortunate to grow up in that environment."

It's what Sorensen wanted to hear.

"OK, that's a home run," Sorensen told. Hall. "Let's go."

XIV. Epilogue: The Cows Don't Care if We End Up Like Maple Grove, Minn. But I Do.

I don't know what Clay Jenkinson's ACT score was, but I'm guessing it was double digits better than mine. He has a way of taking a subject, putting sense to it, and explaining reasons why. His weekly guest appearance on the Mike McFeely talk show on WDAY-AM radio in Fargo is a must-listen segment. I had several questions for him on the attitude of the state when we sat down at a Bismarck coffee shop on a cool August morning. I wanted to pick his mind because he has a pulse on North Dakotans. He also had a question for me.

Is North Dakota still tough?

My response: Not as tough as it used to be.

"There's something different about this state," I said.

"Why?" Jenkinson asked.

"I think it's changing," I said, "but a lot of people grew up not expecting handouts."

"Is it because we're rural?" Clay asked. "But there's rural Arkansas and rural Mississippi."

Hard to answer that in one or two sentences.

"I don't doubt what you're saying, but I'm trying to figure out what it is about us," Jenkinson said. "It was easier to be a nice North Dakotan when we knew that I probably knew somebody who knew somebody who knew your brother. And now the degrees of separation are much greater on average. I think it still works in small towns."

The fear is the exodus of the small communities and the intensive growth of the state's larger cities like Fargo, Bismarck and Grand Forks leaves behind a legacy of the work ethic.

"Our connection with the farms has really eroded," Jenkinson said.

Low population and relative isolation made it a simpler lifestyle. As the end of 2018 approaches, things are changing. Jenkinson called it the Fargo Effect.

"Do we get to maintain that character or does it slip away?" he said. "These are the hard questions, and no one is asking them."

I grew up in central Fargo. The Fargo I knew in the '70s and '80s is nowhere near the Fargo of 2018. It's now the Fargo and West Fargo of 2018, with the population continuing to swell southwest like a thunderstorm across the prairie. People call it progress. I call it a cause to be concerned. On Sept. 25, 2018, I saw three stories of separate murder cases on the front of my local newspaper: a son who apparently shot his father, a 20-year-old who was shot outside a fast-food restaurant on Main Avenue, and the trial of Savanna LaFontaine-Greywind, a Fargo woman who died from a gruesome "womb abduction."

Nothing works better than western North Dakota to get away from these news clippings. In 1987, my brother Dave and I hiked the Badlands in the Theodore Roosevelt National Park. It was so North Dakota.

It's so North Dakota to not like the below-zero weather in the winter, yet don't give one thought to moving somewhere warm. It's so North Dakota that dinner means 6 p.m. with everybody around the table. It's so North Dakota not to care what others around the country say about you.

The challenge is to teach our children or grandchildren the meaning of doing a job. I'm just as guilty as anybody. Put the video game down, son, and mow the lawn. Have your child do it, even if you can afford a lawn care service. In the North Dakota of old, nobody needed "Farm Rescue" to help the farmer. Now we do. The people in the rural communities aren't there anymore.

Jenkinson took issue with Attorney General Wayne Stenehjem's comment on the crime rate spike of recent years.

"He was essentially saying welcome to the world; it's just the way it is," Jenkinson said. "First of all, I don't think it's true, and we shouldn't allow that kind of thing to be true. If you went to every North Dakotan and said, is North Dakota better? Equal? Or in decline? Almost every North Dakotan would say it's better. They may tell you things like we have better air traffic, we have better satellite television, we have better restaurants, whatever they would say. We have a nationally-important set of sports teams at NDSU and UND."

But at what cost?

"Most people would say, no real cost," Jenkinson said. "So maybe it just is better. Maybe we want to be Maple Grove, Minnesota. Maybe we don't want to be that old North Dakota anymore. I don't think you can maintain the qualities from North Dakota that are the best qualities if we cease to be connected somehow to agriculture and small towns and the land."

The reason we live here, Jenkinson said, is not because of great boutique restaurants. If you want that, move to Seattle. The reason to be here has to be you love this place.

What is it, then, about this place? Winter makes it a real hassle.

"The compensating reason to live here is there is a quality of life you can't have in other places," Jenkinson said. "What is that quality of life? It's access to hunting. Access to recreation – water in the summer. A neighborliness and a friendliness that's not like Minnesota Nice but a deeper niceness of character. When I was growing up, we lived here because it was safe. If we're joining the real world and the benefit is prosperity but the cost is what was uniquely wonderful about North Dakota, I think that's a conversation worth having and I'm not sure I want to live here. Then I might live in the suburbs in Minneapolis."

It's highly doubtful anybody is riding a horse to school. That was Dave Osborn. Or a junior high kid walking 2.5 miles in the middle of winter to get to wrestling practice by 7 a.m. That was Virgil Hill.

That was Norval Baptie, the most legendary North Dakota sports figure nobody knows. He was a world champion speed skater in the 1890s who grew up in Bathgate, N.D., located in the northeast corner of the state. He was born in Canada but lived there only a year before his family moved across the border.

"Although North Dakota produced him; Canada claims him and almost nobody in our state has ever heard of him," said Dick Johnson of Drayton.

It still boggles Johnson's mind that Baptie is a forgotten champ. He dominated speed skating for almost 20 years. He was one of the inventors of the ice show, touring with famed skater Sonja Henie. In 1913, Baptie switched to figure skating and convinced the owners of the Sherman Hotel in Chicago to build an indoor ice rink so Baptie could produce the world's first indoor ice-skating show. His acts included singles, pairs and ballets. His legendary career can be found at the Pembina County Historical Society museum. Baptie was so good a speed skater that as a local North Dakota kid he beat his competition skating backwards. He was nicknamed "The Flickertail Flyer."

In the mid-1930s at the age of 58, Baptie told a reporter he could still skate as fast as he did when he was 16. The reporter, and other writers, joined Baptie at a rink the following day. Baptie finished three-fifths of a second off his former world record.

"Maybe it's time we take Norval Baptie back from Canada," Johnson wrote. "He was a North Dakota boy after all."

The persistence shown by Norval Baptie is still alive in this state. NDSU football makes a living on in-state players with a hard work ethic. UND is a national pulse of college hockey. Both programs operate at the highest levels of their divisions.

But I'm with Clay Jenkinson

I'm nervous about what the future holds.

I do not want to be Maple Grove, Minn.

About the author

The family on a non-winter coat Christmas day in a downtown Fargo alley. Jeff, Ruby, Brandt, Leah, Ben

Jeff Kolpack started a career in journalism on March 14, 1964 – the day he was born. His father, Ed Kolpack, was a sportswriter and sports editor at The Forum of Fargo-Moorhead newspaper for 39 years. His mother, Idamarie, was an English teacher. Jeff took his first position at The Forum in 1990 and started covering North Dakota State athletics in 1995. He had a behind-the-scenes seat to NDSU's five straight Division I FCS football national championships and wrote a book about it in 2016 called "Horns Up: Inside the Greatest College Football Dynasty," which will always be available on Amazon.com.

He is married to Ruby Kolpack and they are the parents of three children: Ben, Leah and Brandt. Jeff is a tenured member of the B Team Bicycle Club in north Fargo, where a few members invented the Fargo-to-Zorbaz Metric Century Ride to Detroit Lakes, Minn.; the GD Cooking Club and the Edgewood Golf Course men's club. He is half of the Kolpack & Izzo multimedia tandem and hosts the WDAY Golf Show on Saturday mornings from April through August on Fargo radio station WDAY-AM.

Made in the USA
Middletown, DE
28 January 2019